THE ROBUST FEDERATION

The Robust Federation offers a comprehensive approach to the study of federalism. Jenna Bednar demonstrates how complementary institutions maintain and adjust the distribution of authority between national and state governments. These authority boundaries matter—for defense, economic growth, and adequate political representation—and must be defended from opportunistic transgression. From Montesquieu to Madison, the legacy of early institutional analysis focuses attention on the value of competition between institutions, such as the policy moderation produced through separated powers. Bednar offers a reciprocal theory: in an effective constitutional system, institutions *complement* one another; each makes the others more powerful. Diverse but complementary safeguards—including the courts, political parties, and the people—cover different transgressions, punish to different extents, and fail under different circumstances. The analysis moves beyond equilibrium conceptions and explains how the rules that allocate authority are not fixed but shift gradually. Bednar's rich theoretical characterization of complementary institutions provides the first holistic account of federal robustness.

Jenna Bednar is an associate professor of political science at the University of Michigan. Her work crosses disciplines, addressing constitutional questions using the methods of complex systems analysis and game theory, and has been published in law reviews as well as journals in economics, political science, and sociology. Professor Bednar received her Ph.D. from Stanford University in 1998.

POLITICAL ECONOMY OF INSTITUTIONS AND DECISIONS

Series Editor

Stephen Ansolabehere, Massachusetts Institute of Technology

Founding Editors

James E. Alt, Harvard University
Douglass C. North, Washington University of St. Louis

Other books in the series

Alberto Alesina and Howard Rosenthal, *Partisan Politics, Divided Government and the Economy*
Lee J. Alston, Thrainn Eggertsson, and Douglass C. North, eds., *Empirical Studies in Institutional Change*
Lee J. Alston and Joseph P. Ferrie, *Southern Paternalism and the Rise of the American Welfare State: Economics, Politics, and Institutions, 1865–1965*
James E. Alt and Kenneth Shepsle, eds., *Perspectives on Positive Political Economy*
Josephine T. Andrews, *When Majorities Fail: The Russian Parliament, 1990–1993*
Jeffrey S. Banks and Eric A. Hanushek, eds., *Modern Political Economy: Old Topics, New Directions*
Yoram Barzel, *Economical Analysis of Property Rights,* 2nd edition
Yoram Barzel, *A Theory of the State: Economic Rights, Legal Rights, and the Scope of the State*
Robert Bates, *Beyond the Miracle of the Market: The Political Economy of Agrarian Development in Kenya*
Charles M. Cameron, *Veto Bargaining: Presidents and the Politics of Negative Power*
Kelly H. Chang, *Appointing Central Bankers: The Politics of Monetary Policy in the United States and the European Monetary Union*
Peter Cowhey and Mathew McCubbins, eds., *Structure and Policy in Japan and the United States: An Institutionalist Approach*
Gary W. Cox, *The Efficient Secret: The Cabinet and the Development of Political Parties in Victorian England*
Gary W. Cox, *Making Votes Count: Strategic Coordination in the World's Electoral System*
Gary W. Cox and Jonathan N. Katz, *Elbridge Gerry's Salamander: The Electoral Consequences of the Reapportionment Revolution*

Continued at the back of the book

THE ROBUST FEDERATION

Principles of Design

JENNA BEDNAR

University of Michigan

CAMBRIDGE
UNIVERSITY PRESS

CAMBRIDGE UNIVERSITY PRESS
Cambridge, New York, Melbourne, Madrid, Cape Town, Singapore, São Paulo, Delhi

Cambridge University Press
32 Avenue of the Americas, New York, NY 10013-2473, USA

www.cambridge.org
Information on this title: www.cambridge.org/9780521703963

First published 2009

Printed in the United States of America

A catalog record for this publication is available from the British Library.

Library of Congress Cataloging in Publication data
Bednar, Jenna.
The robust federation : principles of design / Jenna Bednar.
p.   cm. – (political economy of institutions and decisions)
Includes bibliographical references.
ISBN 978-0-521-87899-9 (hardback) – ISBN 978-0-521-70396-3 (pbk.)
1. Federal government.   2. Federal government – United States.   I. Title.   II. Series.
JC355.B43 2009
320.4'049–dc22
2008037679

ISBN 978-0-521-87899-9 hardback
ISBN 978-0-521-70396-3 paperback

Contents

List of Figures

List of Tables

Acknowledgments

Some books seem to write themselves. Ideas spring out of the author's mind, arguments fully formed, as the fingers race to capture them on paper. This is not one of those books. The arguments in these pages were shaped by workshop audiences and colleagues who generously took the time to offer suggestions. Thanks to the graduate students and faculty at the Santa Fe Institute, Texas A & M, Michigan, Rochester, NYU, Chicago, George Mason, Penn State, Washington University, University of Wisconsin, Wilfred Laurier University, UCLA, and Stanford for your reactions; I hope that many of you find your fingerprints on this book. Thanks to Bob Axelrod, Cliff Carrubba, Bill Clark, John Ferejohn, Barry Friedman, Liz Gerber, Anna Grzymala-Busse, Daniel Halberstam, Don Herzog, Simon Hug, Jim Johnson, Orit Kedar, Ken Kollman, Larry Kramer, Rob Mikos, Burt Monroe, Scott Page, Sunita Parikh, Jonathan Rodden, and Craig Volden, my kind colleagues who provided detailed comments: I have finished this project now and am ready to return the favor. I am also grateful to John Ferejohn and Barry Weingast, whose writings inspired my approach to constitutional analysis, and Jack Rakove, for introducing me to James Madison and encouraging me to use my skills in formal analysis when reading his writings.

For superb research assistance I am indebted to Carolina de Miguel Moyer, Olesya Tkacheva, Colleen Castle, and three intrepid first-year Michigan undergraduates: Zeke Daniels-Shpall, Christina Spallina, and Alexandra Tilén. And thank you to the University of Michigan's Center for Local, State, and Urban Politics for the funds to pay for this assistance.

In addition to the transformative effect it has had on my research, the Santa Fe Institute provided warm hospitality over several summers of intense writing. Stanford's Hoover Institution generously provided me with space and financial support while I worked on the final revisions to the manuscript.

Despite all this support, this book would not be possible without the distracting love of my three boys: Orrie, Cooper, and Scottie.

I

Constituting the Robust Federation

How can a federal constitution—mere words on paper—produce a government that is strong, flexible, and resilient? A federal constitution creates distinct governments endowed with different responsibilities. The boundaries between national and state governmental authority are set with goals in mind; to be effective, these boundaries must be maintained. At the same time, the constitution is not written to satisfy a single moment, but needs to remain relevant in perpetuity. Over time, owing to changing circumstances and intentions, the authority boundaries sometimes must be redrawn. The tension between strength and flexibility, commitment and mutability, creates a conundrum inherent to federal constitutional design. Making the problem all the more vexing, the safeguards that uphold the boundaries depend on humans, acting as both individuals and collectives, and are thus flawed. How successful federations overcome this apparent contradiction, enforcing the rules while maintaining flexibility—and do so with imperfect components—is the focus of this book.

This book builds a logic of robust federal design. I offer a set of general principles of constitutional construction and institutional performance that can be adapted to fit local conditions. I diagnose the inherent weakness of federalism: the temptation for constituent governments to exploit the union for their own gain. I show how the constitution constructs safeguards to prevent these transgressions, but each is imperfect and none is sufficient. As a collaborative system, however, the safeguards overcome one another's weaknesses to protect the federal boundaries against manipulation while admitting beneficial adjustments. By explicitly acknowledging the context dependence of institutional performance, we can understand how safeguards intersect to fashion a robust system: strong, flexible, and able to recover from internal errors.

Whether measured in population or gross domestic product, the world has grown increasingly federal,[1] making the need to understand federalism, and its constitutional design, ever more urgent. Emerging democracies turn to federalism with hope, as the solution to bind together diverse populations. But federalism is not a panacea: the federal structure is often blamed for political crisis, where observers complain that the federation is either over- or undercentralized. In many countries, federalism is touted as the solution to fiscal mismanagement, while in others—notably Argentina's 2000 economic collapse—federalism takes the brunt of the blame. What makes the problem interesting is that all ring true. Unlike its unitary cousins, a federation suffers from structural deficiencies that challenge its robustness: the very features that make a federal structure appealing for a heterogeneous society—decentralization and regional semi-independence—also build in new opportunities for transgressions.

To develop principles of robust federal system design, we need to understand what undermines a union from reaching its potential. Observations confound analysis because internal competition can lead to many different outcomes. The federation can grow too centralized, or spin out of control; pieces may secede, or the whole federation can crumble into autonomous entities. The center can grow so forceful that the subunits either rise up in challenge or wither into nonexistence, legally or in practice. A study focused exclusively on the United States would be tempted to conclude that the national government is the main threat to federal harmony, swallowing the states' authorities (what I will call encroachment). The U.S. federal government, after all, holds the lion's share of the purse strings and controls the military. But both factors are present in Argentina, with the opposite effect: paradoxically the provinces are both chokers and the choked, and they often cannot escape their own collective stranglehold. Americans begin to see that what is particular about their federation, the apparent overcentralization, might not be a universal tendency of federalism. The tendency of state governments to overstep their authority should not be overlooked. In federations there is no unique

---

[1] See Table 2.1. The 33 countries that were federal or quasi-federal in 1990–2000 made up about 50% of the world's population and contributed 61% of the world's GDP in 2000. Acknowledging China's quasi-federal *practice*—it has partially devolved significant authority, including economic planning, growth strategies, and welfare provision—the numbers leap to 70% of the population and 65% of GDP.

culprit that prevents the union from achieving its goals, no single cause of poor performance.

Nor do we observe a single recipe for success. While all federations are more institutionally developed than an alliance, none is designed identically, and even those with nearly identical constitutions grow informal institutions and evolve wildly different political cultures, as with Argentina and the United States. Despite the observational variance, there are properties—forces induced by the structure of federalism—common to all federations. Focusing on the common underlying forces, lessons learned studying the United States, Argentina, Canada, and Australia might prove instructive for Russia, Iraq, South Africa, and the European Union. To understand the general properties, we need to get to the root of what ails a federation; in the midst of such institutional variety, we need a fundamental understanding of how the constitution contributes to the well-being of its member governments.

The federal structure is adopted for a reason (often several, which vary from country to country); to achieve these ends, authority within the federal system is deliberately distributed between federal and state governments. This distribution may fail for two reasons: noncompliance and inappropriateness. Governments may fail to respect one another's authority; this opportunism throws the federation off balance, depleting its potential, perhaps even destroying the union. Transgressions are tempting when the rules are costly for the governments to follow. Therefore federal design cannot stop with the distribution of authority: it is also necessary to engineer a system to uphold the rules.

A second challenge is the match between the distribution of authority and the federation's needs and potential. The rules regulating federalism's boundaries may be poorly conceived from the start, a product of political compromise or asymmetric bargaining power, or they may become inappropriate over time, as the environment or public demand changes. The federal system needs a procedure for adapting the distribution of authority even as it upholds the existing rules.

Notice that federalism's second problem of adaptability contradicts the first, of compliance. Constitutional design faces a dilemma: the federation needs sufficient structural integrity—solving the compliance problem—to work in the short run, but the rules upheld must adapt to changing needs. Compliance maintenance makes the robust federation effective; adaptability keeps it relevant. Robustness requires both commitment and flexibility. A robust system of safeguards is strong enough to bind member governments to the rules, but also sufficiently supple to adapt the rules. It is also savvy; it resists opportunistic manipulation.

To understand how a constitution overcomes this conundrum to create a thriving federation, one must look beyond the rules to the *system* created by the constitution. A constitution prescribes the government's formal structure, describing how the executive, legislative, and judicial powers will be implemented, whether there will be regular elections, and who counts as a citizen. Informal elements rise up as a product of these formal institutions, including the party system and political culture. Federal constitutions add a wrinkle of complexity: they replace the unitary government with multiple independent-willed governments, set within a hierarchy including one central government. All of these elements—including the governments themselves—act as safeguards of the rules.

Safeguards sustain rules in two ways: through coordination or force. When the only barrier to compliance is a common understanding of the behavior required, rules are upheld by institutions that publicize the meaning of the rules. Often the meaning itself is not clear and so the safeguards can serve double duty, aiding a deliberative process of determining the meaning of the rule (and so also allowing it to evolve, if necessary) and then publicizing it once determined. Sometimes rules prescribe behavior that a government would rather not follow; in these cases, compliance is upheld through safeguards that reward desired behavior, or more often, punish undesirable behavior.

Safeguards are not robotic, but staffed by humans, and so will reflect our tics and inconsistencies. The imperfection of these safeguards is the source of federalism's third challenge. Each safeguard forms its own judgment about what governmental behaviors to tolerate. When a safeguard is particularly intolerant it punishes frequently, making the union less beneficial to its members. On the other hand, when safeguards are overly tolerant they punish rarely, reducing the incentive to comply, again reducing the benefit of federation. The federal system of safeguards needs sufficient redundancy to recover from the errors made by its components.

The heart of the book is dedicated to understanding how the safeguards operate. It will not offer an ideal design—there is no "perfect" constitution in an appendix—but it does offer design principles. I offer a perspective that sees the safeguards as varying in their capacity to respond to different transgressions, varying in the force of their response, and varying in the causes of their own failures. These heterogeneities provide an opportunity to overcome the apparent dilemma of force and flexibility while providing insurance against misjudgment. The key lesson of this book is that safeguards must be understood within their institutional context. Each has a role to play in the recovery from another's failures, in bolstering another's powers, and through their diversity, to provide a space for policy experimentation. It is their interaction that generates the strong, adaptive, and ultimately robust federation.

1.1 FEDERALISM AS MEANS

Resolved that the Articles of Confederation ought to be so corrected & enlarged as to accomplish the objects proposed by their institution; namely, "common defence, security of liberty and general welfare." —James Madison, *The Virginia Plan*, 1787[2]

Governments are designed to pursue society's goals. Most constitutional preambles remind the reader of this purpose, and James Madison's draft of the U.S. Constitution, *The Virginia Plan*, is no exception.[3] People form political communities for security (common defense), to ensure their rights (liberty), and to strive for widespread benefits such as a common market (general welfare). Some federations are founded with all three of these purposes in mind, while in others an initial concern births the union, and over time others are added. The European Union is an excellent example of an evolved federation; the union's purposes have expanded over time, and as the goals of the union expand, the institutions are adjusted to accommodate the changing goals. In Chapter 2, I explore the purposes of federalism in more depth and include an overview of the European Union's development. Following is a brief overview of the purposes.

---

[2] Madison (1999:89).

[3] Throughout this book, I build on the thinking of James Madison because Madison approached the design of federations as a problem of incentives: how to structure institutions to induce desirable political behavior. Madison may have invented modern federalism, but in a very real sense he had no alternative: a unitary government was out of the question, and the looser confederation had proven unsuccessful. His goal was to devise a system of government that would make the union thrive. Simultaneously he was concerned with the problem of democracy, since the early American experience with it had left many disgruntled. Therefore Madison began his study of federal design with a puzzle: to design a government to serve the people, specifically, to meet their goals and perform well over time, sometimes by overriding their immediate desires.

Just as Madison had no real alternative but to recognize state sovereignty, this book begins with the premise that federalism has been selected as the governmental form and thinks about the principles for constructing a federal constitution. For more on the origins of federalism, see Riker (1964) and Ziblatt (2006).

Military Security: With military power centralized, a federal union is better able to defend itself than a confederation or looser alliance of states. The strength that comes from an expanded territory and resources, as well as the improved coordination of effort, makes members of the federal union more secure against foreign invasion than they are on their own (the *Federalist*, Riker 1964, Ostrom 1971).

Economic Efficiency and Innovation: The science of fiscal federalism studies the design of taxation and expenditure policies between governmental levels in search of efficiency or to maximize total utility (e.g., Musgrave 1997, Oates 1999). With market-preserving federalism, decentralization coupled with other conditions such as decentralized fiscal control and hard budget constraints enables a state to commit credibly not to expropriate all rents (Weingast 1995, Parikh and Weingast 1997, Qian and Weingast 1997, Rodden and Rose-Ackerman 1997, Rodden and Wibbels 2002). Also, decentralization may spur beneficial government policy experimentation (e.g., Kollman et al. 2000). Intergovernmental competition, enabled through decentralization, may make government more efficient (Tiebout 1956). At the same time, a federation has a central government, often lacking in a confederacy, and centralized regulation of trade permits a polity to enjoy the benefits of a common market (e.g., the *Federalist*) as well as other financial standards, including common currency and interest rates.

Effective Representation: Madison emphasized federalism's potential to prevent tyranny and improve the quality of representation in the state and national legislatures, bolstering democracy's performance (the *Federalist*, Elazar 1987, Ostrom 1991). Others cite the value of decentralization: distributing authority at lower levels may serve as a pressure valve, releasing tensions in heterogeneous populations (the *Federalist*, Horowitz 1985, Stepan 1999). In the fiscal federalism literature, decentralization permits citizens to elect politicians who will tailor policy to meet local preferences or to provide an opportunity to move to states that better match their interests (Tiebout 1956, Inman and Rubinfeld 1992, Peterson 1995, Donahue 1997, Oates 1999).

1.2 DISTRIBUTING AUTHORITY

Among the numerous advantages promised by a well constructed union, none deserves to be more accurately developed than its tendency to break and control the violence of faction. ... Complaints are every where heard ... that our governments are too unstable; that the public good is disregarded in the conflicts of rival parties; and that measures are too often decided, not according to the rules of justice, and the rights of the minor party; but by the superior force of an interested and over-bearing majority. —James Madison, *Federalist* 10[4]

Even as he relays complaints (and to be sure, he agrees with them), Madison's optimism prevails. To say that the performance of government falls short is to measure it against a greater potential. Madison implies that a well-constructed government might respect political minorities, might be reliable, might reflect local interest while generating the efficiency of a centralized government. The design of government affects its ability to accomplish citizen goals. A federal structure gives constitutional designers the opportunity to fragment government geopolitically into independent governments, with direct governance of the citizens at each level.[5] Authority can then be distributed between levels of government. A federal structure becomes a tool that can be used by the people to craft a more effective government, with some authorities assigned to the national government and others to the states.

If the distribution is flawed, then the government cannot perform well. It can be flawed for a number of reasons. First, social science is imperfect. Designing the allocation of authority is a great problem in social engineering. People are not atoms; their actions and reactions surprise the institutional engineer. A perfect design would demand a perfect understanding of how people will react to complex, interdependent incentives, but for all of its advances, the scholarship to date has only an imperfect understanding of the relationship between the distribution of authority and the union's ability to reach its potential.[6] Second, any distribution of authority implies compromise. Not all objectives are complementary; pursuit of some ends compromises a union's ability to pursue others. If the union is evaluated only along the dimension that is sacrificed, its performance will appear lackluster. The third reason is a natural extension of the second: with heterogeneity in the population, some will prefer one distribution over another because of the asymmetric consequences. Subgroups within the population would rank potential distributions of authority differently. A fourth reason for poor design further extends this

---

[4] Madison (1999:160).

[5] See Chapter 2 for a complete definition of a federation.

[6] For two thorough evaluations of the relationship between decentralization and social goals that reach opposite conclusions, see Triesman (2007) and Inman (2007).

thought: the adoption of the distribution of authority may be affected by power asymmetries.

The second through fourth points underscore the delicacy of adapting federal boundaries of authority. Most studies of institutional effectiveness assume that players willingly enter into the incentive environment established by institutions. Moe (2005) warns against this overly rosy view of institutions because players subject to an institution's incentives may be forced to play according to rules chosen by another. There is reason to believe that in many cases the initial adoption of the federal constitution, including the distribution of authority, is voluntary. The history of many federal unions reveals holdout cases: Buenos Aires in Argentina, British Columbia and Prince Edward Island in Canada, and Great Britain in the European Union. In these examples, the federal subunits waited to sign until the federal arrangement was redrawn to their liking, or until they had more confidence that the distribution of authority would be respected, without endangering local interests. Moe's cautions about power become particularly important once the federation is established. The voluntary nature of the federal union dissipates after constitutional adoption. Exit, while possible, arguably grows costlier after joining, which makes exploitation more likely when power asymmetries are present.[7] Adaptation is critical to the robust federation, but the process should be able to discriminate against the dominance of particular interests over the societal whole, a crucial problem addressed in Chapter 7.

In short, the allocation (and exercise) of authority matters. In the preceding paragraphs I have described the need to make adjustments to improve the functioning of the government, but adjustments may also be opportunistic, to serve a subset of interests (back to Madison's factions), at the expense of the whole. Distributing authority requires rules, and rules may be broken.

1.3 OPPORTUNISM

The great desideratum in Government is, so to modify the sovereignty as that it may be sufficiently neutral between different parts of the Society to controul one part from invading the rights of another, and at the same time

---

[7] However, even here one may find examples of successful subunit resistance to changes to the federal arrangement. Consider the 2005 French and Dutch rejections of the European Constitution.

sufficiently controuled itself, from setting up an interest adverse to that of the entire Society. —James Madison, letter to Thomas Jefferson, October 24, 1787[8]

A federation is more than divided authorities; it also requires independent wills and the power to exercise them. It is not sufficient to divvy up authority between governmental units like any corporation, where the real power is exercised by one unit alone, which might at any moment reorganize or recapture the devolved authority. Should this happen, and the balance of authority be tipped in one direction or another, tyranny becomes a problem, and the society's other goals—security and the economy—may also be sacrificed. When the federation does not perform well, it is vulnerable to break-up, revolution, coups, and invasions. Respect for the distribution of authority will come when power, not just authority, is shared. It requires severing the dependence between governments and defending the union against the temptation of opportunistic behavior.

The distributional battles in a federation are symptoms of an underlying public good provision problem. The federal benefits often require that the member governments, both state and federal, put general welfare above their own apparent self-interest. This transformation is not going to happen by luck or divine intervention; it must be engineered through institutional design that can align self-interest with common interest. Chapter 3 describes why opportunism is an unavoidable threat to federal unions. A robust federation minimizes opportunism to maximize productivity. Opportunism is described in detail in this chapter, with examples. The federal government may *encroach* on the authority of the states; states may *shirk* on their responsibilities to the union; and states may *burden-shift*, imposing externalities on other states in the federation. Figure 1.1 captures the logical essence of federalism's compliance problem.

Notice how opportunism also interferes with adaptation, federalism's second problem. The federation needs to be able to experiment with new policies to adapt the distribution of authority optimally. But the temptation of opportunism makes toleration of experimentation hazardous. Opportunistic transgressions may be punished extra-constitutionally through revolt, but at a high cost; it is risky, and it requires significant coordination and a high level of consensus. It does not guarantee any improvement in outcome. Finally, popular revolt is virtually incapable

---

[8] Madison (1999:152).

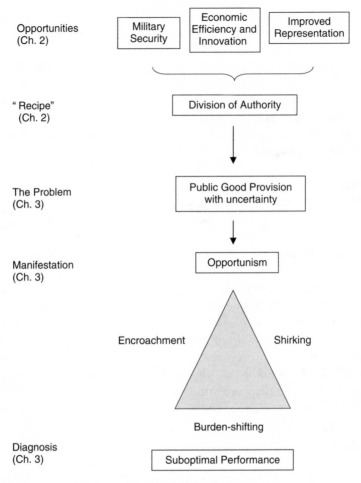

Figure 1.1. The Problem of Federal Robustness

of punishing burden-shifting—transgressions of one state on another. If this were the only control mechanism available to citizens, the government would have a wide berth before punishment through revolt would become likely. How can the citizens control their government without resorting to such extreme measures? It may seem unlikely that a paper document (if the constitution is written) could make a difference, but this book will break down federalism to its basic components to examine how a thoughtfully designed constitution may provide an institutional enforcement aid to the citizens.

Setting aside revolution, federalism's disaggregation of government creates a second primitive defense: intergovernmental retaliation. The model developed in Chapter 3 examines this mechanism, and the model becomes a baseline for later chapters. The primary means of sanctioning (and therefore encouraging compliance) is by intergovernmental threat of retaliation, and ultimately, the threat of the union's dissolution. Intergovernmental retaliation is an inefficient mechanism, limited by its costliness and the availability of outside alternatives. Robustness might be improved if other safeguards were available.

1.4 SAFEGUARDS

A dependence on the people is no doubt the primary control on the government; but experience has taught mankind the necessity of auxiliary precautions. —James Madison, *Federalist* 51[9]

We are now prepared to turn to the theory of the safeguards that sustain the federal structure. Political actors and the governments they lead respond to incentives: political agents will be drawn toward actions that offer rewards and move away from actions that incur punishments. Hamilton writes of the necessity of sanctions in *Federalist* 15:

Government implies the making of laws. It is essential to the idea of a law that it be attended with a sanction; or, in other words, a penalty or punishment for disobedience. If there be no penalty annexed to disobedience, the resolutions or commands which pretend to be laws will in fact amount to nothing more than advice or recommendation.

While a constitution can define rules, and a court can interpret them, these recommendations alone do not alter governmental behavior. What transforms the constitution from platitudes to expectations?

A half year after his important letter to Thomas Jefferson—an excerpt from it opened the last section—Madison published *Federalist* 51, laying out the argument for institutional supplements to popular control. Clearly, a federation that has to resort to threats of interstate war will not be harmonious or productive; despite being the primary force backing most international treaties, intergovernmental retaliation is an unacceptable exclusive defense of federal unions. A democratic federation relies

---

[9] Madison (1999:295).

upon the people to punish errant governments, but as Madison understood well, popular management is flawed and therefore insufficient. While in the aggregate the nation is harmed by opportunistic behavior, opportunism often can be framed as constituency service, hampering direct popular control. To sanction transgressions requires consensus, common information, and even common perceptions of governmental action. At the same time, a diversity of viewpoints and perspectives may contribute to the overall health of the union (Page 2007). To aid their coordination without eliminating their diversity, the citizens need institutional safeguards, Madison's "auxiliary precautions."

This book describes five categories of safeguards. Intergovernmental retaliation is the baseline enforcement mechanism in any union (including international organizations), but it tends to be difficult to control. Institutional safeguards include structural features (e.g., fragmentation of powers and incorporation of the states in federal decision making), political safeguards provided by the party system, and the judiciary. Finally, popular safeguards—where the public directly responds to governmental transgressions—is an elusive but important safeguard.

Chapter 4 begins with the Madisonian structural safeguards, and then proceeds to more modern theory, including political and judicial safeguards. While most of these safeguards are initially cut from the pattern designed in the constitution, politics is the tailor, making adjustments that influence the capacity of the safeguards to maintain the division of power. The chapter points out the strengths and weaknesses of each safeguard, ultimately arguing that no institution is a self-contained remedy for federalism's opportunism problem. Each is incomplete, imperfect, and insufficient. Effective laws require credible sanctions, and no one of these safeguards is credible.

Despite the impossibility of any single ideal safeguard, multiple safeguards may enhance one another, together approximating an optimal mechanism to sustain a robust federation—one that upholds compliance, recovers from shocks, and adapts to change. Chapters 5, 6, and 7 explore the functional heterogeneity of the different safeguards to develop a three-part thesis of how the safeguards interlock to transform governmental behavior. The safeguards vary by which transgressions they target, by the severity of their punishment, and by the role that they play in making the federation resilient. When implemented together, their functional diversity creates a robust system. Figure 1.2 illustrates the theory of a federation's remedies.

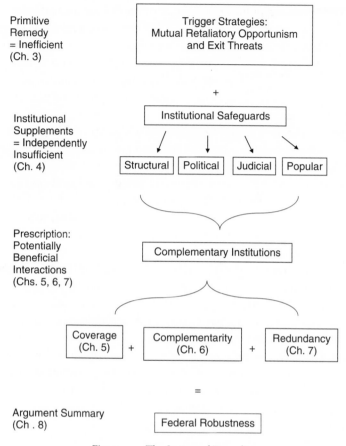

Figure 1.2. The System of Remedies

1.5 ROBUSTNESS

Robust system design has three properties: *compliance*, to dissuade transgressions; *resilience*, an immunity to design flaws and external shocks; and *adaptation*, an ability to adjust the rules to meet changing needs. Traditional institutional analysis has focused on structuring incentives to induce compliance in equilibrium. The equilibrium-based approach considers the problem of institutional design to be one of balancing incentives to produce stability.[10] Although important, incentive compatibility considerations ignore the dynamic nature of a federal bargain. The system

---

[10] Mathematical appendices to Chapters 3, 4, and 6 provide the equilibrium-based analysis that I used to derive the insights contained within those chapters.

must be able to adapt and be resilient to shocks. Thus, end-state analysis must be complemented with analysis of the processes of reaction and change. Chapter 7 completes the theory by including the design principles for resilience and the process of adaptation.

Compliance

Chapters 5 and 6 focus on compliance. As Chapter 3 argues, federalism is a complicated form of a public good provision problem, with two types of actors and three broad types of violations. Transgressions range from mild to moderate to severe, depending on the significance of their deviation from the existing distribution of authority. To uphold compliance effectively, the system of safeguards must successfully deter (or minimize occurrences) all types of transgressions, at all levels of severity. Chapter 5 describes what type of transgression each safeguard "covers"— what each attempts to deter. Ideally, the system will provide complete coverage. Incomplete coverage may exacerbate tensions.

Chapter 6 shows how institutions of varying sanctioning force work together. With safeguards that have different capacities to punish, a remedy can be sensitive to the extent of opportunism. The more egregious the transgression, the greater the punishment. At the same time, severe punishments should be rare. More frequent, but milder, punishments may deter moderate transgressions. The chapter also describes the consequence of incompatible sanctioning capacities.

Resilience

Chapter 7 addresses the problem of institutional imperfection, where a safeguard misidentifies a situation. Safeguards may fail to sanction when they should or they may sanction too frequently. Either flaw leads to frustration. The chapter explores how to design a system of safeguards to overcome these contradictory problems. If it is possible that a safeguard might fail to sanction, back-up safeguards may be added as insurance that duplicate the coverage and punishment capacities of the first. On the other hand, if a safeguard punishes too frequently, additional safeguards may be added to confirm the observation before any safeguard is permitted to sanction.

While each solution is intuitive, insurance and confirmation contradict one another, implying that federal design forces a choice between the two. But let us return to the observation that transgressions, and punishments, vary in severity. Overly frequent severe punishments are much more damaging to the federation than extraneous mild sanctions. For safeguards with severe consequences—particularly intergovernmental retaliation—the system should have confirming redundancy before the safeguard is triggered. For mild sanctions—structural, political, and judicial safeguards—letting them trigger independently increases the likelihood that moderate transgressions are sanctioned, without adding intolerable costs. By exploiting the variation in transgression severity, we can overcome the apparent contradiction between insurance and confirmation to make the federation more resilient to flaws.

Adaptation

The federation also needs to adapt in response to changing desires and needs. A society may change its mind about its goals, and appropriate amendment procedures are necessary to reflect changing preferences while preventing manipulations. But even if goals do not change, the best method of pursing them—the optimal distribution of authority between governments—may change. An overly rigid authority distribution may snap when pressured by new circumstances, from technological developments to globalization to societal drift. Rules should be bendable (subject to constraint) and changeable.[11]

After a shock to the system, a robust federation does not necessarily return to the same way of distributing authority, but it may adapt to find a better balance. A robust federation is flexible, not rigid. The system should have a mechanism in place to accept—even promote, through exploration—beneficial adjustments, while inhibiting harmful ones. Multiple overlapping safeguards are, through their inconsistency, a means for exploring the policy space. Safeguards can tolerate experimentation that involves minor transgressions. In this method, the federation continues to explore the appropriateness of policy and of the distribution of authority, and the union may adopt beneficial changes. Adaptation may occur in practice, through an understood evolution of rule interpretation, or happen more formally, perhaps with a constitutional amendment that reassigns authority.

Multiple judgments serve a secondary purpose: they provide a forum for deliberation when ideal policy is unclear. Diverse arguments are made

---

[11] See Volden (2005) for an argument about the conditions where flexibility is beneficial.

about the constitutionality of a governmental action; sometimes, since these safeguards are triggered at different moments (structural safeguards are almost always *ex ante*, judicial safeguards are mostly *ex post*) a policy may be tried out and later rejected, so the deliberation involves experimentation as well. This public conversation about federalism—although never described in those terms—helps to form a common vision in the public about the shape of their federation and its importance. Public reaction, in the form of popular safeguards, may lie latent. In fact, popular safeguards are most likely to be dormant when the system is otherwise working well, because transgressions are effectively deterred by the structural, political, or judicial safeguards. Chapter 7 describes how the mild safeguards work with, and on, the popular safeguards. It develops a theory of the federal culture, the practice described earlier, as the emergence of public consensus about constitutional procedures and, ultimately, rules that allow the public to be an effective safeguard of federalism.

1.6 DISCUSSION

A robust federation needs firm constraints, upholding the distribution of authority between federal and state governments. It needs a method to recover from error, and a way to deliberate, experiment, and ultimately adjust the distribution of authority. In this opening chapter, I have provided a preview of what this book offers: a theory of how the system of safeguards can fulfill these needs. I offer a perspective of federalism as a means to achieving social goals, where the problem of federalism is ensuring production of these goals by creating a robust system of safeguards. Robustness implies compliance, resilience, and adaptation. No single safeguard is sufficient, but a system of safeguards may work. The people can manage their federation, but their effectiveness is greatly improved through an accompanying system of safeguards. The federal culture, where the populus develops the consensus necessary to act, may lie latent, as other safeguards react more immediately to any challenge to the distribution of authority. A network of institutions, complementary in their functional capacity, may supplement the intergovernmental retaliations. In short, the theory built in this book exploits the superadditive properties of institutional safeguards.

This thesis generates corollaries with implications for empirical analysis. In evaluating federal performance, focusing on a single measure—for example, growth—may miss other social priorities that differ from federation to federation. It is independent of both the particular distribution of authority and the safeguards that protect it. That is, a robust federal structure does not imply a particular ratio of national to state authority, even in fiscal responsibilities. Nor does the robust federal system imply particular safeguards: since I argue that no safeguard can be understood in isolation, it is improper to posit a linear relationship between the presence of any one safeguard and a federation's robustness. Safeguards are, to use Madison's word, *auxiliary*, something appended to the basic model of central and state governments. Finally, the latency of the public interest in federalism does not mean that the popular safeguard has disappeared. It may decay, but normal observation of political life will not reveal its status conclusively because other safeguards are more likely to intervene first.

In short, in this book I present a theory of federal design based on a system of collaborative safeguards. A successful system fills three functions: coverage of all transgression types, complementarity of one another's punishment capacities, and redundancy in case of human failure. Three principles guide robust design: compliance, adaptation, and resilience. When these functions and principles are met, mere words on paper can foster security, prosperity, and liberty.

2

Federal Structure and Potential

This chapter lays two foundational blocks, both necessary precursors to the development of a theory of federal safeguards. First, I propose criteria that define a federal structure and provide a list of federations during 1990–2000. Second, I review the current science regarding how the distribution of authority should be calibrated to achieve social goals. In a third section, I trace the European Union's development from a treaty organization to a federation as its purposes evolved.

The main arc of my thesis begins in Chapter 3. Those who are comfortable with the purposes of federalism might choose to skim this chapter.

2.1 DEFINING THE FEDERATION

A federation is defined by more than internal geopolitical boundaries. Those boundaries separate *independent* governments, a status that distinguishes the federation from a decentralized but unitary government. Furthermore, in contrast to the confederation or treaty organization, each level of government, whether state or federal, enjoys a *direct* relationship with its citizens. The federation is a unique relationship between governments and the people.

A government is federal if it meets the following three structural criteria:

1. *Geopolitical Division:* The territory is divided into mutually exclusive states (or provinces, lander, etc.). The existence of each state is constitutionally recognized and may not be unilaterally abolished.
2. *Independence:* The state and national governments have independent bases of authority. In general, this independence is established

constitutionally through electoral independence, where each government is held accountable to its constituents, although nondemocratic forms of independence may be available.

3. *Direct Governance:* Authority is shared between the state and the national governments: each governs its citizens directly, so that each citizen is governed by at least two authorities. Each level of government is sovereign in at least one policy realm. This policy sovereignty is constitutionally declared.

Decentralized unions that fail to meet one of the three criteria are quasi-federations.

These criteria define federations in law; they do not guarantee that a system is federal in practice. Each of the components in the definition of federalism depends on a constitutional statement or other commonly recognized declaration. These declarations may be only erratically followed, or never be realized at all. In order to understand the effect of an institutional incentive structure on making the boundaries of federal-state authority stick, I include in the definition constitutional declarations even if they are not followed, so the theory might speak to failed federations as well as successful ones.

Geopolitical division insists that the primary political divisions be territorial. The definition excludes consociational organizations that divide authority between segments of society, such as in Lebanon. Although one might allow exemptions for special territories and national capital regions, if the primary territory is not exhaustively divided into autonomous regions it fails to meet this criterion. Some partially decentralized countries, such as the United Kingdom and Ukraine, are quasi-federal. Minimally, federations have two levels; a few do recognize the autonomy of municipalities.

The second criterion, independence, reflects Madison's thesis: governmental self-control may be induced by creating competition between governments. Independence creates distinct political wills, and distinct wills can lead to confrontations between governments. With independence, governments can challenge one another in ways that administrative units are unlikely to do. When policy is conceived and implemented perfectly, decentralized union may be sufficient. But if there is any uncertainty about what policy should be, or how it should be implemented, or any concern that a single government may fail through incompetence or corruption, then it is important to have true federalism rather than administrative decentralization.

To meet this criterion, one level of government may not appoint all political leadership at the other level. If interlevel appointment occurs, then other political leaders derived entirely from the state (or federal) selection method must be able to veto the decisions made by the appointee. For example, in the United States prior to 1913 (the adoption of the 17th Amendment to the U.S. Constitution), senators were appointed to Congress by the state legislatures. However, Senate-originated legislation is subject to House of Representatives' concurrence.[1]

When the legislative process is complex, determining whether or not the independence criterion is met is a judgment call. The European Union (EU) is an excellent example. In most policy domains, the Commission, composed of delegates from the member states, proposes legislation, with significant oversight from the Council, the member states' ministers responsible for the relevant policy portfolio. The only directly elected body—and therefore the only unit directly accountable to the people—is the European Parliament, which for the first few decades of union had only a consultative power. Recent treaty revisions have expanded its role, and in many EU policy competences, the Parliament has the power to amend or even reject legislation.[2]

With direct governance, the third criterion, actions taken by the governments at each level directly affect each one's constituents. Both federal and state law implies obligations and rights for private citizens. When the laws of both levels of government apply directly to its citizens, then the citizens have rights under those laws and may pursue those rights in court. This criterion excludes countries where the national level operates as an oversight board or coordinates state activity, such as confederations.

Note that the definition does not include a particular assignment of authorities, either in substance or ratio. It is possible—although not

---

[1] At a federation's founding, compromises are often made in institutional design to appease hesitant parties. State appointment of U.S. senators was a compromise engineered to placate those fearful that the states would be overwhelmed by the national government. Several other structural features are engineered to make the central government more "federal" than "national" (as Madison described it in *Federalist* 39): the electoral college, organized around the states, elects the president, and many appointments, including all judicial appointments, must be confirmed by the Senate. See Section 4.1 for a discussion of structural features designed to incorporate state preferences in federal decision making.

[2] It is not always included in EU policy making: neither establishment of the common customs tariff and determination of breach of the budget deficit limitations require its approval. Hix (1999) has a comprehensive appendix listing the legislative procedure for all components of the treaties.

prudent—to have one level of government collect all revenue, as long as the transfers are not subject to its discretion. But if expenditure independence is compromised, so is the division of authority.[3] Again, reference to the European Union is instructive, where the budget is a poor indicator of governing impact: although the EU's budget is small,[4] it sets 80% of the rules governing exchange of goods, services, and capital within the member states (Hix 1999:3). The relative sizes of the state and federal budgets alone cannot tell us anything about the health of the federal system.

The federal criteria also do not include any institutional details about the system of safeguards, but the system transforms a *de jure* federation to a *de facto* federation when it can protect the independence of the governments and uphold the distribution of authority. When the safeguards fail, one government is able to manipulate the distribution in its favor because it can dominate the other governments. If federalism helps citizens to control their government, then when federalism falters through system failure, citizen control is weakened. A good example of federalism's failure in practice is President Putin's 2004 alteration of the Russian federal arrangement: by appointing regional viceroys to control subnational governments, independence is violated. The move was widely condemned as a weakening of democratic control. Canada provides a good contrast: despite federal–provincial bickering, including two secession referenda in a generation, the federation is in relatively good shape, in large part to public discourse about the distribution of authority between federal government and the provinces (see Chapter 7). Federalism and democracy are closely related, although neither one requires the other.

These criteria exclude the many polities that have delegated responsibilities to lower levels of government; this administrative decentralization may be economically efficient, but the lower level enjoys its powers as long as it is politically expedient for the national government to permit them. If the national government can dissolve the boundaries of the subunits

---

[3] I further discuss budget independence in Section 7.3. See also Diaz-Cayeros (2006).

[4] Its budget in 2005 was 116.5 billion euros, compared to Germany, with a 2005 budget (estimated) at 258.3 billion euros. The German population is about one-fifth of the European Union. The European Union has a ceiling on own resources—the maximum that member states will contribute to the EU budget—set at 1.24% of EU gross national income (GNI). For comparison, the state of Michigan is one of the few U.S. states with a revenue cap; its constitution limits state government revenues to 9.49% of state gross personal income. Its budget is about 10.8% of the gross state product, and the U.S. budget is about 22% of GNI.

or abolish its governmental organization, the polity is not federal. China, for example, has experimented with policy decentralization, and in some regions operates like a federation, but the central government may rescind the devolved authority.[5] In the United States, most municipal governments are chartered by the state governments; in law they may be dissolved, although in practice, where political costs are weighed, it is unlikely. On the other hand, if the states may terminate the national government's authority, then the union is an alliance, not a federation (Ordeshook and Niou 1998).

Table 2.1 lists all federations for the period 1990–2000.[6] During that decade 25 countries were federal, with 17 democratic federations and another 9 authoritarian federations.[7] The table also includes quasi-federations, which meet at least two of the three conditions: (1) geopolitical division, (2) independence, and (3) direct governance. They may or may not meet these conditions in practice. Those coded "F" fit all three criteria of federalism and are democratic; nondemocratic federations are "NDF."[8] "QF," for quasi-federation, meets two of the three criteria. Should a country qualify for quasi-federation status, the condition violated is included in parentheses following the coding. The quasi-federations are included for comparison, and because some appear to be federal in practice (e.g., India). Finally, "NA" represents countries that lacked a written constitution or codified legal structure. Although this list includes only federations and quasi-federations, some transitioned within the decade from a unitary state, noted by a "U."

---

[5] Referring to China's apparent commitment to a *de facto* practice of federalism, some scholars have treated China as a federation as they analyze its political economy (e.g., Montinola et al. 1995, Qian and Weingast 1996, Qian and Roland 1998). Since there is no distribution of authority in the Chinese constitution, it cannot be classified as *de jure* federalism, despite its practice. When power is decentralized in practice, the lessons of this book help an analyst to determine the credibility of a central government's commitment to devolution, as well as potential of the polity to reach its potential. That is, although China may not be a federation *de jure*, it is hard to explain the persistence of its devolution of authority—the self-constraint apparently exhibited by the central authorities—unless one recognizes the benefits of devolution to the health of Chinese economic growth.

[6] Thanks to Carolina de Miguel and Colleen Castle for research assistance in compiling this list.

[7] Note that Mexico appears in both categories.

[8] The coding as democratic (D) or nondemocratic (ND) of the following federations or quasi-federations is based on the polity index from the Polity IV dataset (Codebook Polity IV Project: Dataset User's Manual:13). If the polity index has missing values for specific countries and/or years the coding is based on the Freedom House Index.

Table 2.1. *List of Federations, 1990–2000*

Country	Years
Argentina	F
Australia	F
Austria	F
Belgium	QF (2) (1990–1993)
	F (1994–2000)
Bosnia and Herzegovina	NDF (1995–2000)
Brazil	F
Canada	F
Comoros	NA (1990–1991)
	QF (3) (1992–1995)
	U (1996–1999)
	NA (2000)
Czechoslovakia	F (1990–1992)
Ethiopia	U (1990–1994)
	NDF (1995–2000)
European Union	QF (2) (1990–1999)
	F (1999–2000)
Germany	F
India	QF (1)
Italy	QF (3)
Malaysia	NDF
Mexico	NDF (1990–1995)
	F (1996–2000)
Micronesia	F
Nigeria	NA (1990–1998)
	F (1999–2000)
Pakistan	NDF (1990–1999)
	NA (2000)
Russia	F (1992–2000)
South Africa	U (1990–1992)
	F (1993–2000)
Spain	QF (1)
St. Kitts and Nevis	QF (1)
Sudan	NA (1990–1997)
	QF (1) (1998–1999)
	NA (1999–2000)
Switzerland	F
Tanzania	ND-QF (1)
Ukraine	NA (1990)
	U (1991–1995)
	QF (2) (1996–2000)
Union of Soviet Socialist Republics	NDF (1990–1991)

(*continued*)

Table 2.1. (continued)

Country	Years
United Arab Emirates	NDF
United Kingdom	U (1990–1998)
	QF (1) (1999–2000)
United States of America	F
Venezuela	F
Yugoslavia	NDF (1990–1991)
Yugoslavia (Serbia and Montenegro)	NDF (1992–2000)

This list varies somewhat from others because my definition does not imply anything about the practice of government. It is not a straightforward task to list all federations in existence. Definitions are often vague. For example, Riker's (1987:101) definition is often used, despite its ambiguity: "a political organization in which the activities of government are divided between regional governments and a central government in such a way that each kind of government has some activities on which it makes final decisions." Many works eschew formal definitions altogether, arguing that federalism has an intuitive quality that formally cannot be defined but is recognizable. Elazar (1987) argues that federalism is a process as well as a structure (see also Ostrom 1991, Beer 1993, Ross 2003). Therefore, most political theorists agree that a polity must be federal in practice as well as form, but defining federal practice is elusive. It quickly degenerates into a you-know-it-when-you-see-it science, and the variation in the lists of federations manifests this controversy. While many agree on about a dozen cases of federalism, including the United States, Canada, Argentina, and Germany, another two to three dozen cases are contentious, including Spain, Italy, India, Venezuela, the USSR, Russia, China, Great Britain, and the European Union.

One should not reject a structural definition of federalism because it fails to guarantee federal practice, because to do so risks missing a clue that could help to identify what makes a federation successful. Another word for practice is behavior, and the positive theory of institutions[9] explores the role that institutions play in affecting behavior. We may examine

---

[9] The approach deduces how individuals interacting in strategic settings respond to incentives. Defining work in the "New Institutional Theory" or "Positive Political Theory" includes Schelling (1978), Williamson (1998), Shepsle (1989), North (1990), and Milgrom et al. (1990). For a terrific methodological primer, see Diermeier and Krehbiel (2003).

how the institutions that surround a federal structure compel behavior that is federal: respect for the integrity and authority of the component governments. Therefore it is important to include as federal all cases that meet a structural definition of federalism, rather than weeding out those that do not "feel" federal because they are not federal in practice.

2.2 THE PROMISE OF FEDERALISM

Three primary goals of governance are security, economic efficiency, and liberty. While it is often argued that federalism is a means to any of these ends, it is not the federal system itself but the way that authority is distributed between the independent governments that determines how well the government achieves these goals. Some goals are best realized through nationalization of policy, while for others, decentralization is best. One might ask: should the government do *X*? With the study of federalism, we must ask additionally, if so, *which* government should do it? The distribution of authority forms the basis of the "boundaries of federalism." A careful assignment of authority can help a federation meet its potential, but if the authority is misassigned—or if the boundaries are ignored—the federal structure will not help a society to reach its goals.

This section examines the current science that calibrates the authority distribution to meet these goals. The literature is extensive but each work tends to focus on a single benefit of federalism.[10] In reading, bear in mind three points: (1) any one union may be designed to achieve multiple goals, not just one; (2) the purpose of a union may evolve over time; and (3) the objectives sometimes contradict one another, necessitating trade-offs, and sometimes they complement one another. Table 2.2 (appearing later in the chapter) summarizes the prescriptions.

Military Security

In general, security is promoted through command coordination, implying centralization of foreign policy and war-making. A federal union is better able to defend itself than a confederation or looser alliance of states. The strength that comes from an expanded territory and resources, as well as the improved coordination of effort and commitment to implement decisions, makes members of the federal union more secure against

---

[10] One important exception is the work of Inman and Rubinfeld, described throughout this section.

foreign invasion than they are on their own (the *Federalist*, Riker 1964, Ostrom 1971).

In the early papers of the *Federalist*, John Jay writes passionately about the dangers of foreign invasion. The American states had hostile neighbors on three sides and faced aggressive navies overseas.

> It is too true, however disgraceful it may be to human nature, that nations in general will make war whenever they have a prospect of getting anything by it; .... Leave America divided into thirteen, or ... three or four independent governments—what armies could they raise and pay—what fleets could they ever hope to have? ... A good national government ... instead of *inviting* war, will tend to repress and discourage it. (Jay, *Federalist* 4)

John Jay endorsed the U.S. Constitution because it could eliminate the confederation's main vulnerability, its defensive weakness. This concern was cited often by many other Federalists, even leading off James Madison's celebrated notes on the "vices" of the Articles of Confederation.[11] Military insecurity derived from lack of organizational vigor was also a complaint of some Anti-Federalists, and fear of future invasion, and the belief that a strong government might repel invasion, is the chief cause of their support of the federal union.

Many federations were created under the pressures of foreign invasion. Included in the list, in addition to the United States, are Argentina from the various Argentine provinces, Canada from the two British colonies Upper and Lower Canada, Switzerland from independent cantons, and Germany from the German sovereign states. Whether the units were European feudal states or American colonies, the act of federation required abdication of sovereignty, a costly price. It was commonly assumed that independent states would pay such a price only if forced to by external circumstances.

Military security is the fundamental priority for any sovereign polity, because sovereignty depends on its ability to resist foreign invasion. It is unsurprising that many theorists of federalism have followed Jay's lead in emphasizing the role that military security plays in the creation and maintenance of federalism. In a wartime essay considering the exigency of world government, Maddox (1941:1122) writes that the most important motivations for creation of a federation out of independent states are "fear, a calculated expectation of advantage, and a response to some unifying ideal or myth" where fear, or "a sustained and profound feeling

---

[11] "Vices of the Political System of the United States," April 1787, in Madison (1999:69–80).

of insecurity," is the most important. Insecurity may be political—a fear of invasion—or economic, a fear of "panic and starvation." A stronger polity can intimidate the first, capitalizing on its insecurity to coerce it into a federal union. Finally, the power of the common enemy binds together a union: "Unity is cemented by specific, external opposition." The more real the external threat, the more it is named, rather than imaginary, the more likely that otherwise opposing forces will perceive their common interests and entertain a union. And the more pervasive the insecurity, the more sacrifices (in sovereignty, in protectionism) each state will be willing to make to ensure its security.

To sustain the coherence necessary for mutual guarantees of protection and security, the central government needs an independent basis of power. Maddox (1941:1125) argues that the government's power must come from direct election and direct power of taxation and military recruitment. In other words, it must be a federal government, rather than a confederacy, because in the latter the relationship between the people and the central government remains indirect.

Riker (1964) translates the argument into the language of modern political science with the claim that insecurity is a *necessary condition* for federalism. A federation is created when willing parties strike a "federal bargain." Two conditions create willing parties: an *expansion condition*, where a strong power wants to expand its territorial control, usually to prepare for an external military threat, and a *military condition*, where a second party is sufficiently insecure about its defense that it would agree to the first's offer. The stronger nation is not quite strong enough to take the second by force, and so proposes a federal union; the second accepts if the terms are agreeable.[12]

But why is the entanglement of political union necessary? Why not enlist in a defense alliance, where union is confined specifically to the dimension of insecurity, and the remaining elements of public policy may be left in the sovereign hands of the separate states, such as NATO? Membership in a defense alliance may make the small state feel more secure, but maintenance of the pact is problematic. In particular, the credibility of each member's promise to mutual defense is suspect. If this commitment problem remains unresolved, alliance members might be tempted to shirk on their responsibilities to defend one another, believing that others might do the same to them.

---

[12] See McKay (2004), particularly pp. 170–5, for a qualification of Riker's theory.

Defense alliances have often proved disappointing because of their inherent collective action dilemma, but federalism does not automatically eliminate vulnerability. While confederations generally increase the dimensionality of the joint policy space over defense alliances, and federations are usually even higher dimensional policy relationships than confederations, it is not the policy entanglement that makes the bond more secure.[13] A poorly designed federation is no more stable than an ill-conceived defense pact. When the federation works—when its potential is reached because member governments comply with the distribution of authority—then the additional policy domains may sweeten the pot by rewarding costly commitments of mutual defense.

Economic Growth

The federation's potential advantages over a unitary state or the completely decentralized state extend along a number of economic dimensions, all related to growth: efficiency, innovation, intergovernmental competition, externalities management, and market preservation. The design prescriptions are more ambiguous with economic benefits than they are with military security (and political representation grows even more controversial). The theory often proposes mixed solutions, where the central government is needed to carry out part of the policy program and the state governments another.

Efficiency. Theories of economic efficiency—the optimal allocation of taxing and spending authority, often to spur growth—are typical in offering mixed prescriptions, weighing the centralization's advantages in returns to scale against the demands of district diversity.[14] To understand why the prescriptions are mixed, we will begin by simplifying the problem of authority allocation. Imagine a population of citizens with identical preferences: everyone wants the government to do exactly the same thing, provided at exactly the same level. Governments require money to operate, so intuitively, it may seem optimal to make a single government responsible for collecting all revenues and managing all resources. But even this society of clones might prefer decentralization.[15]

---

[13] See Rector (2005) for a related argument.
[14] The mature field of fiscal federalism is excellently summarized in Inman and Rubinfeld (1996), Musgrave (1997), and Oates (1999).
[15] This literature often does not distinguish between federalism and decentralization, and sometimes uses the word "federalism" when what is meant is "decentralization."

Decentralization can take advantage of informational asymmetries; that is, lower levels of government may have local knowledge that allows them to tax and spend most efficiently (Oates 1993, Mueller 1996:77–83). The classic example of this informational asymmetry is the property tax; local governments have a keener sense of market value and can more appropriately devise a formula to calculate tax rates than a central government. Decentralization can also allow for revenue specialization based on different characteristics of the regions. A region especially endowed in natural resources with extensive mining operations might best rely on severance taxes, while in another, tourism offers opportunities for licenses and user fees. If we restore preference diversity to our society, and assume that there is some clustering of desires, then it is easy to see why we might want to decentralize policy making.

Peterson (1995) offers an intuitively appealing guide to authority distribution based on a policy's function: developmental or redistributive. Developmental projects are most efficiently handled by the local governments who know local needs and conditions, while higher levels of government are necessary to coordinate redistribution effectively. Unfortunately, many policy domains are both developmental and redistributive. Consider K-12 education: in the United States, local governments have traditional responsibility for raising funds to pay for schools. The inadequacy of funding potential in many school districts created an educational inequity intolerable for many voters. To insure adequate funding, redistribution from wealthy to poor school districts is required. In many states, financing has shifted to the state, either as a purposeful act of the voters (e.g., Michigan's Proposal A of 1994) or as a consequence of other local tax limitation initiatives (e.g., California's Proposition 13 of 1978).

Redistribution also does not fit a straightforward heuristic. The public often disagrees sharply about the structure and extent of many redistributive programs, and local differences in resources may also exist. This diversity, if clustered regionally, may suggest decentralization of the policy domain.[16] But most welfare programs are endangered when decentralization is coupled with a mobile population and income inequities between subunits. For example, China has devolved significant economic policy to the local and regional governments with apparent success in efficiency

---

[16] In the United States, the current welfare-to-work incentives under the federal legislation Temporary Aid to Needy Families (TANF) is an example of a redistributive policy that is arguably best handled locally, or at least at the state level, rather than federally.

and productivity (e.g., Montinola et al. 1995, Qian and Roland 1998).[17] However, China has also devolved responsibility for redistributive policies (Park et al. 1996, Zhang 1999, Saich 2002). This move flouts Peterson's logic and begs the question: is China's welfare state sustainable, particularly as the population becomes more mobile? One might ask the same question about the European Union, which also maintains decentralized welfare programs.

These analytical challenges complicate the recommendation about authority assignment. Nevertheless, economic recommendations about federalism's boundaries are specific, derived from careful analysis. The federation's advantages—reaping economies of scale, minimizing costs, and promoting general welfare—can only be met if the distribution of authority is heeded.

Innovation. In 1932, the U.S. Supreme Court agreed to consider the constitutionality of an Oklahoma statute that regulated ice plants as a public utility. In a time without refrigeration, all justices agreed that ice production was vital to human life, as essential as meat and potatoes.[18] But while the majority argued that it made as little sense to declare ice to be a public utility as it would cattle ranching, Justices Brandeis and Stone had a different perspective. Recent technological innovations had fundamentally altered the production of ice and this had implications for potential imbalances in production and consumption. Without aggressive regulation this could lead to inconsistent employment, an odious possibility during the Great Depression. Expressing great faith in the social sciences, in dissent Justice Brandeis argued that new circumstances may make old policy obsolete. The court should not stand in the way of societal progress. His dissent famously concludes:

There must be power in the States and the Nation to remould, through experimentation, our economic practices and institutions to meet changing social and economic needs. ... It is one of the happy incidents of the federal system that a single courageous State may, if its citizens choose, serve as a laboratory; and try novel social and economic experiments without risk to the rest of the country.[19]

---

[17] On the other hand, China appears to be following a typical path of industrialized economies, with a growing inequality between rural and urban areas.

[18] The majority opinion acknowledged that "ice is a family necessity. So are meat, bread, sugar, coffee, tea, and potatoes." *New State Ice Co.* v. *Liebmann*, 285 U.S. 262, 52 S.Ct. 371, 76 L.Ed. 747 (1932).

[19] Judge Louis Brandeis, dissent in *New State Ice Co.* v. *Liebmann*, 285 U.S. 262, 52 S.Ct. 371, 76 L.Ed. 747 (1932).

Social science works in largely "uncharted seas"[20]: Judge Brandeis championed the states' role as policy laboratories to discover the effect of new policy in response to the evolving technology of the manufacture of ice, and his logic grows more relevant as the governing environment becomes more complex.

Despite the intuitive attractiveness of policy experimentation, we want to attach some conditions on the recommendation to decentralize. Decentralization benefits policy development by stimulating innovation and containing damage, but state experimentation is not a prescription to be applied to every circumstance. The benefit of experimentation will depend on the similarity of states' goals as well as the differences in the policies they try (Volden 2003). If policy is decentralized but all states try the same policy, the benefits are lost. If states try different policies but have different goals, transferrable lessons are limited. When states share goals but try different policies, the potential for policy decentralization to stimulate beneficial innovation is maximized.

Brandeis raises a second advantage of decentralized policies: it reduces scope of policy gone awry. Writing in the midst of the depression, Brandeis certainly did not need to remind anyone of the cost of government failure. It is cheaper—to the total society—to fail in one state than to fail in the whole nation. Consider California's energy crisis of 2000–2001. The wave of planned "rolling blackouts" could be traced back to the 1996 deregulation of the state's energy market and ensuing speculation on energy futures, and inefficient generation of energy supplies.[21] President Bill Clinton and his energy secretary Bill Richardson ordered other western states to sell energy to California, a temporary patch while California could work to repair the legislative cause of the problem. Contrast this pointed national intervention against a general reluctance to bail out all states during their fiscal crisis of 2002–2004, including California Governor Schwarzenegger's appeal for national government assistance based on the imbalance between what Californians pay in federal income tax

---

[20] The phrasing is from Brandeis' dissent *in New State Ice Co.*

[21] California's legislation was implemented to correct an earlier problem: in the early 1990s, Californians were paying nearly 50% more for energy than residents of other states. Deregulation passed without opposition in the hopes that an open market might engage the benefits of price competition. But by engaging market forces, the legislation also created a disincentive for firms to build new power plants. Since energy cannot be easily stored, private firms had little incentive to invest in power generation that would only be tapped during periods of unusually high demand, since at other times the plants would not be needed.

and what the federal government returns to the state in spending. In the first case, the national government responded to cover the consequences of a failed policy experiment (while limiting its response and admonishing California to fix its flawed laws); in the second case, general state government fiscal struggles without a specific source are not covered.

When the national government's policy is ineffective, decentralization can be a useful source of new ideas. Oates (1999:1132) cites examples of U.S. federal policies that started at the state level but percolated up, including unemployment insurance and market approaches to environmental regulation. Current state experiments in health-care coverage may provide inspiration for federal policy. Concurring with Volden (1997), Oates suggests that this may be the primary justification for the American experiment in welfare decentralization that began with the 1996 Personal Responsibility and Work Opportunity Reconciliation Act, which put much more control in the hands of state governments to determine eligibility for welfare as well as benefit levels.[22]

Kollman et al. (2000) add a third criterion: problem *difficulty*. They isolate the importance of the search process—experimentation—by focussing attention on a world where the states have similar goals but some problems are more complicated than others. Straightforward problems require little experimentation to solve. As the problem becomes more difficult, experimentation becomes more useful, to a point. For the most difficult problems, the relative sophistication of the search process—one might think of this as the rigor of the research arm available—outweighs the importance of independent experiments. If we assume that a national government, with its much greater budget and research infrastructure, is more capable of basic research than state or local governments, then as problems become quite difficult, centralization of policy is preferable to decentralization. This relationship is captured in Figure 2.1. Complicated problems have many interacting variables: decentralization's advantages may be outweighed by the cost of reduced research capacity.[23]

---

[22] The legislation also altered the fiscal mechanics of the program by shifting from matching funds to block grants, motivated states to reduce spending on welfare. Innovation was encouraged because the states could reap most of the benefits of cost efficiency: AFDC was a matching grant program, where the national government provided 50% to 65% of each dollar spent (depending on the state's wealth); under TANF, the national government allocated a block grant to each state. Any marginal increase or decrease in spending was kept entirely by the state. Under a matching grant program, states would save as little as 35 cents of each dollar cut; under the block grant, they save it all.

[23] Multiple searches may add to the problem's complexity as state policies generate externalities.

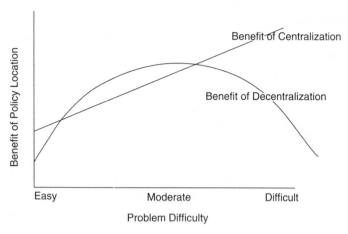

Figure 2.1. The Trade-Off between Centralization and Decentralization (Adapted from Kollman et al. 2000:123)

Naturally implied by these three conditions is a fourth: knowledge diffusion.[24] When policy is decentralized, before a new idea can take hold elsewhere, other states must hear of it. Patterns of information flow may correspond to policy needs: neighboring states are more likely to hear of one another's policy successes, and also to share policy problems.

If the exchange of information is facilitated by proximity, then federalism may be counterproductive to governmentally-spurred research because it encourages state-oriented pork practices, where federal research dollars are spread across the states. With a different organizational structure, independent laboratories could be built near one another and where it makes most sense, given preexisting infrastructure, researchers, and complementary research. However, a contradictory hypothesis also resonates intuitively: perhaps federalism *improves* research productivity by introducing geographical barriers. Proximity might decrease independence. When laboratories share ideas, one might copy too much from one another at just the wrong moment, dampening its own creative potential. To the extent that research progress requires independence, interstate competition could be beneficial because it tends to disperse the laboratories. To the extent that this problem and solution are real, we see the benefits of Congressional oversight of research agencies, where a norm of

---

[24] The roots of the current policy diffusion literature are found in Walker (1969) and Gray (1973).

pork sharing tends to spread out national investments.[25] Congress spreads research dollars for purely distributive political reasons, not because it has developed a model of the optimal independence of research, but innovation may be a positive side effect of pork.

There is a second way that the timing of policy diffusion affects innovation. Innovation often requires upfront investment of significant fixed costs. Decentralization only increases the weight of the costs by diluting the net benefits. States may enter collective-action paralysis, waiting for one another to innovate (Strumpf 2002). Unfortunately, breaking the stalemate may be even worse. Given the costs of innovation and the uncertainty of improvement to the policy, the states that most want change are most likely to innovate. But they are also the most likely to be preference extremists. If the outliers are the innovators, then the projected benefits of decentralization are limited. Decentralization may even decrease overall utility when policy innovations have externalities that spill across its borders. Decentralization does not produce innocuous experimentation; it is not "without risk to the rest of the country," as Brandeis argued. Brandeis's "courageous" state may be an opportunist, and even in effect set policy for the rest of the country.[26]

It is evident that authority assignment designed to optimize innovation cannot be reduced to a simple calculus. But one can see that the distribution matters; in optimizing the governmental role in innovation (in public policy as well as publicly funded private research), we do not want to make a blanket recommendation to decentralize. We can treat the location of authority as a tool to optimize innovation, and we will want to design that distribution of authority carefully, mindful of the variables

---

[25] Although I know of no formal requirements, nor have I seen any controlled study, grant proposers have shared anecdotal evidence supporting the inclusion of research collaborators from universities in other states to improve the likelihood of success in acquiring national government funding. Due to fiscal considerations including a hard budget constraint, states are less likely to fund basic research, although they do make investments in research with more immediate applications. A prominent counterexample is the recent initiative in several states to fund stem cell research, which has a side benefit of spurring economic development in the communities hosting the research laboratories.

[26] Innovations in environmental regulation are a prime example. In the United States, California, a preference outlier, has tended to be the major innovator in a variety of areas, most notably fuel emissions standards. Its strict standards, coupled with its market dominance, has made consumers in other states subject to the will of the median Californian.

that affect innovation. Clearly, intergovernmental competition and externalities are important to the analysis. We turn to these topics in the next two sections.

Intergovernmental Competition. Governments compete with one another to the benefit of their citizens, eliminating waste and encouraging growth. Taking the theory of the firm to government, Tiebout (1956) described consumer-voters who shop around for favorable governmental policies, voting with their feet by moving to communities that suit their tastes. The savvy voter generates two benefits: diversification and efficiency in service provision. First, governments diversify their services to attract clusters of like-minded voters into their community. In the classic Tiebout example, some local governments will boost their school quality, hoping to attract families. Other examples abound of city services targeting particular categories of citizens, from taxi service for seniors to attract older residents to comprehensive curbside recycling for the environmentally minded. Some blur into economic development programs: intracity busing or low-cost parking, city beautification projects, and police patrol on foot, bike, or horseback. Larger governments compete with one another as well, setting tax rates and development plans with one eye on their neighbor's policies. Intergovernmental competition for residents leads to specialization and diversification in public good provision from one community to another, similar to the diversity found in an open market. Competition for capital leads to optimal growth policies, outperforming the unitary system without such competition (Hatfield 2007).

Tiebout imports a second principle of consumer theory to government: the pressure to provide services efficiently, similar to price competition. Efficiency is enhanced as governments streamline the translation of tax revenue into service provision. This efficiency differs from the one we discussed above, where governments could be assigned revenue and expenditure responsibilities based on inherent capacity; here, we are interested in the interaction between governments as they compete for voters, and this competition, like a market with many sellers, encourages governments to pare down their costs. When local governments are like firms in a competitive market, voters shop around for the best fit at the best price.

We might ask why states do not distinguish themselves as broadly as local governments. The answer has a lot to do with mobility. Just as market efficiency depends on a lack of transaction costs, with intergovernmental competition, citizens can only vote with their feet if they are able to move, or find the move worthwhile. It is relatively easy for a family to move 10 miles to relocate in a community with better schools, but a move from one state to another is of a different order, unless it is within the same metropolitan area (e.g., the boundaries of "Chicagoland" include communities in Illinois, Indiana, and even Wisconsin).

There is a second reason for more fierce competition between localities than states. While the market mechanism spurs both diversification and efficiency, these two dynamics are somewhat at odds: the more heterogeneous the population, the more the governments will compete on diversity; the more homogeneous the population, the more the governments compete on efficiency grounds, because voters select their communities based not on a menu of services, but instead based on price. The stuff that distinguishes voter preferences—desire for dog parks and recycling programs—has marginal effects on a voter's overall satisfaction with a government; for most people, to walk a dog off-leash, although one of the finer pleasures of daily life, just is not worth the cost of moving great distances. However, most voters would rather pay less tax than more, especially for the same services. The less a government can target segments of the population, the more it will compete on price.

At the statewide level, the high cost of household interstate movement drowns out the marginal improvement to voters of moving even to satisfy major desires. Many of California's public schools have declined in quality since the passage of Proposition 13 in 1978, but instead of moving out of state, wealthy parents send their children to religious or private schools. In areas where we do see state policy diversification—banking rules and higher education subsidies come to mind—we do have highly mobile populations: investors (i.e., their money) and college students.[27] Therefore, the Tiebout principle is about both efficiency and representation; as long as the voters are sufficiently mobile, then by employing the market mechanism, decentralization encourages beneficial diversity and reduces waste and corruption.

The benefit of intergovernmental competition hypothesized by Tiebout is one of the linchpins of fiscal federalism, but a solid case can be made against decentralization of economic policy on the basis that interstate competition can be counterproductive. In their competitive zeal states

---

[27] Note that this analysis is U.S.-centric, where states compete with one another to attract residents: it focuses on a fairly uniform distribution of population diversity. In federations with distinct regional identities, we would expect to see state government diversification not to attract residents but to satisfy their existing ones. We will discuss this further below, in the section on representation.

may give away too much. To attract firms, states (often in conjunction with local governments) will offer incentives such as low-interest loans, tax credits, a variety of regulatory exemptions, and workforce training. They also engage in policies that are not targeted at a specific firm, or industry, but are designed to make the state more attractive to a variety of investors. These policies include right-to-work laws, looser environmental standards, and infrastructure and education investments. In the past two decades, locational incentives have skyrocketed when measured as price per job. A classic example is Alabama's successful bid for a Mercedes plant in 1993. The state granted Mercedes $253 million in concessions for a promised 1,500 jobs, or $169,000 a job.[28] One might point to the net increase in jobs nationally to justify this cost, but not all interstate competition can claim this benefit. For example, Chicago paid $63 million to lure the Boeing headquarters away from Seattle.[29] Unlike the Mercedes case, which created new jobs and opened new plants, the Boeing deal was a straight transfer of Boeing executives, who all had to move from Washington to Illinois. While Chicago gained 500 jobs, at a cost of $126,000 per job (less than the Alabama price tag), the Boeing Headquarters competition is a net loss nationally, with no new jobs created and fewer government revenues.

Such spectacular per-job costs have spurred some economists to suggest that interstate economic competition generates a winner's curse as well as a net loss to the federation. When states offer tax reductions and other incentives to attract firms, they sacrifice known revenue sources for the uncertainty of economic spillovers.[30] Some object to these tax abatement incentives altogether, arguing that firms should not receive special treatment at the taxpayers' expense. But there is sound logic to "paying" a firm more than its direct costs to locate in an area. When a firm moves in, the local or state economy hopes that the firm will attract other related

---

[28] While at the time Alabama was criticized for capitulating to corporate demands, it looks as though the investment has paid off by creating a "southern Motown." Despite these gains, Alabama's economy still suffers, and it remains at the bottom of many national rankings of state performance, such as health care and education.

[29] The package included $41 million in state tax credits, including 10 years of income tax grants for Boeing's employees, $20 million in job training, technology, and capital improvements, and $2 million in improvements to hangars at Midway airport (Saiz and Clark 2004:430).

[30] Calculating the positive/negative externality ration is extremely complicated and governments are likely to misestimate. Academic research suggests a small but statistically significant positive effect from locational incentives on a county's economy (Greenstone and Moretti 2003).

firms, or have other positive effects. These benefits to the community are not included in the firm's calculation; from a perspective of making the location decision that benefits society most, we would want the firm to *internalize* these benefits in its locational calculus. The most straightforward way to do this is to provide locational incentives in excess of what it costs the firm to move to (or stay in) the area.

Political considerations may exacerbate overbidding. States that enter into competition with one another find it politically costly to lose the competition. Electoral incentives may spur a politician to ignore sunk costs: once they enter the race, they must compete to win because of the demoralizing effect of losing. Finite terms further distort their perspective, causing them to favor quick gains over long-term investments. When revenues are sacrificed, corresponding cuts must be made in expenditures, perhaps leading to an underprovision of other public services.[31]

Given how detrimental interstate competition may be to a state's citizens, naturally many have called for national intervention to end the self-destructive rat race. The phenomenon has resulted in calls for the judiciary to "save the states from themselves" (Enrich 1996), and for congressional regulation of the "economic war among the states" (Burstein and Rolnick 1995). Ironically, these analyses suggest that the best way to allow market forces to prevail is through national regulation, by preventing the interstate competition that may tend to overvalue firm presence. As Burstein and Rolnick argue, when states exhaust their resources competing for a single firm they are unable to attract other firms, thereby leading to a dispersal of firms and preventing the accrual of the positive externalities of industrial clusters. The Enrich and the Burstein and Rolnick arguments boil down to essentially the same recommendation: the national government, empowered constitutionally through the commerce clause to regulate interstate trade, should stop the state practice of locational incentives because it endangers the prosperity of the union.[32]

There may be a silver lining as we aggregate from state prosperity to national prosperity that contradicts calls to limit interstate competition. When states overcompete, while the "winning" state's citizens may suffer, the national economy could benefit. In countries with high per-capita incomes and relatively low unemployment, a state's stiffest competition

---

[31] However, Oates (1999:1135–6) reports that the evidence of public sector underprovision due to locational incentives is not prevalent.

[32] A very important question is raised by this discussion: What institution should regulate? Who should determine the extent of the national government's reach into interstate commerce—Congress or the Court?

is not domestic, but global, with the nation-states that have cheaper labor. As states compete with one another, the overall cost of doing business in the federation falls, possibly below what a centralized government could justify politically. The miscalculated exuberance of one state could bolster the economy of the nation.

Externalities Management. States do not automatically take into account the effect that their policy has on the citizens of another state. Policy effects spill across borders, sometimes harming and sometimes helping the people living in neighboring states. Industrial policy that encourages factories near borders with little environmental control harms all downwind, while a state that builds a new airport near a border provides easier access to another state's residents.

The spillover effects of policies are known as *externalities* because they are consequences of a government's policy that the government does not consider—they are external to its calculus. Much of public economics is devoted to devising mechanisms to "internalize" the externalities. Both kinds of externalities are problematic to the decentralized state: policies with negative externalities are implemented too often for society, and those with positive externalities are less likely to be provided than society would want.

The distribution of authority can be adjusted to manage these externalities. The central goverment can be given full control of a policy domain, it can regulate it, or it can encourage beneficial behavior. For example, in most federations the central government maintains a common market between states by prohibiting state-led industry protection that generates negative externalities. In environmental policy, a government has two primary approaches to regulation: setting standards (what is sometimes referred to as "command and control") and employing market mechanisms (e.g., "cap and trade"). Both incentivize pollution control; the first, through sanctions should the polluter fail to reduce output, and the second, by pricing pollution, to motivate polluters to reduce their output without the threat of penalties.

Environmental regulation in the United States is an excellent example of a transformation in policy that shifted across levels of government and across regulatory schemas: three decades ago, environmental policy was centralized in response to the apparent insufficiency of the states' efforts. It was clear that the problem of externalities—pollution flows across state borders—was too much for the states to manage on their own. While no state legislature wanted pollution, they had to weigh the benefits of clean air against the needs of their state economy. By reducing environmental standards, states could attract and retain industries seeking lower cost manufacturing environments. This competitiveness led to problems beyond inefficient standards: other states suffered doubly, first by losing out on the competition, and secondly, by the cross-border pollution effects. Through legislation including the Clean Air Act (1970) and the Clean Water Act (1972), and the establishment of the Environmental Protection Agency (1970) to aid monitoring (and therefore compliance), the national government enacted a series of laws designed to overcome the inefficiencies of federalism by setting national standards on pollution emissions, something that the states had not been able to achieve uniformly on their own. The national government is currently transitioning some of its environmental regulation from set prescriptions to a market-based approach called "cap and trade," where firms can sell pollution permits. Positive externalities generated by self-induced pollution control measures are priced. This system might allow a return to decentralized regulation as long as the market crosses state lines. Policy innovation opens new possibilities in the optimal division of authority.

Welfare provision is another policy domain with externalities. Decentralization of welfare is controversial because of the fear of a "race to the bottom" in welfare provision. Externalities, generated by mobility, trigger the race. The logic works as follows: a state sets welfare levels according to the preferences of its voters, the needs of its citizens, and within the constraints of its budget. But the neighboring state establishes a less generous policy, perhaps because its voters are less interested in care for the poor, or perhaps because it simply cannot afford to do more. A subset of the population in the neighboring state regularly come up short in their weekly budgeting, and some of them will hear about the better deal next door and choose to move. Demand for welfare benefits increases in the more generous state, while the supply of tax dollars to pay for it stays constant. Or not. In fact, some of those paying into the system may become frustrated with their state's generosity, or its priorities overall, and move out. As long as that state's welfare benefits remain more generous it will be a "welfare magnet," attracting the poor and perhaps repelling the wealthy.[33] As each undercuts the other, the race to the bottom is on.

---

[33] Volden (1997, 2002) argues that the evidence is more optimistic than some fear: people do not tend to move for better welfare benefits. But Peterson (1995) argues

Positive externalities can also detract from policy decentralization. In the language of economics, governments tend to *underprovide* policies that generate positive externalities because they do not consider the broader impact to society when weighing their costs and benefits. A national government can encourage positive externalities through aid or induce them through regulation. Sometimes national governments fail to intervene when it would be helpful. We see this problem with infrastructure development and maintenance. While he was president, James Madison consistently vetoed public works projects, justifying his rejection by arguing that these are essentially local affairs. As a consequence of the national government's early noninterventionist stance, the United States has little in the way of a national infrastructure plan.[34] However, with the expansion of the domestic markets, as well as the growth of trade worldwide, movement of people and goods has become increasingly important for the economy. Quality roads and railways built and maintained by state and local governments generate positive externalities that the states do not take into account when determining their budget priorities.

Externalities limit the efficiency of decentralization; they constrain local or state governments' abilities to be effective in redistribution or regulation. There do seem to be a few rules: centralize to manage negative externalities; centralize if you need to encourage positive externalities, decentralize otherwise. Oates' Decentralization Theorem captures this

that the mere perception of movement could create political demands to reduce benefits. Besley and Case (1995) note that "yardstick" comparisons of leaders may provide the same force as mobility. On the other hand, while a fully federalized policy can overcome the problems of externalities, its efforts to reduce poverty have stalled since the advances of the Great Society programs. With decentralization, there is hope that somehow the states, acting as policy laboratories, will discover a program that is more efficient than what the national government could generate.

[34] Although the U.S. national government heavily subsidized development of the rail system by giving incentives to the railroads, including free land, the government is now out of the business of promoting passenger rail. The national highway transportation system emerged from Cold-War concerns for national defense, not efficiency in infrastructure design. While national cost sharing is available for the construction of new highways, or major reconstruction and expansion projects, most maintenance comes from state and local funds. Cash-strapped state and local governments tend to defer maintenance; unless the potholes are breaking suspensions, road deterioration does not attract the same attention as crime or unemployment.

notion exactly:

> In the absence of cost savings from the centralized provision of a [local public] good and of interjurisdictional externalities, the level of welfare will always be at least as high (and typically higher) if Pareto-efficient levels of consumption are provided in each jurisdiction than if *any* single, uniform level of consumption is maintained across all jurisdictions (Oates 1972:54).

Advances in the three decades since this theorem was first phrased have taught us just how important it is to be mindful of the conditions sprinkled throughout the theorem: cost savings, externalities, efficient policy design (and implied responsiveness to local demands). In the absence of externalities, decentralization is better for the citizens as a whole. From this discussion, we see that externalities often complicate the application of the theorem. It is clear that economic efficiency requires flexibility, multiple levels of government, and a process that will assign and maintain the distribution of authority between those levels, mindful of the complexity raised by externalities.

Market Preservation. An open economy—or common market—is a goal of most contemporary federal unions, despite its hazards. A market requires firmly established and credibly defended property rights. Uniform governmental regulation can establish rules governing property ownership and transfer, as well as provide a forum to adjudicate disputes. But centralized regulation introduces a second-order problem: how to prevent the government from stealing from its citizens. In this section we examine the market-preserving federalism literature, which argues that decentralization and fragmented authority enable a state to credibly commit not to expropriate all rents, when coupled with other conditions, such as a decentralization of fiscal control and hard budget constraints (Weingast 1995, Parikh and Weingast 1997, Qian and Weingast 1997, Rodden and Rose-Ackerman 1997, Rubinfeld 1997, Qian and Roland 1998, Rodden and Wibbels 2002).

Economic gains may be pursued in one of two ways: by stealing or by trade. Bandits arise in the world without constitutions, where collective action problems make coordinated resistance practically infeasible. Without secure property rights, people have little incentive to produce anything worth stealing, and the economic society remains at subsistence levels. A constitution can create a central institution, or government, that will coordinate a common understanding of property rights and organize their defense (Hardin 1989). Goods may be traded meaningfully as ownership can be transferred through voluntary exchange, without fear of plunder.

Governmental regulatory power introduces a hazard: the state strong enough to prevent us from stealing from one another is strong enough to steal from us. Even the stationary bandit cannot resist the "grasping hand" and takes all surplus wealth from his citizens, reducing their incentive to produce (Olson 1993). To overcome this problem, federal systems may be useful as a "market-preserver," subject to several conditions laid out by Weingast (1995): (1) subnational governments with primary responsibility over the economy, (2) a common market assured through the national government, so that the states do not erect trade barriers, and (3) the states face a hard budget constraint with no potential for national bailout.[35] We need to add to this list the critical ingredient of citizen mobility between states. With an arrangment meeting these conditions, the central government establishes the property rights and market, but the states bear primary responsibility for any intervention, including taxation. States are put into competition with one another for citizens and capital. They will no longer tax more than necessary to satisfy local demands for fear that Tiebout-empowered citizens will pack up and move to greener pastures. By enabling intergovernmental competition, federalism may solve the problem of the state that steals from its citizens.

Market-preserving federalism leaves open one problem. It defines a strict division of authority, where the states set economic policy and the national government guarantees property rights. But what prevents the national government from encroaching upon the states' authorities? It is a return to the original problem, the threat of opportunism from the center, this time "stealing" from the states, rather than the citizens. We now have a higher level transgression game, where the states are put in the position of defending one another against federal opportunism. A remedy must solve two problems: agreeing on the definition of a transgression, and coordinating to punish. In Weingast's model, the first problem, agreeing on a definition, is established through the constitution, or some regular practice when no constitution exists. (In fact, two of the three cases that Weingast discusses do not have a written federal constitution: England and China.) The second problem, punishment coordination, involves a transformation in citizen perception, a development of sympathy. Citizens

---

[35] See Inman (2001) for a list of institutional subconditions necessary to support this condition, including responsive and well-informed capital markets and an independent judiciary.

must see any transgression, regardless of target or personal gain, as equally bad. When the citizens do, they can coordinate to punish central government transgression, maintaining the balanced federalism that maximizes a nation's growth potential.

Market-preserving federalism is one of the clearest examples of a potential benefit of federalism that mere decentralization cannot offer. It also underscores the importance of adherence to the distribution of authority. This book focuses on the design of a system of safeguards to prevent central government encroachment, and uphold the distribution of authority more generally. In Weingast's models, the people—what we will call popular safeguards—defend federalism's boundaries. This book develops a theory of how combinations of institutional safeguards complement citizen-initiated sanctions.

Effective Representation

We turn now to the relationship between federalism and representation, a set of arguments that lie almost entirely distinct (with exceptions noted below) from the economics literature. I have divided the discussion into five parts: political participation, satisfaction of diversity, improved accountability, defense against tyranny, and higher-quality representatives.

Political Participation. Effective democracy depends on citizen participation. As more people become enfranchised or enter the political arena, a wider variety of perspectives contribute to public deliberation. As diversity increases, all else equal, collective decision making improves (Page 2007). This diversity often takes the form of dissent, a cornerstone of the democratic process (Sunstein 2003). If democratic outcomes improve as more people participate—from a representational perspective and perhaps even in mustering collective wisdom—then if we could design a political system that increased participation it would improve citizen welfare. Federalism is widely touted as better than a unitary system at encouraging electoral participation (Inman and Rubinfeld 1997a, 2000, Borck 2002) by relying on the straightforward logic of the pivotal voter: with decentralization comes smaller populations in each district, and with smaller populations, any one voter is more likely to be decisive. All else equal, people are more likely to vote the more their vote matters.

But with federalism all else is *not* equal: generally, the power of the national government continues to dominate the subnational governments, despite decentralization. Participation increases with the stakes; setting aside the addition of expressive, noninstrumental considerations, the basic calculus of voting is a calculation of expected utility where the probability of being pivotal is multiplied by the benefit to the voter of a different outcome minus the cost of voting. Higher stakes in national elections may cancel out a low likelihood of being pivotal.[36] This factor may be sufficient to explain the contradictory turnout evidence, where in general voting rates in national elections are significantly higher than in local elections.[37] Other explanations of the gap between the theoretical prediction and the empirical evidence include voter fatigue—local elections are often scheduled more frequently than national ones—and lower mobilization with local elections, with less media involvement and less party activism, lowering the cues available to voters to make informed decisions. The lesson is clear: distribution of authority to the states must be preserved to keep the electoral stakes high enough to encourage participation. Federalism may boost participation not because it adds small-scale elections, but because the robust federation adds small-scale elections that *matter*.

Managing and Satisfying Diversity. "As long as the reason of man continues fallible, and he is at liberty to exercise it, different opinions will be formed," writes Madison in *Federalist* 10. Socioeconomic equity does not eliminate diverse opinions; they are inherent to humanity, whether from the logical errors that Madison mentions, or different histories, or different ways of viewing the world. We cannot eliminate diversity—whether born of social differences or just different opinions—nor would we want to. Diversity is beneficial when states serve as policy laboratories. Diverse perspectives and desires may lead to new ideas, solutions that can be transported to other domains and territories.[38] Federalism may help us to manage diversity's detrimental effects so we can harness its benefits.

Federalism eliminates the need for a one-size-fits-all policy. Governmental competition for Tiebout's mobile voter brings more than efficiency: the competition diversifies the menu of services that governments provide. Just as market forces have not reduced us to a single choice of breakfast cereal, but instead the options fill a grocery aisle,

---

[36] High stakes may also boost satisfaction under the expressive theory of voting, just as viewership is much higher for the Superbowl than regular season play.

[37] For example, Morlan (1984:462) reports a 10% to 15% turnout gap between municipal and national elections in West Germany and a 29% difference in the United States.

[38] See also Page (2007).

intergovernmental competition will lead to diversification. Citizens can "sort" into havens of like-minded communities. With decentralization, residency becomes a matching problem; citizens select a community based on how closely it matches their own desires and priorities, be they good elementary schools, a new fitness facility, a thriving urban center, or bare-bones services with the lowest tax rate.

Decentralization may also create more services over all (Cooter 2000, Borck 2002, Bueno de Mesquita et al. 2003, Persson and Tabellini 2003). Many public goods are "congestable"—that is, they are subject to crowding, where their benefit declines with the number who use it. A pleasant stroll along a riverside path, where one might happily say hello to the occasional fellow traveler, becomes stressful when it seems that the whole city has had the same inspiration, never mind when one is elbowed by streams of joggers or mowed down by mountain bikers. Efficient provision of local public goods requires sensitivity to local desires and conditions. Local public officials are more likely to possess information to make appealing choices, as well as to be held accountable for providing the goods in sufficient quantities that congestion does not become a problem (Hayek 1939).[39] A national official holds neither advantage and the goods are likely to be underprovided. Empirical analysis by Bueno de Mesquita et al. (2003:207–8) confirm their hypotheses that large-population republics do not provide as many public goods, including civil liberties, education, and health care.[40] Federalism minimizes the depressing effect of population by empowering smaller governments to provide these goods.

When national legislators represent particular districts, there is a potential for overprovision. Pork, or public goods targeted to defined jurisdictions, goes up as the marginal cost of provision declines (Weingast et al. 1981), an endemic effect of the U.S. Congress (e.g., Ferejohn 1974). Rather than contradict the theory and evidence that federalism increases social spending, pork is the exception that proves the rule: Congressmen have the local information and local accountability to increase public

---

[39] Folding together participation and public good provision, Lindert (1996) and Mueller and Stratmann (2003) find a positive correlation between voter participation rates and social spending, particularly redistribution. If participation increases with decentralization, then their finding would provide further support for the present argument. Mueller and Stratmann also find that participation is negatively correlated with economic growth.

[40] Persson and Tabellini (2003:52) find a less clear correspondence between federalism and social welfare.

spending, without the strict budget constraint of local jurisdictions. To counter this inefficiency, Olson (1969) recommends a "principle of fiscal equivalence," where fiscal responsibility is borne by the beneficiaries. Federal subsidies to local jurisdictions are justifiable to the extent (and amount) of spillover of positive effects.

Tiebout invokes benign diversity: if Community A has twice-a-week trash pickup, apart from gravitational Tiebout forces, it has no effect on residents of Community B with once-a-week pickup. But some diversity creates clashes. Most significantly, identity diversity—racial and ethnic—can be tindersticks, ready to flare given a small excuse for conflict. Secession haunts the ethnically divided state. Territorial divisions create natural breaking lines for secessionist claims that might not be threatened otherwise.[41] Often secession attempts are met with militarized resistance and are the grounds for civil war.

Federalism is often promoted as a remedy to the problem of governing heterogeneous societies—dubbed "peace-preserving federalism," but with cautionary notes (Horowitz 1985, McGarry and O'Leary 1993, Linz and Stepan 1996, Stepan 1999, Bakke and Wibbels 2004, Gibson and Falleti 2004, Brancati 2006). Empirical support is mixed. Sometimes federalism, by entrenching decentralization, defuses conflictual time-bombs, but other examples show no effect, or even a negative influence of federalism when intergovernmental tensions are fueled by long-standing rivalries or, as Brancati (2006) finds, spurs creation of ethnically based parties. Despite the lack of statistical evidence, a fascinating collection of case studies written by specialists of territorial cleavages shows that in general federalism effectively manages conflict and accomodates territorially clustered minorities (Amoretti and Bermeo 2004).

Some scholars have begun to unpack the conditions most favorable to peace preservation. In reviewing the case studies mentioned above, Bermeo highlights the creation of "linkages," where central decision making incorporates ethnic or regional interests (Bermeo 2004:465-6), a structural safeguard that I describe in Chapter 4. Horowitz (1985) proposes crosscutting cleavages to diffuse tension between states as well as to give voice to subethnic groups. Hale (2005) invokes this tool to explain the balance in center-state power in the Russian Federation; in sharp contrast to the USSR, dominated by a single ethnic state, in splintered

---

[41] Religious secession is an exception, perhaps because religious doctrine often provides an alternative social code, justifying dissent from the existing rule of law.

Russia the Russian ethnicity does not threaten other ethnicities. Chandra (2005) dispels conventional wisdom that ethnic parties are necessarily bad for democracy. Ethnic parties can polarize society, thereby reducing the moderating effect of competition between parties. But as Chandra points out, this is true only if the parties are single issue. If their platforms are multidimensional—a characteristic that the state can encourage through other institutions—then voters will continue to shop around between parties, restoring competitive democracy. The principle is pure Tiebout.

Accountability. Representation and accountability go hand-in-hand: elected leaders are more likely to represent their constituents faithfully when they know they are held accountable for their actions. Accountability is impossible without transparent responsibility. Therefore, it is claimed that authority decentralization improves accountability because citizens are more likely to see the effects of government action at the local level and respond accordingly in the ballot box (Cross 2002, Frey and Stutzer 2004).[42]

If accountability depends on reliable information about responsibility, then it follows that the lines of responsibility be clear cut. In any decentralized system, true responsibility is often ambiguous. Voters may punish local politicians who are only fulfilling the central government's commands, as when the central government commandeers state and local governments. When a federal system cannot defend the boundaries of authority, it will not improve accountability. In essence, this was the U.S. Supreme Court's logic in the *New York* decision,[43] and it is the cause for concern in the increasing practice of attaching conditions on intergovernmental transfers in the United States.

Locational choice gives citizens a nonelectoral method of maintaining accountability, as they vote with their feet, Tiebout-style. Therefore if mobility is hindered, then accountability suffers. Legal obstacles to relocation stymie Tiebout forces, but so do apparently beneficial interventions, such as when state boundaries are traced around territorial clusters because citizens grow reluctant to leave their state. The benefits of federalism that depend on mobility cannot be fully realized. Here again we

---

[42] Cross's argument is more complex: he questions the extent to which federalism can be said to decentralize to the local level more than a unitary government. State governments absorb much authority decentralization in a federation, leaving less for local governments than in a unitary state. Therefore, Cross rejects the argument that federalism improves accountability because he rejects the premise that federalism decentralizes authority to local governments more than unitary governments.

[43] *New York* v. *United States*, 488 U.S. 1041 (1992).

see the advantage of Horowitz's advice: to combine the positive aspects of ethnic clustering with the benefits of mobility, break apart ethnic enclaves. That is, each significant ethnicity should not have only a single state to call home, but instead, several to choose between, to regain the mobility necessary to spur beneficial interstate competition. Accountability is augmented when citizens have feasible choices about where to live.

Anti-Tyranny and Rights. Federalism is often cited as an antidote to tyranny, but its effectiveness is less straightforward than its popularity would make one think.[44] A tyrant consolidates power, so intuitively the more obstacles to consolidation are mounted, the more difficult it will be for the tyrant to assume power. Federalism's inherent fragmentation is well-suited to block tyranny; when decision-making power is subdivided, the tyrant cannot easily gain full control. But how much should power be devolved—should the center be weak or strong?

Given the consolidated force of the tyrannical government, it is intuitive to believe that liberty is best protected by establishing a weak government and preventing it from ever becoming strong. Hamilton chides those who equate minimal government with liberty; when the government is not effective, it cannot prevent the emergence of the tyrant.

[I]t will be ... forgotten that the vigor of government is essential to the security of liberty .... [A] dangerous ambition more often lurks behind the specious mask of zeal for the rights of the people than under the forbidding appearance of zeal for the firmness and efficiency of government .... [O]f those men who have overturned the liberties of republics, the greatest number have begun their career by paying an obsequious court to the people; commencing demagogues, and ending tyrants. (Hamilton, *Federalist* 1)

---

[44] Two other dimensions to rights provision and protection bear mentioning: group rights and substantive rights. Group rights enable a subpopulation to express their common identity in ways meaningful to them, such as language, holidays, education, and incorporation of cultural symbols and priorities into governance. When subpopulations are geographically clustered, lines may be drawn to enable these subpopulations sufficient autonomy to pursue important cultural priorities. This advantage of federalism over a unitary organization we described above, in diversity management.

Evidence suggests that federalism is successful at combating tyranny: Buena de Mesquito et al. (2003) find that federal regimes have less corruption and provide more public goods, and Boix (2003) finds that under certain conditions, it makes democracy more secure. Whether this translates into provision of substantive rights, or the privileges that come from living in an organized state, is less clear: one might argue against common support for redistribution because of the political recognition of local identification may create a preferential bias against supporting citizens in another state.

Hamilton speculates that the tyrant more often cloaks himself in the language of the minimal government because it is undefended from his ambitions; the Weimar government is a classic example. A federation's firm, efficient, and self-limiting government provides a liberty robust to the challenges of a would-be tyrant.[45]

A federation's decentralization threatens rights it has the potential to protect. Riker ultimately condemns federalism for enabling racism: "[I]f in the United States one disapproves of racism, one should disapprove of federalism" (1964:155). While federalism is good at protecting and facilitating the representation of minorities who are regionally clustered, or who can relocate, Tiebout-style, it may be worse than a unitary government at protecting and organizing the interests of those who are distributed throughout the country because the organization must be reestablished in each state. And a states' rights philosophy can cause citizens who might otherwise want to protect rights or prevent racism to look the other way. Gibson (2004) and Mickey (2009) call this an authoritarian enclave. Federalism becomes a method of supporting tyranny within a democracy.[46]

One may also argue exactly the opposite, that new rights have greater likelihood of recognition in a federation. When expansion of rights conflicts with existing norms, the unconventionality of the rights may deflect any reasoned argument in favor of the new right. One state may be more prepared than others to challenge existing norms and experiment. Belief

---

[45] See Myerson (2006) for a formal analysis that supports this argument, and *Federalist* 9 for a similar argument about federalism as a better organization to counter domestic insurrection. The European Union met with initial resistance not because it was viewed as too strong, but too weak. A proposal rejected earlier, Pan-Europa, was suggested by aristocratic elites. And when Austria and Germany proposed a customs union in 1931, it stirred concerns about being the first step toward unification and the spread, rather than elimination, of fascism (Dinan 2004:3–4). It is not the federation that prevents tyranny; it is the well-balanced federation that does. Recently, the ability of federalism to counter tyranny has been tested in Russia.

    Drawing again on the theme of competing affections, Hayek (1939) makes a slightly different argument. Federalism better resists the tyrant because the nation's identity is fragmented by dividing the citizens into separate states. The tyrant cannot simultaneously woo all because federalism makes the establishment of common values difficult. See also Levy (2007).

[46] Again we might favor the strong over the weak center: with the latter the national leadership may enlist political support from regions by tolerating their antidemocratic or discriminatory practices. The strong center will not need to pander.

change is spurred by experience; in time, with the benefit of observing the first state's practices, other states may adopt the new right as well.

Higher Quality Representation. To Madison, federalism was a solution to a vexing problem: how to make representative democracy feasible. That is, he wanted an effective government (the energy Hamilton wrote about) that would not tyrannize the people. In his assessment of the deficiencies of the Articles of Confederation,[47] Madison dedicates Notes 9, 10, and 11 to the problems of representation. Particularly in Note 11—a precursor to *Federalist* 10—Madison describes the two types of representatives who tend to fill the state houses: inept sops and conniving opportunists. Their legislation was of such poor quality that it endangered future support for the democratic "experiment."

At first thought, Madison's solution—two levels of representative democracy—seems odd: if representation is of poor quality with just one level of government, then surely two levels would compound the problem. But the levels can work together, each insufficient, but when combined presenting a solution. Both centralization and decentralization are important for federalism to improve the quality of representatives. With two levels of government, people can gain experience with their local leaders. Accountability is easier at this level, so voters are more likely to make the right decisions about voting poorly performing politicians out of office while retaining better ones. They will promote only the best to higher levels of office (presuming political ambition drives upward). Also, the higher-level representatives are less likely to serve a single interest because the influence of factions are diluted when the constituent pool expands. Local elections may help a fledgling democracy take off: Ordeshook's (1995) work on Russian democracy emphasizes the interaction between levels of government, where a multiplicity of elections could give citizens experience with holding politicians accountable and promote a bottom-up development of political parties.[48]

Federalism is often criticized for biasing representation in favor of clustered minorities or low-density regions (e.g., Stepan 1999, Dahl 2002). To preserve state autonomy, sometimes states are allotted equal voice in

---

[47] James Madison, "Vices of the Political System of the United States," (April 1787) in Madison (1999:69–80).

[48] For further discussion, see Rakove (1996:218–25), Elazar (1987, esp. at 29), and Ostrom (1971, 1991).

one legislative chamber and often have power in other roles dispropor-
tionate to their population distribution (such as the U.S. electoral college
or the First Ministers' Conference in Canada). These accommodations
distort the equality principle of democracy by favoring the citizens of
small states over those living in larger constituencies. While the shorthand
identification of this problem is to disparage federalism in favor of a
unitary system, the criticism is not about federalism, but about the particular construction of the national legislature that usually accompanies
federalism.

Federalism's Engineering Problem

One theme repeats through all of the objectives: benefits depend on the
division of authority. The distribution is an instrument of public policy
that can be calibrated for social benefit. Designing federalism's boundaries
of authority is a problem in social science engineering.

Often the primary determinant of the distribution of authority is
not social science but politics. Many of the prescriptions are contradictory, requiring prioritization, and prioritization leads to politics. For any
one objective it is relatively straightforward to know whether to centralize or decentralize, or what mixed combination is needed. (For an
overview, see Table 2.2). But no federal union is unidimensional, and
when objectives are combined, some prescriptions conflict. Economic efficiency and political participation are often at odds,[49] and even military
security presents difficult constitutional choices when centralization of
force threatens states that prefer to maintain some independence. On the

---

[49] Size is limited by diversity, or the scope of conflicting demands (Bolton and Roland
1996, 1997, Alesina and Spolaore 1997, 2003, Alesina et al. 2000). Inman and
Rubinfeld (1997a,b, 2000) find that political participation increases with decentralization but that the benefits of decentralization to economic efficiency are not
monotonic. As a system initially moves away from unitary government, or completely centralized control of the economy, there are benefits, but at some middling
point, further decentralization of economic control starts to decrease economic efficiency, when negative externalities generated by local economic policy overwhelm
decentralization's other advantages. When one considers the inefficiencies of complete localism for economic performance, some sacrifice in participation may benefit
overall citizen utility.

  Börzel and Hosli (2003) write of the European Union's need of a "double rebal-
ancing" of political and economic authorities, with greater strength in economic
policy making, particularly macroeconomic stabilization and redistribution, but at
the same time, more direct accountability to European citizens.

Table 2.2. *Prescriptions for Centralization or Decentralization by Objective*

	Centralization	Decentralization	Mixed	Summary Comments
Military security	X			• Strength in numbers thesis. Examples of federations founded on this principle include Switzerland, Germany, United states, EU (ECSC, Euratom), Argentina, and Canada.
Economic benefits				
Efficiency			X	• Centralize for administrative efficiency; decentralize for informational advantage or to capture/accommodate diverse revenue potential or essential expenditure need.
Innovation		X		• Decentralization engages multiple laboratories and contains failure; works best when problems are moderately complex and innovation costs are manageable.
Intergovernmental competition		X		• Tiebout's mobile voter brings the market mechanism to government service, promoting specialization and minimizing waste.
Externalities management	X			• Centralized incentives to encourage production of positive externalities; centralized regulation to minimize the adverse effects of negative externalities.

(continued)

Table 2.2. (continued)

	Centralizaion	Decentralizaion	Mixed	Summary Comments
Market preservation			X	• Central governments establish property rights; intergovernmental competition between state governments inhibits government exploitation of citizens.
Efficient representation				
Political participation		X		• Decentralization improves efficacy of vote; nevertheless, participation is generally higher in many national elections.
Managing and satisfying diversity		X		• Tiebout mobile voters sort into like-minded communities; important "peace-preserving" potential when decentralization defuses tension from conflicting policy goals.
Accountability		X		• Decentralization improves electoral information by boosting voter's ability to assess local effects; mobility enhances government responsiveness as voters can compare government performance.
Anti-tyranny and rights			X	• Decentralization fragments authority, limiting a tyrant's reach, but sufficient centralized protection of rights is necessary to prevent an authoritarian enclave.
Higher quality representation			X	• Local electoral opportunities give voters experience with politicians as well as practice with voting; national offices enlarge the pool of potential candidates.

other hand, some benefits may be complementary.[50] The federation can be a forum for linking issues where one group accepts a compromise on one dimension to attain goals in another dimension, making possible cooperation that was not otherwise feasible. Where this is the case, it is the multidimensionality of the federal union that makes it more compelling than the single-dimensioned defense or trade alliance. Therefore federalism is a problem not only of optimization but also of feasibility: where potential bumps up against the reality of interdimensional trade-offs and the politics of compromise.

Since it is not possible to maximize performance on every measure, evaluating the performance of federations requires sensitivity to each one's particular goals. While it is clear that some federations are not thriving, ranking the relative performance of others is less straightforward. Is the United States outperforming Canada? Given Canada's territorial cleavage, it is meeting different challenges than the United States. If we focus exclusively on a single measure of success—say, economic productivity—a particular federation may fare poorly compared to others, but if evaluated instead based on an alternative criterion, such as preservation of ethnic heritage, it may do much better. Every federation makes trade-offs with the hope that overall, each member of the union is better off within it than out.

Given the connection between the distribution of authority and the federation's goals, the distribution needs to be defended. First, deviations from it may be unintentional, but it is also possible, given the controversy in determining priorities, that governments will purposefully try to manipulate the distribution of authority to their own advantage, or deviate from it when the opportunity presents itself. Production of federalism's "goods" is hard to monitor. How does one know if each government is doing what it ought to do, if it is complying fully with the terms of the federal bargain? Second, the science behind optimal distribution is still young. Is the federation underperforming because it is inadequately designed, or instead because its rules have not been followed? Third, the division of authority itself can be ambiguous. How

---

[50] Public projects create many positive complementarities: Yellowstone's preservation is worth more to a public who can travel to it once the highways are constructed. Page (1997) considers how governments compare packages of projects. If governments considered either project independently, its costs might outweigh the calculated benefits. But by examining them together, they become worthwhile.

might we define the terms of the bargain and confidently identify trans-gressions? If the distribution of authority matters—which a significant literature, summarized in this chapter, argues that it does—then federal unions come closest to their potential when the distribution of authority is heeded.

Even as the federation should aim for compliance by its member governments, the boundaries should be allowed to evolve. Preferences for decentralization or centralization change, sometimes because the conditions that led to the initial distribution have changed, sometimes because a better approach is discovered, and sometimes just because there is a general feeling that the national government is too strong (as in the United States during the 1990s) or that the state governments were out of control (the Canadian founders' perceptions of the United States during their founding in the 1860s). The science of distributing authority is developing, and as social scientists uncover new causal relationships, we may begin to map authority to performance with more confidence. In the meanwhile, the purpose of this book, as a parallel study, is to offer principles for constitutional design that protects the distribution from manipulation while allowing beneficial adjustments.

2.3 BUILDING INTUITION: THE EVOLUTION OF THE EUROPEAN UNION

The European Union provides us with a very good example of a union that has evolved both in its purposes and in its structure. It was born a limited treaty in 1951, and did not become a federation (meeting all three criteria) until 1999. (I describe the timing below.) In a brief history of the European Union's evolution can be found several important lessons about federal constructions: first, integration has been pursued for a vari-ety of objectives; second, these objectives have evolved; and third, the institutional structure of the European Union has been adjusted to meet the changing goals.

Five years is very little time for nations to go from enemies to bedfel-lows; nevertheless, in 1950 French foreign minister Robert Schuman used these words to explain France's partnership with Germany:

The contribution which an organized and living Europe can bring to civil-isation is indispensable to the maintenance of peaceful relations .... Europe will not be made all at once, or according to a single plan. It will be built through concrete achievements which first create a de facto solidarity .... [T]he

French Government proposes that action be taken immediately on one limited but decisive point: it proposes that Franco-German production of coal and steel as a whole be placed under a common High Authority, within the framework of an organisation open to the participation of the other countries of Europe .... The solidarity in production thus established will make it plain that any war between France and Germany becomes not merely unthinkable, but materially impossible .... this proposal will build the first concrete foundation of a European federation which is indispensable to the preservation of peace .... [51]

Security concerns motivated the union of European states. Schuman's announcement signaled the conception of the European Coal and Steel Community, established formally under the Treaty of Paris in 1951. If the main industries necessary for war were made interdependent, then France and Germany would be unable to fight one another. Other nations quickly saw the advantage of a common pact to overcome their new vulnerability, in a Europe squeezed between the two growing powers of the United States and the USSR. Although the original justification for integration was security, when a common defense community was proposed concurrent with the planning for the European Coal and Steel Community in 1950, it failed to receive support in France due to fears of German rearmament. That is, it failed not for neglect of security concerns, but because of them.[52]

With experience, the people of Europe noticed other advantages of their union. Even in Schuman's declaration, we get hints of further ambitions: a union established to make Franco-German war impossible laid "a true foundation for their economic unification," the product of which could lead to "contributing to raising living standards" and "with increased resources ..., the development of the African continent."[53] As Dinan (2004:4) writes: "European integration became synonymous with peace and prosperity." Therefore, rather than a deepening of the defense union, the first extensions of the integration were to the European Economic

---

[51] The full text of Robert Schuman's May 9, 1950 declaration, with multiple translations, is available at http://www.robert-schuman.org/robert-schuman/declaration2.htm (December 28, 2006). Similar excerpts from the declaration are included in many treatises on Europe, including John Pinder's (1991:1) introduction to the European Community.

[52] Member state sovereignty was also a significant source of opposition in France. See Dinan (2004:57–62).

[53] The final potential benefit refers to the lingering paternalistic responsibility that Europe felt for African states.

Community (EEC), created by the Treaty of Rome in 1957, which spread the objectives from security to economic efficiency. The EEC established a common market among the six founding member states.[54]

The benefits of a European common market were substantial, and touched even the smallest of issues: standardization of outlets was necessary to make an electronics common market feasible. As the market developed, Europeans found that they wanted more from their union. In particular, they had representational demands: the public wanted more direct influence in the decisions taken by the EC institutions, but at the same time, they wanted to ensure that the union did not become so integrated that it would eliminate local (member state) pursuit of national interests. To improve accountability, the union increasingly shifted from indirect control to direct control by empowering the directly elected European Parliament.[55] The direct relationship between the citizens and the European government established under the Amsterdam treaty causes it to meet the second criterion of a federation, *independence* (see p. 18), and finally to be classifiable as a federal union.[56]

The European Union also evolved over time—and earlier—to satisfy the third criterion, *direct governance*, transforming it from a treaty organization to something more closely representing a state, structured constitutionally. This mutation was driven by European Court of Justice

[54] A third community, less important than the EEC, was also formed at this time: Euratom, or the European Atomic Energy Community, which merged member states' non-military nuclear capacities. The three communities, initially governed distinctly, were merged in July 1967.

[55] As Hooghe and Marks (2001) summarize, the scope of shared decision making—including more input from the directly-elected European Parliament—has expanded greatly over the past 20 years. Under the Treaty of Rome, in place until 1987, the European Parliament had only a consultative role, but its role has steadily expanded, so that under the Amsterdam Treaty, signed in 1999, the European Parliament has an active decisional role on legislation concerning 33% of the treaty provisions (Hooghe and Marks 2001: 21, Table 2.1).

[56] Identifying the European Union as a federation as of 1999 is controversial in two directions. First, there are those who resist its categorization as a federation. From a separate direction, some might argue that the EU qualified as federal earlier in the decade, arguing accurately that the augmentation in the European Parliament's power expanded steadily from the Single European Act (1986) to Maastricht (1992) to Amsterdam (1997). In fact with Maastricht the co-decision procedure was added, giving the European Parliament the ability to reject Council legislation. But as Tsebelis and Garrett (1997ab) point out, the Council was able to make take-it-or-leave-it offers to the Parliament (see also Crombez 1997). This hitch was repaired with the Amsterdam Treaty, so I date the start of European federalism with the year that the Amsterdam Treaty became effective. See Hix (1999:88–96) for an extended discussion.

(ECJ) interpretations, although one must also acknowledge that member states, and their political leadership, did not mount significant challenges to the ECJ's institutional initiatives. First, the ECJ established the *direct effect* of EU law, where citizens can claim rights established by European law in their national courts.[57] Direct effect of EU law was not sufficient to satisfy direct governance; it took the establishment of the *supremacy* of EU law to prevent national law from overriding it. The combination of direct effect and supremacy—both changes instigated by the ECJ—altered the nature of the union to satisfy the third criterion for federalism.[58]

At the same time, the beneficial fragmentation continues. The European Parliament is not nearly as powerful as the American Congress, for example, or any of the other western federations' national legislatures, such as Germany or Canada. Through supermajority requirements within the executive (the Commission and the executive/legislature hybrid: the Council), the member states retain significant power to reject legislation. Nevertheless, the steady shift from unanimity to supermajority for much decision making has made the European Union a more powerful—and therefore politically salient—force.

European integration is most often recounted as a story of centralization, but a fascinating by-product is the empowerment of regional interests. That is, European integration has led to *disintermediation*: the development of supranational decision making has spawned a parallel process of decentralization within the member states. Regional governments and other local organizations have opportunities unavailable to them prior to integration. First, they have access to developmental financing (structural funds) through the European Union; their petition for these funds can bypass member states, reducing the regional interests' dependence on the national government.[59] Second, the European legal doctrine of subsidiarity stipulates that the European Union is only authorized to act when the member states have determined that maintaining control at a lower level of government is insufficient to meet the union's objectives. In practice, subsidiarity implies a preference for policy devolution, which has

---

[57] The doctrine was established in *Van Gend en Loos V. Nederlandse Administratie der Belastingen* [1963] ECR 1.

[58] For an extensive discussion, see Weiler (1991) or Alter (2001), Hix (1999: 107–13) has an excellent summary. However, see Börzel and Hosli (2003:188–9) for a discussion of the limitations of the EU's authorities.

[59] See Marks (1992: 212–8).

legitimized regional governments' demands for more control. Relatedly, the increasing centralization of Europe has proved increasingly to be a source of empowerment for minority enclaves, who can turn to Europe for minority protection, including discrimination based on sex and ethnicity. Regional government empowerment is an unanticipated consequence of European centralization.

Within the evolution of these broad objectives, bargains struck between the treaties, and even the treaties themselves, represent negotiations over specific goals. As with all federal unions, the key is the balance between resolving disputes about diverse substantive interests and implementing beneficial processes. The scope of EU authority has grown dramatically; sprouting from the initially modest cooperation between two industries, it now touches on virtually every aspect of public policy, including agriculture, the environment, labor movement, public health, culture, and education. Despite fair public support,[60] and the early convergence in objectives, the current state was not inevitable, and the future of the European Union cannot be forecast.

Political integration promotes improved representation, but was necessary for other objectives, particularly economic efficiency. At some point, the common market's development slowed considerably, unable to advance without political changes. Also, as the common market grew, it created divisible goods, which needed to be redistributed. So the two objectives of political representation and economic efficiency are intertwined in Europe: one need not choose between them, as they support one another; and pursuit of one—economic efficiency—may introduce new problems, which may be remedied by pursuit of another, in this case, improved representation and further political integration. Institutional structure and political patterns had to adapt to fulfill the new objectives. Each significant institutional shift, marked by the primary treaties of integration, was not just a matter of renaming the union; each new treaty defined new safeguards to render the union possible. Later in the book, we will return to this case to consider how the safeguards were modified to accommodate the advancing complexity of the European Union.

The summer of 2005 brought what many believed to be a serious setback for the European Union: the French and Dutch rejected a constitution

---

[60] See Bednar et al. (1996) for an analysis of the variance in public support across member states.

for Europe. Some speculated that this setback portends a crumbling apart of the union. We can use the framework of federalism-as-means to consider the implication of the failed constitution. It was proposed to reallocate power to better fit the union's needs. If the distribution is not allowed to evolve structurally, but instead is frozen at the current distribution of authority, one might think that the worst that can happen is that EU governance continues as it is now. But that is not the case: it has evolved over time in response to changing needs and circumstances, and it must continue to evolve or lose its efficacy. So to best evaluate the potential loss from the rejection of the Constitution, we should consider the argument that the union will continue to evolve organically, piecemeal, and focus on the changes to its environment. In terms of military security, Europe is under no new state-based threat, and it has more experience with stateless terrorist threats than the United States. It is under a growing trade threat from Asia, especially as China and Vietnam extend their markets. To maintain growth, immigrant populations are needed to replenish an aging native workforce. Also, the citizens are increasingly demanding clarity and accountability in European representation, and the party system has begun to adapt, placing new demands on the political components. The economic and political changing circumstances would be difficult enough to meet under the current membership. But the planned extension of the EU to include even more of eastern Europe means a diversification of member state needs and capacities that may impair its ability to adapt under the current decision-making regime. A static federation is not a healthy one.

Skach (2005) provides a corroborating argument. Examining three justifications for a formal European constitution, she sets aside two: popular legitimacy and clarification of the competences (the distribution of authority), in favor of a third, policy improvement. A written constitution improves policy because it coordinates perceptions about the union's goals. The European Union's objectives have evolved dramatically over its 50-odd year life span; its purpose could be clarified, and rendered focal, by a formal constitution. Once the purpose is more cleanly established, the mechanics of design will follow. Form follows function.

The European Union's development encompasses the three general benefits that a union might hope to obtain: military security, economic efficiency, and improved representation. European integration is motivated by the goal of producing common goods. It was not created to divide Europe's riches, and while redistributive concerns are always an issue (as the Common Agriculture Policy pithily demonstrates), its evolution is fueled primarily by pursuit of common objectives, evolving over time. The distribution of authority is set, and adjusted, to help the union meet these goals.

3

The Federal Problem

A federal constitution distributes authority between governments. If the distribution has been made with goals in mind—rather than randomly, or to satisfy personal ambitions—its maintenance is crucial to a federation's success. Any changes to it must be managed with care. This chapter develops a thesis about what causes governments to deviate from their assigned authorities.

My central claim in this chapter is that the incentive to deviate from the division of authority is inescapably built in to the federal structure. Member governments—federal and state—may try to manipulate the division of authority to their own benefit, an activity I will refer to as *opportunism* or *transgressions*.[1] Intergovernmental rivalry is inevitable and therefore transgressions are a normal part of any federal practice. However, careful design of the federation, mindful of this inherent tendency, can reduce the scale of the transgressions. Governments may punish one another to increase compliance with the distribution of authority, but the tools of enforcement are blunt and productivity limited when this is the only means to induce governmental agents to comply with the constitution. I will use this thesis to develop a theory of federal institutional design in later chapters. When managed, this inherent opportunism may become a benefit.

---

[1] Opportunism is a behavior somewhat the opposite of "federal practice," which, although undefined in the literature, seems to mean a cooperation between governments that comes from the respect for the terms of the federal constitution, treating it like it is a covenant. While we cannot hope that federal practice will emerge spontaneously, institutions can affect it, by converting incentives to behave opportunistically into a motivation to cooperate.

Table 3.1. *State Compliance with Requisitions for Troops (1777–1783) and Money (1784–1789)*

State	Number of Soldiers Supplied	Compliance (% of quota)	Amount Paid	Compliance (% of quota)
New Hampshire	6,653	65	107,305	18
Massachusetts	33,008	63	995,741	42
Rhode Island	3,917	69	18,571	5
Connecticut	21,142	75	196,473	14
New York	12,077	77	706,655	64
New Jersey	7,533	66	35,486	4
Pennsylvania	19,689	49	1,086,190	51
Delaware	1,778	45	103,249	46
Maryland	13,275	50	348,109	22
Virginia	23,503	48	962,522	38
North Carolina	6,129	26	45,226	4
South Carolina	4,348	26	71,871	8
Georgia	2,328	56	0	0

Source: Dougherty (2001), Tables 5.1 and 5.3.

To frame the problem, consider the performance of the American federal union under the Articles of Confederation. The union was formed for mutual defense; it was believed that the colonies would be better able to defend themselves against the British (and other potential invaders) if they banded together. In order for the defense union to be successful, the independent states needed to make two types of sacrifices: sovereignty loss, permitting the creation of a common defense strategy, and economic and social contributions, in providing money and troops for the defense effort.

The states did make sacrifices, but not as much as requested. Usually deviations are difficult to measure, but state compliance with Congressional requisitions offer two quantifiable measures: troops and money. Dougherty (2001) calculates that during the revolutionary war, none of the states complied fully with the Congressional requests for troops, with highest compliance percentages of 75% and 77% from Connecticut and New York, and lows of 26% apiece from the Carolinas (see Table 3.1). Postwar fiscal transfers were even worse, with compliance percentages ranging from New York's high of 64% to Georgia's null. And although the amount ultimately contributed appeared sufficient, as the Americans did defeat the British, this hold on independence was far from secure, and other threats loomed. Furthermore, the union was viewed as insufficient for pursuing other objectives, such as establishment of a common market and effective representation.[2]

James Madison was concerned, as were his compatriots, about the efficacy of the union. While compliance had been sufficient to win one war against Britain, there was limited confidence that the act could be repeated. To evaluate what was wrong with the union under the Articles of Confederation, Madison first identified the symptoms of weakness, or what he called "vices." He compiled his list in April of 1787, after a careful study of the history of confederacies from around the world and relying heavily on his own observations of the Continental Congress. The "Vices"[3] is an account of a variety of dimensions upon which the Articles of Confederation are ineffective, illustrated with examples. He lists 12 problems, annotating 11. The first four describe rivalry between the states and rebellion by the states against their responsibilities to the union.[4] In these notes, Madison describes the states' opportunism—burden-shifting and shirking—that plagued the union under the Articles of Confederation.

The data contained in Table 3.1 must have been painfully familiar to Madison; the first item in his list was "Failure of the States to comply with the Constitutional requisitions," which he described as "fatal to the object of the present System" (Madison 1999:69). In the second item he criticizes the "Encroachments by the States on the federal authority," which are "numerous" and "may be foreseen in almost any case where any favorite object of a State shall present a temptation" (Madison 1999:69). After a third citation that continues the theme of state shirking from the first and second, he develops a fourth: "Trespasses of the States on the rights of each other" (Madison 1999:70). This burden-shifting he said was "alarming" but could be "daily apprehended." The states could not

---

[2] In the American case, the federation was not formed to redistribute goods; it was formed to create benefits to its citizens that could not be obtained otherwise. The American case is not unique; this motivation for federation is general. And although internal rivalries are natural—along governmental lines as well as along many other divisions within the society—it is important to concentrate on solving the problem of production rather than hoping to solve redistributive battles "once and for all." This time will never come.

[3] James Madison, "Vices of the Political System of the United States" (April 1787) in Madison (1999: 69–80).

[4] Note 5 describes the coordination problem between the states and Note 6 the inability of the states to control internal violence. Note 7 is diagnostic; I discuss it further below. Note 8 questions the legitimacy of the Articles of Confederation, since it was not subject to popular approval. Notes 9, 10, and 11 are dedicated to the problems of representational democracy. Note 11 sketches arguments that appear later in *Federalist* 10.

coordinate where necessary, and the national government was too weak to compel them, and could not count upon them, even in its most desperate defensive need, when fighting the British.

These symptoms are all examples of the states engaging in individually beneficial but collectively counterproductive behavior. While the division of authority under the Articles of Confederation was spare—largely empowering the common government, the United States in Congress, with foreign affairs, including treaties and war, and requiring that the states allow free circulation of the people of other states and not enter into special treaties with one another—even under these skeletal terms the states were in violation, as Madison enumerated. Madison was preoccupied with opportunism, believing that it weakened the union, making it less productive, rendering it vulnerable to internal and external attacks. The elimination or management of these vices to boost the union's productive capacity became Madison's primary concern as he devised a plan for a new governmental organization. Merely enumerating a constitutional prohibition of behavior (or specifying an obligation) is insufficient: Madison understood that the incentive scheme had to change.

Any proposed remedy must begin with a diagnosis. In this chapter, I first identify the three general types of opportunism in federations. I next motivate why opportunism would occur, given its destructive (or at least counterproductive) implications. Finally, the chapter concludes by outlining the basic incentive mechanism available to any union: intergovernmental retaliation. This was the exclusive mechanism available to induce compliance under the Articles of Confederation, and is present in every union.

3.1 A Typology of Opportunism

We focus on the activity of the national or state government; our concern is whether or not its behavior (its statutes as well as their implementation) complies with the terms of the constitution. Governmental behavior is driven by its internal motivations and the external forces that affect its ability to reach its goals. Because of the second criterion defining a federation, I will assume that the any elected officials within these governments are office-seeking and electoral accountability motivates them.[5] Generally

---

[5] To aid intuition, for the moment assume that the federation is democratic. In nondemocratic federations, the decentralized structure ensures that each government has priorities independent from the collective.

speaking (without some institutional mechanism to alter the incentives), elected officials consider interests of their own constituents not just first, but exclusively; they will try to create policy that advantages their voters. Sometimes a policy that benefits their own constituents will harm others.

There are three approaches to understanding how opportunism could cause a federation to falter: inefficient allocation of authority, inefficient allocation of goods, and inefficient production of goods. First, both the initial distribution of authority, as well as its evolution, may not be allocated to maximize union productivity. While work within the fiscal federalism literature is traditionally nonstrategic, combining its insights with a game-theoretic study of incentives instructs us about the hazards of opportunism to the federation's performance. Because opportunism is intended to serve the electoral interests of a particular government, when the distribution of authority is manipulated to serve particular interests it may not—and most often will not—improve the union's productive efficiency.

While fiscal federalism is concerned with the generation of goods, a second approach focuses on the distribution of any divisible good that the federation produces as a by-product of its success (Crémer and Palfrey 1996, 1999, 2002, Hafer and Landa 2007). A member government's evaluation of the allocation may be absolute or relative, and subsequent jealousy from the latter concerns much of the political science of federalism; we see it in Riker's (1964) concern for the integrity of the "federal bargain," echoed in Lemco (1991), Dixit and Londregan (1998), and Watts (1999), and probed in depth in Filippov et al. (2004). By increasing the pie to be split, efficient production mitigates distributive tension. Acts that reduce production fuel battles over divisible goods.

Third, opportunism may corrupt the incentives to produce. Production involves self-sacrifice, which opportunists attempt to skirt. Each of the federalism objectives invites temptations to free ride. Compliance with the division of authority pinches, sometimes significantly. While everyone wants a well-equipped military, with intelligent, responsible, and well-trained troops, military equipment is costly and military service often is life-endangering. No state would prefer to sacrifice its own money, or especially its own sons and daughters, if money and troops from another state would suffice. Similarly, although all would like to enjoy the productivity of the common market, free trade between the states requires a willingness not to protect home-state industries from competition. Harmony between diverse populations requires a discipline to respect local sovereignty in specified domains even if a national majority disapproves of its choices. And so it goes with virtually all of the potential benefits of federalism: to obtain them requires sacrifice.

If it is difficult or unlikely that any government would be excluded from the benefits, and as long as the benefit would occur without absolutely every member contributing fully—even if it is only partially or suboptimally provided—there is a temptation to let other governments make the sacrifice while the shirking government enjoys the benefits of union. This is the classic problem of public good provision: under these conditions, there is a temptation to free ride. Translated to federalism, it takes several forms. First, governments will tend to focus on the allocative issues in federalism: who gets what, or more specifically, how many benefits flow into the politician's constituency (Filippov et al. 2004), even if it reduces total utility (Bednar 2007b). Second, governments try to position themselves to claim credit for positive outcomes, or distance themselves from negative ones. At times, this will cause them to either skirt the existing federal distribution of power, or even readjust it, as they exercise power that is not theirs. Federal performance becomes a problem of public good provision. If the member governments have a temptation to shirk on their responsibilities, then the public good may be underprovided, and federal performance will suffer.

It will be helpful to identify three types of trangressions (see Figure 3.1). State governments may try to *shirk* on their responsibilities to the federation: they may fail to implement national policy or may take it upon themselves to enact policy that is normally in the national domain rather than respect the division of powers. States may also *shift the burden* of making the union work onto the shoulders (and economies) of other states, for example by creating barriers to trade between the states, or

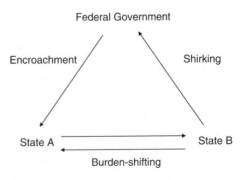

Figure 3.1. Types of Opportunism: The Triangle of Federalism

affecting the mobility of citizens across state borders. National governments may centralize, *encroaching* upon the jurisdictions of the states, or decentralize to shift burdens away from the center.

Of the three forms, federal encroachment most closely resembles tyranny, but state shirking and interstate burden-shifting are also destructive to a federation, and equally difficult to solve.[6] Shirking and encroachment are unauthorized acts of authority migration. They involve one government pulling authority toward itself (or perhaps abdicating it) when it suits that government's interests. Burden-shifting most immediately affects allocations, but because constitutions are often written to empower the national government in realms where states are likely to shift burdens (such as trade), burden-shifting often implies shirking as well. A state's transgression may include both shirking and burden-shifting.

Opportunism may be blatant or ambiguous. In any society there are examples of opportunism that clearly lie out of bounds, but a significant range of actions exists that are less clear-cut: some within the society would call it opportunism, while others would not. As long as the federation is functioning well, probably the majority of opportunism that does occur lies within this range of ambiguity.[7] Consider the differences in examples of shirking. We have already considered a classic example of shirking with the failure of the U.S. states to comply with congressional requisitions under the Articles of Confederation. Another example of shirking comes a bit later in U.S. history, the legislature of South Carolina passed an ordinance in 1832 declaring a federal (national) law to be null and void within the state of South Carolina.[8] Much more ambiguous is the stuff of everyday politics: does Illinois' decision to allow the importation of prescription drugs represent shirking? It was clearly in defiance

---

[6] Madison's diagnosis of the union's "vices" describes only two of the three edges to triangle of opportunism presented in Figure 3.1: shirking and burden-shifting. The common government was so weak—it did not even enjoy the independence of direct election and control necessary to qualify the union as federal—that it had little chance to threaten the states. Once the constitution was proposed, suspicions of the national government's strength forced him, with other Federalists, to dedicate consideration to the third edge, national encroachment. Encroachment did not seem to be a pressing concern when he worked out the principles, and then details, of his plan to remedy the weakness of the union under the Articles, although it quickly became the convention's focus.

[7] The logical argument in the next section will support this assertion.

[8] South Carolina objected to a tariff bill that it believed favored the North. The text of the ordinance is available through the Avalon Project at Yale: http://www.yale.edu/lawweb/avalon/states/sc/ordnull.htm

of national authority to regulate prescription drugs, but this power is not constitutional; it has evolved. Does the popular support for Illinois' decision signal that the power has shifted?

Although the U.S. Constitution enumerates only the national powers, it lists a set of acts expressly forbidden to the states.[9] Included on the list are bans from joining treaties and alliances, coining money, accepting an alternative form of debt payment, imposing tariffs, declaring war, or keeping troops in peacetime without Congressional approval. All have the potential to disrupt the federal union. Should states begin declaring war on their own, or deciding what is legal currency, the union would quickly and radically drop in performance. While this clause may seem redundant, it is a form of insurance that increases the federation's robustness by removing any doubt about whether or not the states have these powers.

It is interesting to note that burden-shifting does not receive the same constitutional attention. Certainly, the commerce clause (granting the national government the right to regulate interstate trade) covers the primary burden-shifting behavior—interfering with the common market to protect local industries. But the states are still given wide rein in generating externalities that would harm one another to the benefit of their own citizens. A clear example of this is banishment. In some states, judges offer convicts a choice between going to prison or banishment. For example, in Georgia, banishment has become a popular sentencing tool, particularly to distance drug offenders from their networks. While the Georgia state constitution prohibits outright banishment from the state, the Georgia Supreme Court upheld banishment from particular counties within the state. County banishment can become *de facto* state banishment, as judges banish convicts from 158 of the state's 159 counties.[10] When criminals leave the state, they immediately become another state's problem. As another example, diversity in marriage law, when a marriage is legal in one state but not another, presents a less clear-cut case. While in general marriages that include an underage party (but of age in the state issuing the marriage license) or marriages between close relatives (permitted in some states) have been honored, interracial marriages were regularly challenged until the U.S. Supreme Court stepped in,[11] and currently, same-sex marriages present a similar controversy.

---

[9] See Article I, Section 10.

[10] The practice is becoming so common that the sentence is known as "158-county banishment." See Teichman (2005).

[11] See *Loving v. Virginia*, 388 U.S. 1 (1967).

Within the United States, the boundaries defining national encroachment recently have changed. While in any federation the limits of national spending power are ambiguous, some acts that would be generally deemed blatant opportunism in the United States are acceptable elsewhere. Recall, from above, the decision by the state of Illinois to allow the importation of prescription drugs. Although the act defies national law, it is unimaginable that the U.S. President would call for the removal of Illinois Governor Blagojevich over it, much less that he would issue a direct order for him to be unseated, and replaced with his own appointee. This degree of national intervention in state affairs is unthinkable to the U.S. citizen but is a regular occurrence in Argentina and India.[12]

While opportunism most intuitively involves a power grab, governments may violate the constitutional division's terms by what they fail to do, or by what they let another government do. We can think of this as opportunistic delegation. If the national government is selecting what to delegate to the states based on its own interests, then it can choose to delegate when it is most able to control state decision making. The thesis parallels the agency delegation literature.[13] Using its spending powers, where it attaches conditions on revenue transfers to the states, the national government can influence state expenditure policy substantially, particularly in the United States, where the national government enjoys broad—that is, little-stipulated—spending powers, abetted by a Supreme Court that to date has supported the national government's muscular use of them.[14] Similarly, the states may engage in opportunistic abdication, where it abandons a policy area, or support a national government's attempt to assume a power. In the United States, states supported the

---

[12] From 1950 to 1995 there were more than 130 interventions in India (Lok Sabha Secretariat, 1996) and 142 interventions in Argentina from 1862 to 2005, with 42 since 1946 (study in progress by Jenna Bednar and Gisela Sin, data compiled from Gomez 1947, Buta 1957, Molinelli et al. 1999, Serrafero 2000).

[13] In fact, it is possible that the national government can control state governments even better than its own agencies. In their study of national delegation to the bureaucracy, Epstein and O'Halloran (1999:153) write that the national government first decides if it should delegate to the states, and then if not, they delegate to the agencies.

[14] The seminal decision upholding the attachment of conditions to national transfers to the states is *South Dakota* v. *Dole*, 483 U.S. 203 (1987). Watts (1999) has an excellent comparative analysis of national spending powers. See McCoy and Friedman (1988) for a criticism of the U.S. Supreme Court's spending powers doctrine. A discussion of spending powers, including data on conditional spending, is found at Section 7.3.

federal Violence Against Women Act, which despite its laudable intentions, duplicated state law (it already was illegal in every state to assault
women). The act shifted prosecutorial authority to the national government, in federal courts rather than state courts, a notable alteration in
the division of authority. The Supreme Court struck down the Act,[15] even
though two-thirds of the states submitted amicus briefs in support of it.[16]
Opportunism need not be resisted to be harmful in the long run.

Multiple reasonable interpretations are available for most clauses in
any constitution, so there will always be flexibility in the division of
powers. Further dimming bright-line prescriptions is that many constitutions also contain implied powers, those that the government needs
to accomplish its enumerated powers. And, as alluded to in the illustrations above, the determination of what counts as opportunism varies from
culture to culture.[17] Given the importance of adaptation for the robust
federation, this flexibility can be useful. But it needs to be channeled:
discretion with oversight. The ambiguous opportunism—where there is
disagreement about the judgment—is also an opportunity to adapt the
system, changing the division of authority to reach greater productive
efficiency. The art of federalism's dispute resolution, addressed in later
chapters, is in the mechanics of distinguishing between beneficial change
and self-interested manipulation.

Although tyranny certainly would violate the distribution of authorities, opportunism is not necessarily corruption. It need not be politicians
using their office to squeeze taxpayers for their own personal gain. To
the contrary, opportunism is often the government using its position
to extract rents from other governments to benefit its own taxpayers.
Paradoxically, in democratic federations, responsiveness to the voters
threatens the performance of its democracy. Credit assignment is inherently ambiguous in the federal structure, where multiple governments
serve the same constituents. Governments want to claim credit for good
outcomes and distance themselves from bad. This electoral instinct can
put them into competition with one another, and even cause them to try
to adjust domains of authority opportunistically. Even in a union that
clearly benefits its members, the electoral independence of the governing

---

[15] *United States* v. *Morrison*, 529 U.S. 598 (2000).

[16] I will discuss this case further in Section 7.3.

[17] Legal ambiguity may be unimportant in the presence of a strong norm against
certain behaviors, perhaps established in the political culture, but we then should
ask: what maintains this norm? Chapter 7 lays out the paradigms for that research
project.

bodies makes each put the interests of its own constituents over the general body. Authority becomes the object in a tug of war between competing governments, and the ensuing authority migration reduces the efficacy of the union (Bednar 2007b).

In fact, some may argue that opportunism is the opposite of corruption, evidence instead of federalism in its fullest glory. Aren't decentralized governments pursuing diverse policies to satisfy diverse populations the very essence of federalism? And at times, can't this diversity even benefit others, when states act as policy laboratories? Under this line of argument, opportunism, construed as policy experimentation, does not limit union productivity, it *drives* it. But even when the opportunistic authority migration is (incidentally) utility-enhancing, it may destablize the union, not because of the outcome, but because of its implications for the robustness of the process. With opportunistic authority migration the federation is altered not by design or by popular amendment, but instead due to self-interest of one or more parties to the federation. The commission of any opportunism fuels the suspicions that the process is not protective of the distribution of authority, and therefore the balance of power within the federation, and these suspicions lead to further acts of opportunism.

Opportunism violates the enumeration of powers, which was designed to maximize the productivity of the union. Therefore, it follows that opportunism reduces the productivity of the union. Why would governments do it, or to put it another way, why wouldn't they be able to resist the temptation? In order to see why, we will now delve further into the theory of federalism as a public good provision problem.

3.2 WHY DO WE SEE OPPORTUNISM?

The answer to this section's title question may seem obvious: people are selfish, so of course governments, composed of people, would take advantage of one another. Madison was a terrific observer of the character of human nature, and kept our tendency to succumb to temptation, even when we "know better," at the front of his thoughts when constructing a government. This section defends his focus; it argues that opportunism is inevitable, but may be minimized (and productivity maximized) through institutional management. This section establishes the difficulties of monitoring compliance in a federation, preparing us for the next section where we evaluate federalism's fundamental safeguard—mutual retaliation—in light of the monitoring imperfection. We will rely on this basic method of analysis in later chapters when formal institutional safeguards amend the basic federal structure.

Although Madison said that if men were angels there would be no need for government, mortals cluster into three categories: selfish wolves, self-sacrificing lambs, and those who are neither; this last camp wishes others no harm, but suspects that some predatory wolves might exist. These wolves may, in Madison's words, be "much more disposed to vex and oppress each other than to co-operate for their common good" (Federalist 10). In this section we will see the consequence on federalism of suspecting that wolves exist, and the difficulty in identifying them by observing actions.

Madison considered this problem in his evaluation of the Articles of Conferation, the "Vices." Once he identified the symptoms of weakness in the governing structure, the next step toward making the union more productive was a diagnosis: why did the states engage in opportunism? The most sustained treatment of this question appears in Note 7, where he makes the following two observations:

1. **Perceived Hardship:** "Every general act of the Union must necessarily bear unequally hard on some particular member or members of it. Secondly the partiality of the members to their own interests and rights ... will naturally exaggerate the inequality where it exists, and even suspect it where it has no existence."
2. **Suspicion Leads to Opportunism:** "[A] distrust of the voluntary compliance of each other may prevent the compliance of any, although it should be the latent disposition of all."

In the first observation, Madison notes that the burden of making the union work falls unequally upon the shoulders of the states; some may be asked to make greater sacrifices than others. All will be sensitive to the hardships of union, and each is likely to believe that it bears more of the burden than the others. In the second observation, Madison laments the inefficient outcome generated by the common knowledge of perceived hardship: each is suspicious that others might shirk—behave opportunistically—in order to deflect some of the burden. If there is a danger that the collective good will not be provided, then suspicious states should shirk. This pairing of observations lead him to conclude that it is impossible to sustain full compliance (FC) within the union of states: "It is no longer doubted that a unanimous and punctual obedience of 13 independent bodies, to the acts of the federal Government, ought not to be calculated on" (Madison 1999:72). Madison diagnosed the union's problem as a collective action problem, where shirking and burden-shifting are its manifestations.

Uncertainty opens the door for opportunism. The uncertainty emerges from the way that actions map into outcomes. Often, actions map into outcomes in a straightforward sense: the Clean Air Act leads to cleaner air. Expressed formally, it looks like this:

$$f(x) = \omega$$

where x is the government's action, the Clean Air Act, and ω is the observed outcome, a change in measurable airborne pollutants. Although everyone observes the action, passage of the Clean Air Act, the public tends to judge the outcome, asking: is the air cleaner?" There are several reasons why the action might not map into the outcome as anticipated. First, there might be an external shock, an event caused by some force completely outside of the system (say, increased industrial production in Canada) that affects the outcome (fouled air blows into the northeast from Canadian smokestacks).[18] While perhaps someone would notice that the Canadians are at fault, a simple measurement of the air quality in New Hampshire before and after the implementation of the environmental regulation would not reflect well on the legislation. In this case, we would want to modify the above equation as follows:

$$f(x, \epsilon) = \omega$$

where the added ϵ indicates influences outside of the government's control affect what people observe as well. Ineffective legislation contributes to undesirable outcomes, but external factors may also tip the balance.

A second factor confounding the translation from action to outcome is misinterpretations, or an inference problem. That is, governments have information that is an incomplete projection of reality.[19] They do not see the full dimensionality of a problem. As such, they may make the wrong inference, both about the appropriateness of their own actions and in judging the actions of others. For example, the effect of the Clean Air Act is dependent not just on the quality of the legislation, but also on its implementation. Improperly executed, good legislation is indistinguishable from bad. In federations, the inference problem is compounded by the multiple governments charged with implementing

---

[18] See Bui (1998).
[19] The inference problem will plague safeguards as well, an issue we will return to later, especially in Chapter 7.

legislation: federal bureaucracies can adhere closely to the legislation, but state governments may implement it loosely (or vice versa). All will affect the quality of the air, but it is difficult to trace the culprit when dirty air is observed.

Finally, a third factor is the complexity of the policy mapping itself. For example, consider President Eisenhower's support of the interstate highway system. It was partly a defense project: during World War II, Eisenhower had seen the military benefits of the German autobahn.[20] In order to get troops, missiles, and other heavy equipment across the country smoothly, each highway was required to have stretches of straight road at prescribed intervals in case an airplane needed to land and minimum heights of overpasses were set in consultation with the Pentagon. Although the interstate was an unprecedented federal public works project, bringing the national government into a realm ordinarily left to local and state governments, charges of potential encroachment might be defended by the security motivations of the project and recast as falling within the national government's jurisdiction.

The jurisdictional implications of the highway system spread much more broadly than better defense. Coinciding with the development of the interstate was the discovery of new oil sources; gas prices dropped even as demand rose. The postwar boom in domestic tourism was made possible by this combination of infrastructure and fuel. The interstate highway system led to increased mobility of people and goods through the United States. It had positive effects including a new interest in preserving American natural parks; negative effects such as the devastation of the economies of small towns bypassed by the interstate, and many unforeseen effects, such as the rise of motel chains and fast-food restaurants, as Americans new to travel sought some familiarity in the course of their explorations. And as far as affecting the division of power, it introduced new possibilities for national government action in realms traditionally left to the states. With increased trade, the national government could engage in social policy, such as desegregation, by linking local activity to interstate commerce.

The complexity of the policy mapping is better represented as follows:

$$f(x_1, \ldots, x_n; \epsilon_1, \ldots, \epsilon_m) = (\omega_1, \ldots, \omega_k)$$

---

[20] Rep. George Fallon of Maryland coined the name National System of Interstate and Defense Highways in the 1956 bill that funded the interstates.

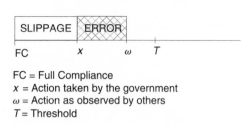

FC = Full Compliance
x = Action taken by the government
ω = Action as observed by others
T = Threshold

Figure 3.2. Slippage and Error in Deviance Space

multiple actions may build upon one another (the interstate and civil rights legislation), combining with exogenous forces, and affect a multidimensional policy space.

Where the mapping contains uncertainty, a government will be able to take advantage of it.[21] Figure 3.2 provides intuition. The axis represents the amount of deviance from full compliance, starting with full compliance (FC) at the left, and with the extent of the transgression increasing as one moves along the axis to the right. If a government takes action x, due to imperfect monitoring others may observe ω. The observation of ω includes some error, but also some intentional deviation from full compliance (FC), since x is to the right of FC. (I will describe more features of this figure in the next section.) The observation does not reveal how much of the deviance is due to error and how much to slippage. Given that error is part of reality, it cannot be eliminated. But can we do away with slippage? That is, can we do away with all intentional deviations from the enumeration of powers?

3.3 INTERGOVERNMENTAL RETALIATION: A NATURAL DEFENSE

With federalism, a good offense may not be the best defense, but it is the most readily available. When a government suspects that another has

[21] Williamson defines opportunism as "self-interest seeking with guile" (1985:47, 1993:97). Whether or not it intends to behave opportunistically, many of its acts will appear to be so, due to the exogenous forces and cognitive dissonance. For this reason it is useful to expand upon Williamson's definition of opportunism; it contains both slippage and error. This expanded definition brings us closer to Simon's, (1985) appeal for institutional design that conceives of citizens as the boundedly rational *Homo psychologicus*. Simon cites Madison: "As there is a degree of depravity in mankind which requires a certain degree of circumspection and distrust, so there are other qualities in human nature which justify a certain portion of esteem and confidence" (Simon 1985:303, quoting Madison in *Federalist* 55).

Table 3.2. *A Standard Prisoners'*
Dilemma Game

		Player 2	
		Cooperate	Defect
Player 1	Cooperate	(1, 1)	(b, a)
	Defect	(a, b)	(0, 0)

transgressed, it has the ability to strike back with retaliatory noncompliance and even threaten to secede. Opportunism can escalate; disputes may even turn into violent, aggressive acts of civil war. Although governments would like to avoid it, the threat of retaliatory opportunism alone is not sufficient to eliminate all transgressions. Opportunism is inherent to federalism. To establish this claim, in this section I will develop a visual intuition and in the appendix, a set of analytical models.

A familiar model, the prisoners' dilemma, shares many features of our problem (see Table 3.2).[22] When the two players encounter one another only once, there is a single prediction: mutual defection. Each considers the incentives affecting the other player's decision. Each knows that no matter what he does, the other is better off defecting, and so he himself will choose his best response to the other's dominant strategy, and defect himself. The mutually beneficial, socially optimal cooperative equilibrium cannot be sustained, and the players each get a payoff of zero instead of one apiece. But if we repeat the game, we have the possibility of sustaining full compliance because players may encourage one another to cooperate by playing a "nice" *trigger strategy*, where each starts by cooperating and continues to do so as long as the other does as well. Any defection "triggers" a punishment. For example, with Tit-For-Tat a player initially cooperates and then conditions subsequent actions upon what the other did in the previous round (Axelrod 1984). Many nice, punishing strategies may sustain full cooperation if the players are sufficiently patient.[23]

With just two possible actions, the players have little choice. Many analysts are interested in understanding the presence of any cooperation and so use of minimal alternatives (such as cooperate or defect) is sufficient.

---

[22] We will assume the usual formal details: let $a > 1$, $b < 0$, and $a + b < 2$.

[23] For infinitely repeated games, the result I have described is known generally as the *folk theorem*. Kreps et al. (1982) prove the potential to sustain cooperation in finitely repeated games as long as players do not know one another perfectly (incomplete information); with even a tiny possibility that the other player is generous, or believes the first to be, cooperation can be sustained even when the game's endpoint is known.

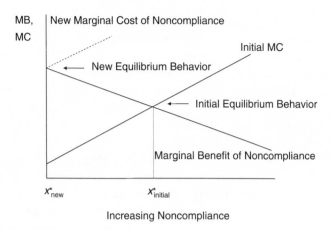

Figure 3.3. Institutionally Influenced Behavior with Linear Marginal Benefits and Costs

With federalism, the problem is different: we want to know how to design the incentive system in a federation to improve its productivity. Incremental increases in compliance are important. In our analysis, governments may choose not to comply at all, to comply fully, or to choose any partial degree of compliance (see Figure 3.3). Deviations from the distribution of authority are represented on the *x*-axis; opportunism is bounded between zero (full compliance) and one (no compliance), but may take any value between these points, to give us a rich span of possible actions unlike the highly constrained prisoners' dilemma.[24]

Most game-theoretic analyses focus on equilibrium to predict the behavioral consequences of institutionally induced incentives. In equilibrium, the system is "in balance": as long as the incentive environment remains constant, no player—our governments—would change its behavior unilaterally. When choosing a course of action, a government weighs the potential benefits of the action against the potential costs. The government's action corresponds to the point where the additional advantage from any further noncompliance (marginal benefit) is exactly offset by the

---

[24] Technically speaking, no folk theorem result exists with a continuous choice set, but there is some disagreement over this statement. The work of Fudenberg et al. (1994) is sometimes cited as an example of a continuous choice space folk theorem result, because although the model assumes a discrete action space, it considers how to enforce mixed—randomized—actions, which lie in a continuum. When the discount factor approaches 1, payoffs may come arbitrarily close to those corresponding to full cooperation, in alignment with a folk theorem result.

anticipated penalty from that additional noncompliance (marginal cost). These elements of utility are represented on the y-axis in Figure 3.3.

It is a standard assumption that the marginal benefit of shirking decreases in the amount of noncompliance—initial deviations from FC are well rewarded, but the additional value of further deviations are incrementally less—represented accordingly in the figure by a downward-sloping line, while marginal costs may remain fixed or increase. Here I have pictured them as increasing, to underscore the most probable scenario: as noncompliance becomes more egregious, it is more likely to be detected, so the probability of punishment accelerates. As with Figure 3.2, the horizontal axis represents the extent of opportunism. With full compliance fixed at the origin, any behavior registering to the right of the origin represents some noncompliance. As pictured, initial equilibrium behavior, at $x^*_{initial}$, shows a sizable deviation from FC.

To improve compliance, players can threaten to retaliate for any transgression. This trigger strategy increases the cost of noncompliance, with a corresponding upward shift of the marginal cost curve, represented by the dotted line and labeled "new marginal cost." In theory, inducing full compliance is simply a matter of increasing the marginal cost of noncompliance enough that the marginal costs equal or exceed the marginal benefits of shirking at full compliance. With trigger strategies that credibly threaten to punish, the players can eliminate transgressions, with equilibrium behavior at x^*_{new} as labeled in Figure 3.3. The result is not limited to just two players; increasing the number of players, but holding all other conditions of the problem constant, does not affect the result. Full compliance remains possible.

This theory—the elimination of transgressions by threatening to retaliate—is intuitively reasonable and often used in practice. Even governments in unions as primitive as that created by the Articles of Confederation employ methods similar to the strategies of the players of the repeated prisoners' dilemma to motivate compliance: the threat of retaliatory transgressions should one government fail to abide by the terms of the distribution.[25] The threat may be as severe as breaking the union apart. In theory, through use of these trigger strategies, governments should be able to motivate one another to comply fully, and federations would not have a problem of opportunism. So why, then, does opportunism persist in federations?

The problem lies in the gap between optimality and feasibility, or, more colloquially, between theory and reality. Simple models provide us

---

[25] The identical logic applies to treaty organizations as well.

with core intuitions: the repeated prisoners' dilemma shows how repeated interactions can sustain cooperation. But models can be too simple. By assuming complete information and discrete actions, the repeated prisoners' dilemma oversimplifies the interaction between member states. Although each must make a decision before knowing what the other will do, it always knows what the other one did after each moves. That is, the standard prisoners' dilemma assumes away any problem of monitoring; all transgressions are seen and never misunderstood. Therefore, punishments are only meted out when someone actually deviated, and given sufficient deterrence, no one deviates. This is not true in federalism.

Suppose a government suspects opportunism. Perhaps it has measured a disappointing change to an aggregate measure, such as interstate trade volume, or it believes that another government's legislation assumes powers prohibited to it by the constitution. In the simple model, any deviation was recognized and punished. But we have established above that uncertainty obscures observation. Actions taken by the governments rarely correspond so closely to defiance of common agreements as they do in the requisitions data of Table 3.1. Governments do not, usually, have the opportunity to steal from one another outright. Instead, they take actions in a policy space—often its own budget—but outcomes are felt, often, in unrelated domains. This distance between actions and constitutional obligations makes the actions difficult to observe and verify.

Look again at Figure 3.2. Recall the difference between error and slippage: error is a product of imperfect monitoring and bounded rationality, while slippage is intentional deviation from full compliance. In the federalism context, slippage represents opportunism, deviations from the specified distribution of authority. Even if the government complied fully (where $x = FC$), the observed behavior ω may signal a deviation. The observation does not reveal whether the deviation is due to error or intentional noncompliance. This uncertainty means that all punishment is costly: punishments triggered due to observational error harm a government and make it less interested in remaining in the union. When punishment is costly, governments hesitate to punish.

To better fit reality, we will make changes to our assumptions about both the likelihood of being punished and the expected benefit for any action.[26] These changes are reflected in Figure 3.4. First, let's reexamine the punishment mechanism. The simplest institutional design is to draw

---

[26] By Bednar (2006), only one of the two conditions is necessary to render full compliance practically impossible to uphold. In federations, both conditions are likely to be present.

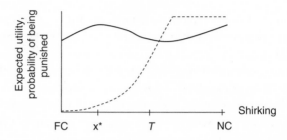

Figure 3.4. Intergovernmental Retaliation Generates Inherent Opportunism

a line, a threshold, that if crossed, triggers the punishing behavior. This trigger mechanism consists of three components: an observed behavior (what we might call the signal), a threshold, and a punishment. With the error (as shown in Figure 3.2), actions that should be tolerated might appear to have crossed the threshold and trigger punishment. Therefore the probability of punishment is no longer zero if to one side of the threshold and one if on the other, but instead increases as the action moves away from full compliance. We will further assume that the probability takes an s-shape, as illustrated by the dotted curve in Figure 3.4. For small amounts of deviation, there is very low probability of crossing the threshold and triggering a sanction, and the curve is relatively flat. For high levels of noncompliance, the probability of crossing the threshold reaches one; additional noncompliance at this point does not alter the likelihood of triggering sanctions. The story is quite different for the middle range of non-compliance. Here, the curve slopes steeply upward; small additional deviations dramatically increase the likelihood of triggering punishment.

The top curve represents the relative expected payoff for any degree of non-compliance, given the benefit of not having to make the sacrifice compliance demands, the anticipated benefit to one government when others are complying, and the likelihood of triggering punishment. Read the curve from left to right. Initially, if everyone is complying fully then a government may increase its payoff by transgressing slightly. At some point this expected utility peaks, but then declines as the likelihood of triggering punishment increases. Notice that the expected utility starts to climb again once the likelihood of punishment reaches certainty: here, the government may as well take as much as it can get in the short run, knowing that punishment is coming.

In examining the graphic, first note that expected utility peaks not when a government complies fully, but when it deviates somewhat. Second, the peak should be compared against the tail to the right, representing the expected benefit from complete noncompliance. If the tail is greater than the peak, the federation is not sustainable because the member governments prefer to be outside of the union than in it, given the benefits that are possible to obtain.[27] Third—and this is not visible in the graphic, but is implied by it—although the equilibrium behavior is marked at x^*, well to the left of the threshold, from time to time the error will cause that behavior to appear to cross the threshold, and punishment will be triggered. All "know" that no one transgressed, but as long as actions cannot be distinguished fully from error in the observation, the players enter a regime of mutual punishment. If they did not, they would create an incentive to deviate, because the likelihood of punishment would drop. Thus bad luck, in the form of a large error, has two effects: states get low utility from the bad shock (if their utility is a function of the signal) and they must punish one other to maintain the incentive to comply.

We should also pause for a moment to interpret how this mechanism upholds the division of powers, which requires a closer look at T, the threshold where the signal triggers punishment. It should be evident that T is "the law" in a sense; it is what the mechanism upholds. But it is not what the governments do. in equilibrium, governments comply *more* than the law requires, because of the chance that random misinterpretations of action will cause the behavior to look like it exceeded T when the behavior was in the range of tolerable noncompliance (see Figure 3.4).

More important, however, is the effect on productivity. We have argued that the distribution of authority determines the productivity of the union, and opportunism diminishes productivity. If T is high, there is a broader range of outcomes that are acceptable, that do not trigger punishment, and so there will be more egregious displays of opportunism the higher T is set. In unions that rely upon interstate triggers to sustain compliance, fairly outrageous opportunism will go unpunished. In this case, federations that rely upon intergovernmental retaliation will be less productive because they tolerate more opportunism. In federalism, the sum is more than the parts. The trigger strategy that emerges in equilibrium is set to maximize *government* utility, not the utility of the citizens as a whole. If the opportunism that goes unpunished decreases union productivity,

---

[27] Note the trade-off in increasing the frequency of triggering the punishment—moving T to the left—and the ability to maintain a cooperative equilibrium: as punishment becomes increasingly likely, the expected utility from any moderate degree of shirking declines, raising the comparative appeal of the fully noncooperative strategy. I describe more comparative statics in the chapter's appendix.

then citizen utility could be increased by reducing it. This becomes our goal in subsequent chapters.

So far in this discussion, we have ignored one final choice available to the governments: to secede from the union.[28] While mutual retaliation is a strategy meant to encourage the continuation of the union (but with different behavior from the members), another threat that governments may naturally make to one another is to leave the union. The value of secession (or for the national government, usurpation of all state authorities) is less than the potential in the federal union—otherwise the union would not have been attempted—but may be higher than the value of a very unproductive union. This external option limits the severity of the punishment.

It has been shown that the efficient punishment mechanism—the one that maximizes utility (but not necessarily compliance)—will punish infrequently (a high threshold, T) but severely (high punishment).[29] But these analyses studied games where the players did not have the ability to exit the system, or any external boundaries on their ability to punish one another. Noncompliance was valued at the productivity of the union in the absence of any cooperation between the members, and through the discussion in Chapter 2, we know that unions can fall short of their potential, in fact harming the member governments (and their citizens) significantly, if the distribution of authority is set inappropriately or is ignored.

So what is the value to members of a federation of having an outside option? The answer is, of course, "it depends." The exit option is a mixed blessing. On the one hand, it is a way to induce compliance, because governments threaten to exit should the union's performance dip too much. On the other hand, it reduces compliance, because it puts a limit on how bad the punishment can be before a government will prefer not to be a part of the union any longer. While an extremely good outside option is of net benefit to a member of a group, and an undesirable exit option has no positive effect, having a moderately attractive outside option might actually generate lower net utility for the member than having no outside option at all. The logic is straightforward: if a member government has a credible outside option, it reduces the capacity of the other members of the union to induce compliance. While some exit options are beneficial, the net effect of a *moderate* exit option is to hurt the productivity of

---

[28] This discussion leans on the formal analysis in Bednar (2007a).
[29] See Green and Porter (1984). For a numerical example, see Kreps (1990).

the union, and potentially to lower not just compliance, but utility, of its members.[30]

3.4 FITTING FEDERALISM'S COMPLEXITY: IMPLICATIONS FOR DESIGN

The potential benefits of federalism—military security, economic efficiency and innovation, and improved representation—have qualities of classic public goods. One government may attempt to improve the welfare of its own constituents at the expense of the rest of the nation. Such opportunism is a natural temptation of any government, and manifests itself as national encroachment, shirking (or state overreaching), and burden-shifting between states. The distribution of authority, the key to a federation's potential, must be defended against manipulation.

A robust system of federal safeguards minimizes opportunism to give the federation an opportunity to reach its potential. The safeguards are trigger strategies: commitments to react in a particular way to observed behavior. Desirable behavior can be rewarded, undesirable behavior punished. With the self-enforcing federation, the rewards are generated internally and punishments meted out by the governments themselves. The intergovernmental retaliation that I have described here is the most primitive of these mechanisms, and crude. Monitoring is subject to charges of bias. Punishments are hard to adjust and often leads to escalation. A federation sustained by intergovernmental retaliation alone will not be very robust; a few years of bad luck, triggering repeated punishments, could cause the union to rupture—assuming it ever got off the ground. In the remaining chapters, we will consider supplemental safeguards.[31]

We can now summarize the main claims of this chapter. Given this problem, the lessons of this chapter are as follows:

1. A federation's decentralized structure creates incentives for member governments to behave opportunistically.
2. Significant opportunism reduces a federation's productive efficiency and exacerbates allocative problems.
3. Trigger strategies—mutual threats of defection—control opportunistic tendencies.

---

[30] See Bednar (2007a).
[31] In a general analysis of federalism with an application to Argentina, Iaryczower et al. (1999) also stress the importance of supplemental institutions, which they call complementary because they complete the governance structure of the federation.

These observations lead to the following main claim:

4. In federal unions, one should *expect* deviations from the constitutional prescription distributing authority between federal and state authorities.

Furthermore, this behavior is *efficient*: it is utility maximizing. Governments can do no better than deviate a little bit from the distribution, tolerate small deviations by others, and punish forcefully when they observe more significant deviations. From this primary claim, the following two corollaries follow:

5. The outside options available to governments sustain some compliance when they serve as threat points, but also reduce the extent of compliance by minimizing the severity of punishment possible.
6. Unions sustained by intergovernmental retaliation may display significant opportunism.

Two comments bear noting. First, although diversity—both interregional and within the population—affects a federation's promise and needs, none of the results in this chapter has depended on diversity. No heterogeneity is necessary for the public good provision problem to be realized: even without net negative redistribution, uncertainty over who has complied with the terms of the union will mean that governments are tempted to free ride off the compliance of others. Opportunism is inherent, even to the homogeneous federation.

Second, while significant opportunism is detrimental to the union, the fact that opportunism cannot be entirely eliminated may be beneficial to the federation. Given the limitations in our understanding of how to distribute authority, as well as environmental shifts that may recommend alterations from time to time, minor opportunism may be a useful way to explore the space of possible arrangements, leading to discoveries of better ways to distribute authority.

This model is a baseline: the most primitive mechanism available to sanction noncompliant behavior is the threat of retaliation, and ultimately, the rupture of the union. The model indicates that opportunism, despite being generally counterproductive, is inherent to a federal union. It cannot be eliminated. Even if the trigger strategy could be set most efficiently, it could not sustain full compliance. So what does this mean for federations? First, the immediate implication: Every federation will exhibit some opportunism. The Articles of Confederation are an excellent example of a union sustained only by intergovernmental trigger strategies: while the union survived, it certainly was not thriving.

It is now appropriate to ask how this inefficient primitive mechanism of intergovernmental retaliation could be supplemented to boost compliance, thereby improving the federation's performance and ultimately, its robustness. The implications of items 5 and 6 on the above list represent the fundamental challenges of a federation. Taking the final point first, toleration of significant opportunism means that the union returns less to its members. Regarding item 5, while the exit option's attractiveness is out of the control of a federal constitution, its *relative* attractiveness is fair game. As the union grows more productive, returning more to its members, exit will be less tempting. So the objective of constitutional design is to build in safeguards that increase governmental compliance to boost productivity. In addition to the primitive, fundamental safeguard of intergovernmental retaliation introduced in this chapter; further safeguards may be structural, popular, political, or judicial.

In the next chapter we will inspect these safeguards, ultimately rejecting theories that deposit their main trust in any single safeguard. The theory of institutional remedies must be expanded to embrace the complexity of federalism to see how safeguards might work together, by complementing one another, to boost compliance levels above that induced by intergovernmental retaliation alone. In the subsequent chapters I present a theory of how safeguards, singly insufficient, may complement one another to improve compliance and utility. The safeguards may supplement one another in one of three ways: coverage, complementarity, and redundancy.

3.5 Mathematical Appendix to Chapter 3

This appendix supplements the graphical arguments within the chapter with a more formal mathematical analysis that provides sufficient conditions for inherent noncompliance. Although this appendix can be skipped without losing the main thread of the argument, it reveals the proximate causes of slippage and how the level of slippage relates to other features of the federation.

The intuition behind the slippage result is straightforward. A constitutional division of powers, and therefore federalism, must be self-sustaining; it cannot rely upon outside forces to maintain it. Any self-enforcing relationship depends on players doing what is in their best interest. That is, results focus on utility calculations (payoffs to players) rather than compliance maximization. And, as we will see, full compliance, in general, does not provide players with as much utility as partial compliance. The cost of maintaining full compliance, in terms of the frequency of punishment, makes member governments prefer to tolerate a little indiscretion rather than seek perfection.

In what follows, we will consider games where government utility is a function of the actions of other governments, its own noncompliance, and any sanctions. These will be games of imperfect information: the constitutionality of a player's action is not directly visible to other players. Instead, all see a signal of the player's action. In specific games signals may be tied directly to a single player's action, or general, as an indicator of aggregate action. For example, in the Green and Porter (1984) context, the price of oil is an aggregate signal of the oil production of each member of the cartel, while in a Gilligan and Krehbiel (1987, 1989) context, the policy realization or outcome is a signal of the intent of the committee that authorized the policy, and would be indexed to indicate the policy source. In each of these games, there is a target effort level from the contributing players: all, in the public good provision game, or any agent, in a principal-agent context. The target effort level is designed to maximize utility by ensuring that a cooperative equilibrium is obtained. We assume that there is a cost for the government to comply, and therefore it prefers to shirk if it believes it will not be punished or if others will shirk as well.

To induce compliance, we will consider trigger mechanisms. Not meeting the target triggers punishment. At this point there are no constitutional safeguards (they enter in the next chapter), so the trigger mechanism is simply intergovernmental retaliation; the other government's response to an action. In general, the trigger mechanism has three components: a threshold, which it compares the signal against, a punishment, and a duration of the punishment. In this model, I collapse the last two elements into a single parameter, a fine, so that the punishment is realized as a utility loss.

To simplify the presentation, we will consider a linear utility function but include curvature in the probability of being punished. Elsewhere (Bednar 2006) I have developed a full treatment of both cases and general proofs of the claims that follow. In accordance with the logic presented within the chapter, I will define opportunism as a continuous variable $x \in [0, 1]$, so that x is an expression of the degree of noncompliance. With costly compliance (it involves sacrifice), each government prefers not to comply, but benefits from the compliance of others. Specifically, here we will assume that each government's utility is a fraction α of the sum of the contributions to the federation plus whatever that member holds back. We assume $\alpha < 1$; otherwise no collective action problem exists. Given these assumptions, the single period utility to member 1 from its contributions and those of others (governments 2 through n) can be written as follows:

$$u_1(x_1, x_2, \ldots, x_n) = \alpha \sum_{i=1}^{N} (1 - x_i) + x_1 \tag{3.1}$$

To model uncertainty, we will assume that the members of the federation see a common signal ω as an indicator of the amount of noncompliance.[32] The value of ω is a function of the sum of the noncompliance of the three members plus a noise term ϵ, $\omega(\sum x_j, \epsilon) = \theta(\sum x_j) + \epsilon$, where θ is an increasing function. Given this formulation, the noise term could increase or decrease the governments' perceived noncompliance. I will assume here that ϵ takes some value between some minimum $\min_\epsilon$ and maximum $\max_\epsilon$ according to a probability distribution F, which, I assume, has an associated density f. To avoid confusion, $\Pr(\omega > T)$ will denote the probability that ω exceeds a threshold, T. If so, then each member is punished some amount Q at the beginning of the next period, that is, punishment occurs if $\omega(\sum x_j, \epsilon) > T$. The probability of this equals one minus the probability that ϵ is less than $T - \theta(\sum x_j)$. I will write this formally as $1 - F(T - \theta(\sum x_j))$.

The threshold T and the bounds on the error term (its minimum and maximum) determine the range of the governments' aggregate behavior, $\sum x_j$ (at least in all interesting cases). Specifically, $\theta(\sum x_j)$ will lie between $T - \max_\epsilon$ and $T - \min_\epsilon$. To see why, consider the alternatives. Suppose that $\theta(\sum x_j) < T - \max_\epsilon$. Then there is no possibility of punishment: even the worst possible error term will not put the signal ω above the threshold. Therefore the governments have an incentive to be more opportunistic. Alternatively, if $\theta(\sum x_j) > T - \min_\epsilon$, then no matter what the error term is, punishment is certain. Here too governments might as well be more opportunistic because they maximize immediate gain knowing that punishment is on its way anyway. Thus, in equilibrium, we will assume that $\theta(\sum x_j) \in [T - \max_\epsilon, T - \min_\epsilon]$.

To complete the model, I need only include a discount rate δ. I will focus on stationary, symmetric equilibrium in which each member makes the same contribution in each period. This allows me to write a recursive equation that gives the value for member i (the present discounted sum

---

[32] I relax this assumption in Chapter 7.

of utilities, denoted V_i):

$$V_i(x_1, x_2, \ldots, x_n) = \alpha \sum_{j=1}^{N}(1 - x_j) + x_i + \delta\left[\Pr(\omega > T)(-Q)\right.$$

$$\left. + V_i(x_1, x_2, \ldots, x_n)\right] \qquad (3.2)$$

Solving for V_i produces:

$$V_i(x_1, x_2, \ldots, x_n) = \frac{\alpha \sum_{j=1}^{N}(1 - x_j) + x_i - \delta\Pr(\omega > T)(Q)}{1 - \delta} \qquad (3.3)$$

Government i chooses x_i to maximize this value. To solve for the first-order condition, I can exploit the fact that $\Pr(\omega > T) = 1 - F(T - \theta$ $(\sum x_j))$. Taking the derivative of this new expression gives the marginal value of opportunism:

$$\frac{1 - \alpha - \delta f(T - \theta(\sum x_j))\theta'(\sum x_j)Q}{1 - \delta} \qquad (3.4)$$

Recall that f is the density function associated with the probability distribution F. If full compliance were an equilibrium, then this expression would equal zero when $\sum x_j = 0$. Our working assumption throughout the chapter has been that small deviations are very difficult to notice. This implies that $\theta'(0) \sim 0$. In other words, at full compliance the marginal increase in the signal from a slight deviation is approximately zero. Given that assumption, the above expression cannot equal zero at full compliance (because $\alpha \in (0, 1)$, a basic assumption of collective action problems). Therefore in equilibrium some noncompliance occurs.[33]

While this is sufficient to show inherent opportunism, by making further assumptions about the distribution of the error term and the functional form of θ which enters into the signal, I can derive comparative statics, using two models. In the first, we will assume a uniform distribution of the error term which simplifies the analysis but the equilibrium

---

[33] Models that sustain full compliance assume linear signals and uniform distributions of the error term. Given these strong assumptions, it is easy to see that full compliance is possible. The first-order necessary condition becomes

$$\frac{-\alpha + 1 - \delta Q}{1 - \delta}$$

If Q and δ are sufficiently large then this expression is negative, which implies that at the margin opportunism reduces the member's value. This aligns with the intuition from the repeated prisoners' dilemma. If punishment is sufficiently severe, no deviation need occur.

does not depend on the threshold T. Therefore in the second model, I relax the uniform assumption but make the signaling function linear in x_i. This second model, although more complicated, will prove useful when we make the comparison between targeted and universal punishments in Chapter 4.

Model 1: Our first modification is to assume that the error term is uniformly distributed—that it is equally likely to assume any value between $-m$ and m. This implies that $f = \frac{1}{2m}$. Recall the realistic assumption that small deviations are less likely to be caught than larger ones. One way to capture this mathematically is to assume that $\theta(x_1, x_2, \ldots, x_n) = (x_1 + x_2 + \cdots + x_n)^2$. Recall that $\omega(\sum x_j, \epsilon) = \theta(\sum x_j) + \epsilon$. What the governments observe about one anothers' behavior is a combination of signal and noise: with this assumption that squares the sum of the noncompliance, small degrees of opportunism produce a very small signal to noise ratio, and therefore the deviation cannot be detected. The marginal value of opportunism can now be written as follows:

$$\frac{1 - \alpha - \delta \frac{1}{2m} 2(\sum_{j=1}^{N} x_j)Q}{1 - \delta}$$

Notice that the noise term, ϵ, drops out of the derivative because its effect is independent of the action taken by the governments. In this formulation small amounts of opportunism pay, but the marginal value of opportunism falls as the degree of opportunism increases (referring back to the figures, moving rightward on the x-axis). In equilibrium, the marginal value of opportunism will be exactly zero. Setting the previous expression equal to zero gives the following symmetric equilibrium level of noncompliance:

$$x_i = \frac{m(1 - \alpha)}{N \delta Q} \tag{3.5}$$

Note that noncompliance does not go to zero, no matter how high the discount factor (as long as it is not greater than one). This contrasts with linear folk theorem results where full compliance is a possibility. Likewise, even very high punishments (high Q) do not eliminate all opportunism. Again, as long as $\alpha < 1$, opportunism is inherent. Slippage—noncompliance—is unavoidable.

We are also now able to compute comparative statics, or the effect of altering parameters on governmental behavior. Notice that the higher α, δ, N, and Q, the less the slippage: opportunism decreases as the return on compliance increases, as patience increases, as the number of governments increases, and as the penalty increases. On the other hand, opportunism increases as the range of the noise term increases (m). These are all intuitive results.

A natural question to ask is whether this slippage is meaningful. As constructed, the federal problem has two sources of disutility: (1) punishment periods to maintain compliance incentives, even though no one deviated from the equilibrium and (2) the loss due to the equilibrium noncompliance. In the example below, the second source is a greater source of disutility than the first.

A Numerical Example: We can plug in specific numerical values for each of the parameters to help us see the relative effects of slippage and incentive-preserving punishments. Suppose there exists a federation of two states plus a central government (so $N = 3$). Recall that in Model 1 $\omega(x_1, x_2, x_3, \epsilon) = (x_1 + x_2 + x_3)^2 + \epsilon$. I will assume that the random error term is uniformly distributed between -1 and 1 so that $m = 2$, and further assume that the discount rate, δ, equals $\frac{9}{10}$, the return on collective action α equals $\frac{7}{10}$, the punishment for triggering the threshold Q equals 2, and that the threshold T equals 1. To solve for the equilibrium, I need only plug these values into Equation 3.5 to find the equilibrium level of opportunism:

$$x_i = \frac{(2)\left(\frac{3}{10}\right)}{(3)\left(\frac{9}{10}\right)(2)}$$

Thus, $x_i = \frac{1}{9}$. Each member contributes $\frac{8}{9}$. This creates a utility loss. If each member contributed fully (and if we ignore punishment), each member would get utility of 2.1 ($\frac{7}{10} \times 3$) each period. However, owing to opportunism, each member only gets $\frac{7}{10}(\frac{8}{9})(3) = \frac{56}{30}$, per period loss of utility equal to $\frac{7}{30}$, or approximately 0.233.

We want to compare this loss from opportunism to the cost of the punishment regimes. To determine the probability of a punishment regime, we will first calculate the likelihood that the signal ω exceeds the threshold T (set at 1). From above, we have that $\omega = \frac{1}{9} + \frac{1}{9} + \frac{1}{9} + \epsilon$. This exceeds 1 if and only if $\epsilon > \frac{8}{9}$. Given our assumptions, this occurs with probability $\frac{1}{18}$.[34] If we add in our assumptions that $\delta = \frac{9}{10}$ and $Q = 2$, we get that the expected per period loss due to incentive-preserving punishment equals $(\frac{1}{18})(\frac{9}{10})(2)$, which equals $\frac{1}{10}$.

Thus in this numerical example, the utility loss due to opportunism (0.233) exceeds the loss due to incentive-preserving punishment (0.1).

---

[34] Given that $m = 2$, the distribution is uniform with a value of $\frac{1}{2}$. Therefore, the probability that ϵ lies in an interval of length x equals $\frac{x}{2}$.

This need not always be the case; if the probability of punishing or the cost of the punishment was to increase, the losses due to opportunism would decrease and the losses dues to incentive-preserving punishment would increase. At some point, the losses due to opportunism would become smaller than the losses due to incentive-preserving punishment.[35]

Model 2: The first model allowed us to write down the pertinent comparative statics with one exception. Owing to the uniform distribution assumption, the equilibrium opportunism was independent of the threshold, T, except in so far that T was set to make the equilibrium feasible. In this second model, I will relax the uniformity assumption on ϵ but assume that the signal is linear in the governments' actions. Formally, this means that $\theta(\sum x_j) = \sum x_j$.

Recall that F is the probability distribution function of the error term. I will now assume that you are less likely to get a large error than a small one, and that the likelihood of an error decreases as ϵ increases (formally, this means that $F(\epsilon)$ is strictly concave and that $f(\epsilon)$ is a strictly decreasing function). With this restriction on the functional form, I can demonstrate that noncompliance increases as T increases—as the trigger grows more tolerant of deviation.

We start with the first-order necessary condition, derived from Equation 3.4:

$$1 - \alpha - \delta f\left(T - \sum x_j\right)Q = 0 \qquad (3.6)$$

Reducing, and solving for x_i^* becomes:

$$\frac{1 - \alpha}{\delta Q} = f(T - \sum x_j)$$

$$\sum x_j = T - f^{-1}\left(\frac{1 - \alpha}{\delta Q}\right)$$

$$x_1^* = T - f^{-1}\left(\frac{1 - \alpha}{\delta Q}\right) - \sum_{j>1} x_j \qquad (3.7)$$

where $f^{-1}(\cdot)$ is the inverse of the density function. Since by assumption $f(\epsilon)$ was strictly decreasing, its inverse is well defined and also strictly decreasing. Equation 3.7 also generates other comparative statics that agree with our earlier results: noncompliance increases in the amount of

---

[35] One could derive sufficient conditions for the first utility loss to be larger than the second, but that investigation goes beyond the scope of this analysis, where we are concentrating on identifying the general problem of federalism and appropriate remedies for it.

tolerance, T, decreases in the size of the punishment Q, and decreases as the union generates less return (denoted by α). The proof follows by inspection. As T increases, so does x_i^*. As Q increases, the value of the fraction decreases, so the argument of f^{-1} decreases, so f^{-1} increases, and the right-hand side value decreases. Therefore x_i^* decreases in Q: confirming expectations, noncompliance falls as punishments become more severe. Increasing α or δ has the same effect on the argument of f^{-1}, and so it follows that as the union becomes more productive (with more valued returns to the governments within it), governments are more compliant.

Our results require one more step. While I have shown that a partial compliance equilibrium exists, it is possible that no union is more attractive than a union where member governments partially comply. Under this assumption about the error term, if a player chose an $x_i > T$ that player would be punished with certainty. Therefore, any government that deviates significantly will deviate fully, at $x_i = 1$. We therefore have to compare the payoff from playing x_i^* and the payoff from shirking entirely. Recall that the payoff from the former is

$$V_i(x_1^*, x_2^*, \ldots, x_n^*) = \frac{\alpha \sum_{j=1}^N (1 - x_j^*) + x_1^* - \delta \Pr(\omega(x^*, \epsilon) > T)(Q)}{1 - \delta}$$

$$(3.8)$$

Alternatively, the player could choose $x_i = 1$. For simplicity, we will assume that this leads to a punishment regime with probability one. If so, the value to the player equals:

$$V_i(1, x_2^*, \ldots, x_n^*) = \frac{\alpha \sum_{j=2}^N (1 - x_j^*) + 1 - Q}{1 - \delta}$$

$$(3.9)$$

The ability to sustain partial cooperation depends on whether Equation 3.9 < Equation 3.8. That will be true if and only if

$$(1 - \alpha)(1 - x_i^*) \quad < \quad \delta[1 - \Pr(\omega(x^*, \epsilon) > T)]Q \qquad (3.10)$$

We can also use this inequality to derive some comparative statics. As long as Q is large enough, it will always be better to partially comply than to deviate. However, increasing Q too much can cause players to prefer to exit—especially at the onset of a punishment regime as the expected utility of leaving the federation can surpass the expected utility of enduring the punishment and returning to partial compliance. Thus, Q needs to be big enough to support cooperation but no so big that it encourages governments to opt out of the union when punishment becomes necessary.

4

The Safeguards of Federalism

In every federation, governments have an incentive to free ride off the sacrifices made by others. The standard method for overcoming compliance problems is to introduce sanctions for noncompliance. Intergovernmental retaliation is the natural sanction available within any federation, but it is costly to implement, making it ineffective at reducing the frequency of minor transgressions, the everyday aggravations of intergovernmentalism. Threats of retaliation can also quickly escalate, leading to a union of threats and holdouts, hardly a recipe for harmonious union. Now understanding the mechanics behind Madison's analysis of the flaws of the Articles of Confederation, we can begin to examine his prescription: effective sanctions. A federal constitution is as much about designing a common procedure for compliance maintenance and systemic adaptation as it is about allocating authorities.

James Madison provided the intuition for a model when he wrote: "A sanction is essential to the idea of law, as coercion is to that of government" (Madison 1999:72). The rule of law transforms society from the unproductive chaos of a Hobbesian world to the order, trust, and then fertility of a society where we are freed to interact with strangers not because the law transforms us into angels, but because to break the law hurts the perpetrator as well. The law is a coordinating force, but the rule of law is dependent on an enforcer that is capable and motivated to defend it. It is natural to blame others for our own shortfalls, while making excuses for our own transgressions. Governments are no less likely to subjectively perceive transgressions of federal boundaries. Therefore, ideally the governments involved in a dispute will not play a role in monitoring and punishment, but instead allow a common system of safeguards to judge action and impose sanctions. This chapter surveys the breadth of safeguards available in federal constitutional design. Through-out the chapter we will return to Madison's theory and rely primarily on the United States constitution for illustration, although the principles of safeguards are general and each type of safeguard is available (although perhaps not incorporated) in other federal unions.

While the criteria defining a federal union are minimal,[1] federalism is typically associated so closely with many institutional features, such as bicameralism, equal representation of the states, and often, an inde-pendent judiciary, that a complex system of institutions seems inevitable, if not integral, to any successful federation. The variety of institutional features of many federations fall into four main categories:

1. *Structural*, including fragmentation of the national government and giving the state a voice in national decision making;
2. *Popular*, when the public regulates the government;
3. *Political*, the role of the party system to bind together through inter-dependence the officials of the two levels of government, as well as from state to state; and
4. *Judicial*, where the court serves as umpire of legislative constitution-ality.

These safeguards are the diverse set of institutions and actors that might react to governmental action (or intentions) in a way that could alter behavior. Along with the primitive threat of intergovernmental retaliation (which we must not forget as the critical fifth safeguard of federalism), they are the *trigger mechanisms* that shape federalism: each safeguard specifies a boundary on behavior and warns of the reac-tion should its boundary threshold be violated. In theory, there is a common understanding of acceptable behavior, and if that threshold is crossed, then a punishment—structural, political, popular, judicial, or intergovernmental—is triggered.[2]

The most intuitive safeguard is the court. It interprets the constitutional and statutory law that regulates governmental behavior, and when asked to review a particular behavior, the court will review it against its interpre-tation of the law, rendering a judgment about whether or not the behavior has crossed the threshold of tolerance. Other safeguards similarly create

[1] See Section 2.1.
[2] In theory, a common understanding exists; in practice, it is very rare. Throughout the text, I make reference to the lack of common understanding and dedicate Chapter 7, to understanding and resolving it.

an incentive environment that affects governmental behavior.[3] For example, the decentralized party system is a safeguard of federalism when local and state parties react to attempts by the national government to overreach its authority at their expense. They may withhold support for the national government's activities and otherwise signal displeasure as a punishment for overstepping the boundaries on national authority. Several of the safeguards may themselves trigger electoral responses: public acknowledgment of tension within a party or (in structural safeguards) of disagreements between the branches or between houses in the legislature may alert voters to attempts to unbalance the federation.

It may be useful to consider how the federal division of authority might be like a game of tennis between the state and national governments. At times, one may try to gain advantage over the other—here we should let go of a literal application of the metaphor, because the "game" need not create a single winner—nevertheless, at times one government will find it advantageous to skirt the rules or even exploit another for its private considerations, perhaps in service to its constituents. Shots to the corners are difficult to defend, as are serves that skim closely to the net. Referees are needed to decide if the shots adhere to the rules of play. Consider the role of the line judge. On a court at Wimbeldon or Roland Garros, the lines are drawn brilliantly white; players, spectators, and referees all agree on their location. Even still, the line judge is needed to declare whether a shot fell out of bounds.

This vision of the safeguard's role, where the division of authority is sparklingly clear, and the safeguard is needed only to determine the legitimacy of the statute (whether proposed or enacted), is unrealistic. Although the constitution might resemble a rule book, each application of a rule requires interpretation. It is much more likely that in judging action the safeguard also draws the line. This is the declaration of T, the threshold, in our baseline model from Chapter 3. Like the intergovernmental retaliation, a safeguard's declaration of law is not the action that would comprise full compliance, but instead, the behavior that triggers a punishment. The safeguard may also determine the consequence for crossing the threshold, although this punishment might also be predetermined, perhaps by being written into the constitution.

---

[3] For legal scholarship on extra-judicial constitutional interpretation, see, for example, Friedman (1993), Dorf and Friedman (2000), Kramer (2004), and Primus (2006). Whittington (1999) describes the extra-judicial constitutional interpretation as "construction": the political actors shape the constitution, and are shaped by it.

In the appendix to this chapter, I make one important modification to the model developed in Chapter 3. In the baseline model, the only safeguard available to the federation was intergovernmental retaliation. While effective, it is costly: the only way to punish other governments is to punish oneself as well. Punishment tends to be reserved for extreme observations. With the addition of institutional safeguards, punishment can be targeted at offending governments, relieving the other governments of assuming equivalent costs to punishment. (There may still be minor costs of punishment, but they are akin to court costs versus the penalty imposed by the court's negative judgment.) The important result (proven in the appendix) is that despite the reduction in costs, full compliance cannot be sustained.

There is, however, one significant difference in the results: holding fixed the ability to punish, and frequency of punishment, institutional safeguards are often more efficient than intergovernmental retaliation. Safeguards may increase utility and increase compliance over intergovernmental retaliation. The result is not surprising, because we have eliminated the cost of punishment and introduced targeted punishment. However, before anyone gets carried away with enthusiasm for institutional safeguards, I need to emphasize a caveat: *Safeguards must be able to punish as severely as intergovernmental retaliation.* This is unlikely: a judicial decision just does not carry the same force as an army at the border. In the remainder of the chapter, I will review the four basic types of institutional safeguards, noting their strengths, but also weaknesses, including their individual insufficiency to maintain compliance.

4.1 STRUCTURAL SAFEGUARDS

The structural safeguards of federalism restrain the national government to prevent encroachment.[4] Three primary forms of structural safeguards are enumerated powers, fragmentation, and state incorporation. I will first describe each component of structural safeguards and then evaluate their collective capacity to induce compliance. Most modern arguments about structural design of a federal constitution rely heavily on Madison's theory, so I will employ his arguments as illustrations.

---

[4] Portions of this section are drawn from Bednar (2003).

Elements of Structural Safeguards

Enumerated Powers. Although at first glance it may seem to be a tautology, the enumeration of authority itself has been proposed as a safeguard of the distribution of authority. The foundation of the theory is that some distributions of authority are self-regulating; therefore, if the distribution is carefully planned, opportunism may be avoided.

Madison provides the most cogent presentation of this argument in dismissing fears that the national government would grow too powerful under the Constitution, overwhelming the state governments. Madison and his colleagues often tried to deflect concerns that the national government would trespass on the rights of states and citizens by suggesting that the national government would have little opportunity or motivation to do so. Writing long before the welfare state was imagined, both Madison and Hamilton argued that the national government was needed primarily to promote the defense of the union,[5] while states held normal police powers and would perform day-to-day government. Madison wrote in *Federalist* 45:

The operations of the federal government will be most extensive and important in times of war and danger; those of the State governments, in times of peace and security. As the former periods will probably bear a small proportion to the latter, the State governments will here enjoy [an] advantage over the federal government.

To this defense he appends an equilibrium-based argument nudging citizens to arm the national government as completely as possible: "The more adequate, indeed, the federal powers may be rendered to the national defense, the less frequent will be those scenes of danger which might favor their ascendancy over the governments of the particular States." He cleverly inverts fears of the national government's power into a call for supporting it all the more: the stronger the national government's defense capacity, the less need there is for defense; therefore, the less need we will

---

[5] By no means did the founders think that defense was a minor function. Riker (1964:20–1) neatly summarizes the urgency of stabilizing the union: external threats from Great Britain and Spain meant that the American hold on the continent was tenuous. If the union could not be strengthened, then its internal divisions would ease foreign encroachment. Citing the first papers of the *Federalist* (written by John Jay, the diplomat), Washington's preoccupation with war preparedness in letters, and Madison's own notes on the Vices, where 5 of the 11 deal with military weakness, Riker argues that the primary motivation for reconstruing the union was external military threat.

have for the national government generally, and the less it will come to dominate the state governments.

A focus on the distribution of fiscal powers shares a similar logic. The distribution of fiscal authority was a primary concern of many Anti-Federalists (Rakove 1996:194–5) and continues to be focal to many federalism theorists (see, e.g., Weingast 1995, Watts 1999, Rodden and Wibbels 2002, Diaz-Cayeros 2006). Interdependence in fiscal responsibilities and powers maintains a balance between the levels. When one level of government gains an advantage in spending or revenue collection, it can use its fiscal dominance to manipulate policy in realms assigned to the dependent level. We will consider this problem further in Section 7.3.

Interinstitutional Oversight. Separation of powers is Madison's most enduring contribution to the theory of political institutions. Breaking with the parliamentary model, Madison advocated the fragmentation of executive, legislative, and judicial power at the national level. In so doing, Madison implicitly acknowledged that the federal system is not self-regulating, for the same reasons that humans find self-restraint difficult. Just as human society needs laws, the federation needs institutional support.

Human innate self-interest makes opportunities difficult to resist; a tendency to compare ourselves against others breeds natural jealousy. Recall the effect of suspicion in Chapter 3: the defenses we construct against opportunists may lead us to self-interested behavior as well. Brilliantly, Madison transforms vice into virtue by manipulating the institutions of government to mimic the forces of selfishness in society: "[A]mbition must be able to counteract ambition." Madison's theoretical trick is to fragment government but make the components partially dependent on one another through checks and balances. The antagonism within governmental parts induces a self-regulating whole.

To Madison, separation of powers was necessary for "preservation of liberty" and the prevention of tyrannical laws.[6] Madison fused protection of the people with maintenance of federalism, and separation of powers could help achieve both ends, dubbing it in *Federalist* 51 a "double security," explaining in a later editorial: "[So] it is to be hoped ... the two governments possess each the means of preventing or

---

[6] See, for example, "Remarks in the Federal Convention on Electing the Executive," July 17, 1787, in Madison (1999:125–7) and *Federalist* 51.

correcting unconstitutional encroachments of the other."[7] While separation of powers might contribute to governmental efficiency because of task specialization, it seems far more likely to stall government action as the distinct interests bargain. For this reason, stagnation is evidence that separation of powers is working according to theory, because gridlock means that no one interest is able to overwhelm another. By frustrating attempts to dominate, separation of powers preserves federalism and protects people from tyranny.

In Madison's theory, separation of powers has two necessary ingredients: distinct but partially overlapping power, and independence. Overlapping power allows one branch to oversee the actions of another (or, with bicameralism, internal division creates a self-regulating organization). In a 1785 reply to questions asked by his friend Caleb Wallace, in the course of agreeing with Wallace that amendment was necessary, he slipped in a comment about the importance of having some remedy available when one branch believes that another has superseded its powers (1999:41): interbranch conflict was on his mind, and rather than promote a unified government, he sought an institutional outlet for internal disagreement. The cousin to separate powers, bicameralism, further unravels the structural monolith of parliamentary government by fragmenting power within the legislature. In the same letter to Wallace, Madison denigrated the design of the existing Senate,[8] but "bad as it is, it is often a useful bitt in the mouth of the house of Delegates" (1999:40). In the Constitutional Convention, speaking on the proposed Senate, Madison argued: "[A]ll business liable to abuses is made to pass thro' separate hands, the one being a check on the other" (1999:110).

In sum, interinstitutional oversight works through a combination of independence and dependence. Structural safeguards should have distinct wills but need one another to act. When this balance is achieved, the national government is less likely to behave opportunistically, whether by encroaching on the state governments or by tyrannizing its citizens.

State supervision. In the pure form of dual federalism, the states and the national government are like layers of a cake: authorities are divided exhaustively between them, with no shared powers. Federalism's

---

[7] James Madison, "Government of the United States", *National Gazette*, February 6, 1792, in Madison, *Papers* vol. 14:217–8.

[8] He joined objections in the Convention to state representation in the Senate (Rakove 1996).

theorists have resoundingly rejected this model, from Morton Grodzins' description of American federalism as a marbled cake, to Elazar's definition of federalism as shared sovereignty. Wechsler (1954) renewed interest in state supervision by noting the states' involvement in national decision making. State supervision shares the same combination of independence and dependence that drives the other elements of interinstitutional oversight, and while it is the least elaborated component of Madison's system of constraints on the national government, it is one of the most cited today, often appearing in the U.S. Supreme Court arguments.

Although history students remember *Federalist* 51 as a defense of separation of powers, in it Madison describes a parallel system for maintaining the power balance between state and national governments: "the different governments will control each other, at the same time that each will be controlled by itself" (*Federalist* 51). "So it is to be hoped," Madison later wrote in a newspaper editorial, "the two governments possess each the means of preventing or correcting unconstitutional encroachments of the other" (Madison 1999:508). States supervise national action from both within and without the national government apparatus because the Constitution has made the national government dependent on them to act. In correspondence with Thomas Jefferson, Madison wrote: "This dependence of the General, on the local authorities, seems effectually to guard the latter against any dangerous encroachments of the former" (1999:147–8).

In theory, the entanglement of state and national interests in the national legislature makes it unlikely that the national government will ignore state concerns. Reminiscent of Madison's earlier assurances that the national government will have no desire to encroach on the states, he submitted in later correspondence that:

encroachments of [state sovereignty] are more to be apprehended from impulses given to it by a majority of the States seduced by expected advantages, than from the love of Power in the Body itself, controuled as it *now* is by its responsibility to the Constituent Body

(1999:774). National encroachment, if it occurs, is likely to be from state capture of the national government.

Within the national government, states have many avenues to express their interests. In *Federalist* 39, Madison describes how the Constitution is both federal and national: by federal he means that the states are involved in the central level decision making, and he cites the Senate (then appointed by state legislatures), the electoral college, and state ratification of the Constitution, as well as the "natural attachment" (*Federalist* 46) that citizens have to their own state, as evidence. Madison continues the theme in *Federalist* 45, adding that House members, although directly elected by the people, will likely have state legislative experience.

In federations outside of the U.S. model, other structural methods of incorporating state interests into national decision making have been tried. In Canada, a convention exists of consultation with the provincial premiers before the prime minister proposes any changes to the distribution of authority. Several unions—Switzerland, the former Yugoslavia, and the European Union—have adopted a power-sharing system that rotates the executive leadership between the states.[9]

States may also stand up for themselves: they will watch what the national government does, and if any one perceives encroachment it will spread a cry of alarm. Madison wrote in *Federalist* 45:

But ambitious encroachments of the federal government, on the authority of the State governments, would not excite the opposition of the single State, or of a few States only. They would be signals of general alarm. Every government would espouse the common cause.

Ignoring any collective action problem,[10] much less the possibility that the national government's encroachment may be welcomed by some of the states, Madison argued that the states would watch national action closely and jointly protest any violation. The 1798 Virginia and Kentucky Resolutions were attempts to trigger this safeguard to resist the Alien and Sedition Acts of the Adams administration.

---

[9] Still others have rotated leadership between other societal subcomponents, including religious groups (Lebanon) and political parties (Colombia). For analysis of the European Union's rotating council presidency, see Kollman (2003), who points out that one significant advantage is innovation: new policies are tried due to the leader's agenda-setting position.

[10] Madison's logical slip is worth noting because he well understood the collective action problem in state financing of war debt. Perhaps he believed protest was costless—that it was in each individual states interest to protest—thereby skirting the collective action problem, or that he still did not believe that the national government would encroach, so given the irrelevance of counterstrategies, he did not devote much thought to the protest mechanism. Or perhaps, a better assumption still is to recognize the *Federalist* for the propaganda that it was; Madison must have known how well this vision would appeal to Publius' readers. Rhetorically, it is brilliant: to refute the claim, one must admit that states would become complacent or are poorly organized, thereby doing more damage to Anti-Federalist arguments than to the Federalists'.

Evaluation of Structural Safeguards

The criticism most often leveled at the structural safeguards, dominated as they are by institutional arrangements designed to fragment authority and incorporate state interests, is that they are undemocratic because they introduce bias in the system of representation (e.g., Stepan 1999, Dahl 2002). In any structural safeguard that gives the states equal (or nearly so) voice, the citizens of the smaller states have greater voting power than those in larger states. This criticism extends to many of the structural safeguards: upper legislative houses, including in the U.S. senatorial confirmations of the judiciary, the U.S. electoral college, and the Canadian norm of provincial consent on constitutional changes affecting federalism (not written into the constitution, but identified as a nonjusticiable norm by the Canadian Supreme Court in the *Patriation Reference*[11]). If the criteria for judgment is purely democratic equality, surely these institutions fall short. But our concern is federalism, and democratic equality may need to be compromised to achieve some of the other potentials that federalism can offer, such as the feasibility of a union with heterogeneous subpopulations.

Our primary concern is with how well the structural safeguards satisfy the conditions of an effective safeguard as established by the above model. Recall our central problem: to ensure the productivity of the union by minimizing opportunism, defending the distribution of power, and ensuring that adaptations to the division are efficient. The structural safeguards fragment the national exercise of power and force the national government to hear the perspective of the states. There are three weaknesses of the structural safeguards as sanctioning devices to prevent counterproductive opportunism. First, they do not affect all opportunism; with rare exceptions, the structural safeguards can only prevent encroachment. Second, even limiting our expectations to the realm of monitoring and sanctioning encroachment, the setting of the threshold, T, may be imperfect. Third, state supervision is suspect: states cannot be counted upon to defend one another *as states*, and fragmentation's creation of independent wills may evaporate in the vertical competitive context. I elaborate on these points next.

Incompleteness. As a prevention of encroachment, structural safeguards may perform well. When the national government's powers are

---

[11] *Re Resolution to Amend the Constitution* [1981] 1 S.C.R. 753 (in the Canadian Supreme Court).

fragmented, and each serves a slightly different set of constituents, then what would be a singular interest in a unitary government becomes internally competitive, with distinct (correlated, but still distinct) interests and each a desire to please its constituents. In essence, internal fragmentation creates veto players. Tsebelis (2002) has modeled the effect of multiple veto players on policy stability. With more veto players, it is harder to adjust policy because it is more likely that any move disadvantages one player. At the same time, it has a moderating effect on policy; extremist policies can be shifted to a more central position, preferred by all veto players. In this way, veto players improve the performance of the union by permitting change to unsuccessful, disliked policies, but tempering the rate of change of fairly successful policies.

Therefore, structural safeguards—increasing veto players at the national level—generate more policy stability from the national government. Does this lead to a more robust federation? Possibly, but probably not, for two reasons. First, when we transplant the theory to federalism, with multiple layers of government, we see that the theory is correct but incomplete. Veto players at the national level may help to prevent encroachment, but can do nothing to prevent shirking or burden-shifting, the opportunism by the states. Clearly, structural safeguards need to be supplemented by another mechanism to prevent state opportunism. Second, the policy inflexibility introduced by veto players may work *against* robustness because it inhibits adaptation. Future chapters address both of these problems.

State Supervision, as States? Many of the forms of incorporation, such as representation in the Senate, or legislators with former state legislative experience, cannot guarantee that a representative would stick up for the states as states. A national representative serves the people of his state, not the state government. Even when senators were directly appointed by the state legislators, Riker (1955) found little evidence that the state legislators were able to enforce their instructions to the senators. Similarly, there is no reason to believe that a representative who has had experience in a state legislature will betray her own interests or the interest of her current institution out of sentimentality for former colleagues. An exemption would be made for systems unlike the United States, where the natural progression of ambition does not set a strict hierarchy between state and national level institutions. For example, in Canada it is a regular feature of a political life for a member of the national legislature to serve later at the provincial level.

A Common Adversary. To prevent encroachment, structural safeguards need to be in competition with one another, motivated to prevent one another from taking action that would cause the federal government to overstep its bounds. "Each department should have a will of its own," writes Madison in *Federalist* 51. The structural safeguards would fail if its components could gain from cooperation. If opportunism is a power tug-of-war, then the federal branches would all benefit by pulling authority away from the states and into their shared jurisdiction. Task specialization is not enough to break the team mentality of the government. Their objectives and incentives must be independent as well. Electoral design may alleviate this problem: electoral separation prevents the coagulation of interests, thereby exploiting institutional self-interest by inducing the branches to be watchful of one another's actions. In a unified government, whistle-blowers lose their jobs when their party is punished at the polls. With separation of powers, constituents are not restricted to such a blunt instrument; they may retain their district's representative while rejecting their president.

Even when the prudence of independence and overlapping powers is seen, it is still difficult to work out in practice a combination of institutions that can carry it off. Certainly, Madison's vision of the government evolved with experience: he seems to have grown more convinced of the necessity to disentangle the branches and put them on much more equal footing.[12] If the mechanisms to provide independence are functioning correctly, a consequence is conflicting interests that need to be aired and reconciled. One feature that the remainder of this section will highlight is different mechanisms proposed to mediate intergovernmental disputes.

While separation of powers promotes contest and compromise, if it is at all imbalanced, it alone does not provide a means to halt interbranch encroachment, nor does it guarantee the constitutional boundaries. A complete institutional recipe must include some method of binding government action through constitutional review. Instinctively, the judiciary seems a likely candidate, but Madison and his colleagues were wary of vesting so much power in an unelected body,[13] and Madison doubted

---

[12] Madison's appreciation for the difficulties in achieving independence grew. Earlier structural schemes do not show this sensitivity: *The Virginia Plan* called for the lower legislative house to appoint an upper, and the two chambers together would appoint the other branches. Staggered terms would "ensure" independence. Following the Convention, he was much more supportive of fragmenting the elections and the constituencies of the separate branches and the two legislative houses.

[13] For the modern edition of this concern, see Ely (1980) and Friedman (1993).

that the judiciary alone would be strong enough to counter the other two branches (Rakove 2002). Instead, Madison was intrigued by an institution in the 1777 constitution of New York, a Council of Revision (1999:41). The Council of Revision joined the judiciary to the executive in a body that would have power to veto national legislation, as well as reject the legislature's vetoes of state legislation.[14]

I am reserving discussion of the judiciary for its own subsection, although properly speaking, it is an element of structural safeguards. Madison left it out of his early theory; it is not even mentioned in *The Virginia Plan*.[15] In later years he was more receptive to its potential, although he remained concerned that the judiciary would not have enough influence to control the state governments.[16] The judiciary does not fit with the arguments of this section because as a (largely) nonpolitical actor, its motivations are different from those of the political branches. But most importantly, it views its role differently; it has a different method and perspective. I elaborate shortly.

4.2 POPULAR SAFEGUARDS

Structural safeguards are but "auxiliary precautions," writes Madison: the primary control of the government is its dependence on the people (*Federalist* 51).[17] But the people are a strange safeguard. Treated as such, they become an independent variable, a way to explain the robustness of a federation. But the popular—and especially electoral—safeguard is also a dependent variable, a product of the system: improving representation is one of the potential objectives of federalism, and democratic competitiveness is one potential measure of robustness. Further compounding the analytical circularity is the conventional intuition that citizen participation depends on public confidence in the political system, but that

---

[14] For more discussion of the Council of Revision, see Bednar (2003).

[15] In point 9 of *The Virginia Plan* he details his conception of the judiciary's role, which includes no powers of review, unless you creatively interpret "questions which may involve the national peace and harmony" (Madison 1999:91).

[16] See the discussion in Rakove (1996:171–7, 2002).

[17] The people's capacity to uphold their constitution has received increasing attention in the legal scholarship: see Kramer (2004) for an exposition of "popular constitutionalism": the capacity of citizens to interpret the constitution themselves, to determine what is acceptable governmental practice according to the constitutional bond between them, and to hold their government to this interpretation. On federalism, see Mikos (2007) who argues that federalism is upheld through "populist" safeguards and Levy (2007), arguing that citizen allegiance to the state minimizes the potential for tyranny.

legitimacy is established with experience, so popular safeguards grow in capacity as the federation proves itself to be robust. In this section, I lay out the argument for popular safeguards while acknowledging the feedback. Resolution comes in Chapter 7.

It may seem odd to talk about citizens safeguarding federalism in a nondemocracy, but as Madison writes, even the tyrant is concerned about his public:

> The stability of all governments and security of all rights may be traced to the same source. The most arbitrary government is controuled where the public opinion is fixed. The despot of Constantinople dares not lay a new tax, because every slave thinks he ought not.[18]

Revolution is enormously costly, but popular rejection lurks in the mind of any leader. Even in democracies, where citizen control may appear more readily available, popular safeguards remain difficult to employ.

Theory of Popular Control

Our goal is to consider whether the people—in democracies, primarily the electorate—might serve as an umpire to patrol the boundaries of federal and state authorities. In Note 11 of the "Vices" and in *Federalist* 10 Madison frankly assesses the capacity of citizens to control their government generally, with the concern of tyranny in mind. When the sphere of influence is too small, citizens cluster into factions of self-interest: government will serve these factions rather than the broader interests of the nation. Citizens are also prey to two types of undesirable representatives: the smarmy charismatic manipulator who pursues "base and selfish measures, masked by pretexts of public good and apparent expediency" and the "honest but unenlightened" representative who frequently becomes the former's "dupe."[19]

Rather than rejecting popular control, Madison sought an electoral system that could alleviate these tendencies. He planned to rescue popular sovereignty by perfecting the means by which people control their government. He was confident that if the people had the right instruments for governance—those that captured their reason while controlling their passion—then no government could better guarantee individual rights than a representative democracy (Madison 1999:532–4). Multiple levels

---

[18] James Madison, *National Gazette*, January 19, 1792, in Madison (1999:503).
[19] "Vices of the Political System of the United States," April 1787, in Madison (1999:69–80), quotations in Note 11, p. 76.

of energetic government, enabled by and accountable to the people, would resist attempts to consolidate power.

Two levels of government bring more political offices, and with them, more opportunities for voters to hone their electoral skills. If elections are episodically distributed, then voting becomes a common part of citizenship.[20] Frequency creates fatigue, true, but before voters can become jaded they acquire experience. The familiarity of the voting booth and the expectation that the act, when all votes are counted, will have an effect, creates first a confidence in the democratic practice, and second, empowerment. In analyzing Russia's developing democracy, Ordeshook and Shvetsova recommended instituting frequent local elections (Ordeshook and Shvetsova 1995, Ordeshook 1996). While they hoped that local elections would seed a system of parties where politicians were dependent on one another across levels (more on their theory of political safeguards comes in the next section), acquiring an ease with electoral practice is an important aspect of democratization.

Secondly, a hierarchy of offices, when combined with progressive ambition—politicians who want to move "up the ladder"—gives voters a chance to gain experience with their politicians locally, learning (ideally) to distinguish the "enlightened statesmen," as Madison calls the ideal public servants in *Federalist* 10, from the would-be tyrants and the dupes who follow them. To the extent that political candidates are equivalent to a gardener's "volunteers," emerging through self-selection rather being planted by parties, federalism gives voters a chance to observe politicians in lower offices, weeding out the undesirables while retaining and promoting the better public servants.

From the hierarchy of offices flows a third potential of popular safeguards. Recall the diversity of institutions involved in structural safeguards. In the democratic federation, these safeguards are responsive to the people, but each one is responsible to a different set or aggregation of people. Therefore to the extent that the structural safeguards depend on conflict generated by distinct interests, the multilevel electoral system samples citizen preferences in various ways and in doing so strengthens the likelihood of separate interests in any one government or component of government (or, equivalently, reduces the likelihood that the structural safeguards share the same interest). In this manner popular safeguards boost structural safeguards. (The next three chapters examine complementarities in much more detail.)

[20] Madison underscores the importance of frequent elections in *Federalist* 52.

Madison reassured constitutional skeptics that directly or indirectly the people controlled all national institutions. Congress' bicameral structure tempered the House's passionate impulse with the Senate's longer view, and the executive might recruit seasoned leadership, but all were subject to electoral review (the Senate and president indirectly). Rather than construct a criticism of the undemocratic judiciary, he optimistically pointed out that the people had indirect control over appointments, and underscored (twice repeating it in *Federalist* 39) that the judges would retain office only in cases of good behavior. The Constitution itself could be amended by the people, although only indirectly (through Article V).[21]

Inarguably, Madison envisioned federal dynamics as pulled by a joint team of national and state governments, but the people held the whip and reins. "The federal and State governments are in fact but different agents and trustees of the people, constituted with different powers, and designed for different purposes" (*Federalist* 46). Federalism, by creating a multilevel electoral system, encourages citizens to think of their governments as tools. Rather than placing all faith and trust in one government, they develop an instrumental view of government: it is meant to serve the people's interest. Citizens then may select the right tool for the job, and if the tool does not work right, replace it.

In order for the electorate to be an effective safeguard of federalism, it must have a threshold that when crossed, triggers a sanctioning reaction. In Volden (2005), voters patrol not constitutional boundaries, but efficient governmental activity, punishing those governments that are inefficient. Where constitutional boundaries are connected to efficiency, Volden's model becomes one of electoral management of federalism. He generates a surprising paradox: despite an electorate focused on efficiency, federalism creates an inefficient overprovision of public goods, compared to a unitary state.

---

[21] He did not support direct popular constitutional amendment. In *Federalist* 49, he criticized Jefferson's proposal for frequent or periodic review of the Constitution by the people, as it implied some flaw in the government and reduced the legitimacy of the Constitution. Madison's fear is not so much with the people's involvement but the method of their involvement: passion may lead to regret. Government should channel passion; passion should not be able to directly influence the structure of government. To reject popular constitutional amendment is consistent with Madison's goal of improving the operation of representative government. However, in the same essay, Madison does admit of the power of knowing that many others share the same view, knowledge that elections may establish. I will return to this thought in Chapter 7.

The informational requirements of a mass action by the electorate are significant; Chapter 7 is largely dedicated to understanding under what circumstances the informational obstacles might be overcome. Setting aside that problem for the moment, we still must be convinced that citizens would be willing to punish their government. To the extent that they have an allegiance to a government they identify with it; rejecting governmental action is akin to selfcriticism. With multiple levels of government, no single government is necessarily identified with the regime or representative of the nation. By breaking citizens free from allegiance to a single government, they are able to view any particular government as an instrument. An indication of this instrumental view of governments may be the extent that voters elect different parties to power at different levels of government. Dubbed "vertical balancing," scholars have empirically identified this phenomenon in the United States, Germany, and Canada.[22]

Evaluation of Popular Control

Despite the optimism coursing through the theory of popular safeguards, it is possible that federalism abets rather than dispels the electoral problem it was designed to overcome: accountability. The primary impediment for popular accountability, regardless of the number of governments, is information: do the voters know what they are voting for? Federalism may (in theory) encourage citizens to view governments as tools, but its complexity may frustrate voters' ability to put their tools to best use. In federalism, patrolling the boundaries of authority means identifying both the constitutional division as well as the government responsible for an action.[23]

---

[22] See Gaines (1992), Soss and Canon (1995), Lohmann, et al. (1997), Erikson and Filippov (2001), Kedar (2004), and Gaines and Crombez (2004). Researchers generally attribute vertical balancing to a desire for policy moderation, extending the divided government hypotheses to federalism. The explanation hinges on power sharing between levels of government in the policy areas most salient to voters.

[23] In their criticism of the U.S. Supreme Court's spending doctrine, where the court has admitted a broad ability for the federal govenrment to attach conditions to money transferred to the states, McCoy and Friedman (1988) point out the obstacles this creates for effective electoral management of federalism. Powell (2000:62–8) argues that federalism decreases accountability: by incorporating the opposition into decision making, responsibility is blurred. Gehlbach (2007) untangles the claim further by investigating the effect of a variety of electoral institutions on local and national electoral control; his analysis agrees with Powell's general principles.

A second problem, tangential to information, is self-interest. When the union distinguishes territorial regions, voters are naturally inclined to support policies favorable to their local interests and pay less attention to the effect on national welfare. Electoral responsibility can augment the opportunism we were trying to escape. Filippov et al. (2004) champion the party system as safeguard because it offers a method for overcoming this inefficiency generated by parochial interests. The next section develops their argument in some detail.

A combination of information deficiency and self-interest leads to a credit assignment problem (Bednar 2007b), where a government exploits voter uncertainty to transgress in its own electoral interest. Although voters do not directly encourage opportunism, they reward politicians who pursue policies that minimize the likelihood of a bad policy outcome or maximize the likelihood of a good one. If politicians are unlikely to win reelection, they may try to associate themselves with a successful policy launched by a different government. In order to claim credit, they only need to be able to point to some minimal action in the policy realm. In this manner, a retrospective electoral retention decision rule creates inefficiencies as well as authority drift.

Finally, we return to the question of allegiance. A reliable safeguard will trigger regardless of which government was perpetrator and which (if any) was victim. If citizens identify primarily with one government, then they may forgive or ignore (or even reward) its opportunistic behavior, or be blind to it altogether. A canonical example is the near-exclusive allegiance of citizens to their states under the Articles of Confederation: voters did not sanction their state governments for shirking in provision of the congressional requests. The union created by the Articles of Confederation was not a federation precisely because there was no direct relationship between the citizens and the Congress; this example emphasizes the importance of a vibrant relationship between citizens and the governments at both levels. Asymmetric allegiance reduces the likelihood that popular safeguards cover all types of opportunism and may even spur more transgressions. Its counterproductive potential makes the problem of federalism more complex: how does the public form a common view of federalism's boundaries, and what conditions make it more likely

In preliminary empirical evaluations, Rodden and Wibbels (2005) find little support for distinct electoral accountability between levels of government in federal systems.

that the public will police those boundaries? Chapter 7 returns to these questions.

4.3 POLITICAL SAFEGUARDS

Political safeguards—the organization of the party system—were not part of Madison's plan for federalism, but have been introduced by modern scholars. Given that the robust federation shifts redistributive tendencies to productive ones, at first blush, the political parties would seem to be an odd method to overcome self-interest. In the United States, politicians woo voters with pork from Washington, and voters respond enthusiastically even as they complain of government waste. It would seem that any system directed by pork addicts cannot move beyond distributional concerns. Filippov et al. (2004) hone in on this weakness of electoral control to develop an ingenious argument about the potential of political safeguards: an integrated party system, where politicians are progressively ambitious but the local and national branches of a party are dependent on one another for their own success, causes politicians to be *imperfect* agents of their constituents.

Theory of Political Safeguards

Apart from the direct effect of the ballot box, the electoral system generates a secondary system, political parties, whose force has the potential to overcome the deficiencies of the popular safeguards. Political safeguards are distinct from popular safeguards: the political safeguard is interested not in the electoral process but instead in the organization that forms to bind together political candidates. The party organization offers many benefits to the candidate, from campaign finance to strategic development to a brand name. In return, the politician supports party-defined goals. In evaluating the ability of the political system to overcome the federal problem of destructive opportunism, again we are asking the question: do these institutional mechanisms create incentives for the policymakers to respect federalism, whether they do so intentionally or not?

States are often fiscally dependent on the national government. Riker (1964) argues that the U.S. federation was always centralized; others, such as Diaz-Cayeros (2006) (examining Latin American federations), say that a natural trend in federations is a steady creep toward fiscal centralization. Politically, a reversal of the tables helps to balance the federation. A decentralized party system can counter encroachment because the national

Table 4.1. *Criteria Defining Integrated Parties*

1.	The party's organization exists at all levels—national, regional, and local—and fields candidates at all levels.
2.	The party's electoral success at the national level facilitates the electoral success of its candidates at the local and regional level. Defecting from the party's coalition, especially if it is successful nationally, is costly to local and regional candidates.
3.	The regional and local organizations and candidates of the party retain sufficient autonomy, nevertheless, to direct their own campaigns and to defect from the national party (or a candidate of the party for national office).
4.	National platforms are acceptable in local terms and are interpreted in local terms by local politicians campaigning on behalf of national parties in national elections.
5.	Every component part of theparty contributes to the party's overall success, so that the defection of any part diminishes the party's overall strength in its competition with other parties for other offices.
6.	Winning nationally requires that the party and its candidates campaign locally.
7.	The offices the party seeks to fill through election at the local and regional levels are meaningful—they control valuable resources and those who fill them can implement policy that can either aid or thwart the policies implemented at the national level.

Source: Filippov et al. (2004:192).

government is dependent on the state party apparatus for support (Riker 1964, Kramer 1994, 2000, Filippov et al. 2004). To overcome the potential imbalance of overperipheralization politically, Filippov et al. describe an *integrated* party system, where the different levels of the political party are interdependent. One method of creating this connection between levels is through the individual politicians; political ambitions cause local and state politicians to imagine themselves in higher public office and appreciate the expanded authority national encroachment would provide. A sympathy develops between the levels of the party system; the hope is that this sympathy translates into mutual respect for authority, and federal productivity. While it is critical that the party organization be integrated, rather than decentralized, it may be difficult to disentangle the two. Table 4.1 presents the criteria offered by Filippov et al. to recognize an integrated party.

Political safeguards theories diverge in their philosophy about the people: are they the root of the problem or its ultimate resolution? This opposition in views is expressed in Filippov et al. and Kramer: in Filippov et al. the role of a party system is to overcome the self-interest inherent to electoral demands by giving the representatives the ability to represent them imperfectly; that is, to ignore them. On the other hand, with Kramer, parties are a means to incorporate the totality of the voters' preferences. Like Madison argued in developing the structural safeguards thesis, since we cannot shake human nature, embrace it. Political officials are self-interested: they want to win office. In accountability theory, this works to focus their actions to satisfy voter preferences; if they do not serve their constituents, then they will not be reelected. But in the problem of federalism as described by Filippov et al., voters are part of the problem: they get too caught up in what they can get from the federation. They want more and more of the public pot for themselves. This rivalry is destructive; those who gain less might just want to leave the union. But the only way to share is for a majority to agree to share.

How is a political official to develop the urge to share? By being ambitious. If public officials have their eye on bigger jurisdictions, they will act to please not just their current constituents, but those in the larger territory as well. Progressive ambition is a way for the larger territories to be served by lower level representatives. When the electoral system offers lots of opportunities for advancement, ambitious public officials will take a broader view; if not exactly keeping the national interest at heart, at least one larger than the parochial interest of their current constituents. But in an open political market, why would voters ever vote for a representative who is distracted by larger horizons? Because they understand that in order to get anything at home some political clout is needed, and that clout can come with a party's support. The party becomes a conduit, nurturing the ambition of the public official as well as the appetite of the locally minded voter.

Whether it works because representatives are freed from the voters (Filippov et al.) or because local and regional interests are taken seriously at the national level (Kramer), as a solution to the allocative problem, an integrated party system is excellent. It ensures that the divisible public goods produced by the federation are distributed throughout the nation, and that both strong and weak party holds are serviced: the strong because the political official is more likely to have gained, through seniority, a position of influence, and the weak, because the party senses that the district is either under attack or vulnerable to falling, and will pump resources into the district to win over the hearts of the voters.

A safeguard's duty is to protect the boundaries of authority to help the federation reach its potential. While the party system distributes the pie, it must work to make the pie grow. How could it do this? Three answers: coordination, patience, and nationalized vision. First, again, it is the nature of the production problem that as the pie grows, everyone is better off because there is more to share, but each individual has an incentive to take just a bit more for himself. The party system, through its organizational structure, may aid the cooperation necessary to overcome the suspicion of others' defection; it may also be more efficient at punishing deviants from within the party, in a form of in-group policing.[24] Second, another element that inhibits cooperation is impatience: the short interval between elections and the "what have you done for me lately?" attitude of retrospective voters causes many political officials to prioritize immediate gains over longer term growth strategies. Here again the party system may help by sufficiently overlapping the generations of candidates within it to stretch out their strategic perspective and promote production.[25] Finally the party system may be an engine that develops a nationalized set of priorities, shifting attention away from the localized concerns that contribute to rivalrous, counterproductive behavior.

The integrated party system addresses some of our main concerns about popular safeguards. But it is not guaranteed to work. The means that the party system might use to translate allocative efficiency into productive efficiency are hypothesized, but not established in the literature. It is easy to generate intuitive counterhypotheses that suggest that the party system might fail to shift attention from redistribution to production.

Evaluation of Political Safeguards

The party system can free politicians from strict adherence to people's wishes. As a safeguard, this has many advantages: not only will it trigger for localistic opportunism, but it might tolerate adjustments that are beneficial overall for the union. On the other hand, there is no guarantee that the outcomes will be beneficial for the whole union. The motivation of the party is to win elections. Some policy domains may be well served by this objective—perhaps the economy, certainly security—but others, such as minority rights, are not. An integrated party system also relies upon a delicate balance between national and local politicians that is difficult to engineer. Ultimately, the weakness of political safeguards is its inconsistency.

---

[24] See a related example in Fearon and Laitin (1996).
[25] In Diermeier (1995), the institutional structure of Congress generates overlapping generations of legislators, enabling coordination despite lawmakers' short-time horizons.

The theory of allocative efficiency is about the distribution of the divisible product of federalism, not inherently about the distribution of authority within it. The theory will attend authority indirectly; authority will be shifted about to improve the allocation of goods. This adjustment to authority may aid the productive efficiency of the federation. But it also may be fruitful for parties to redistribute authority in a way that promotes allocation but corrodes the union's productive effectiveness. For example, if one party controls all institutions within the national government, then the national political officials may encroach upon the states, and this power shift may not be objectionable to the states because they benefit from fiscal returns.[26] The lure of pork is perhaps inevitable; at least political safeguards seem ill-equipped and certainly mount an incomplete resistance to federal encroachment in the pursuit of pork.

We also see that the party system is less effective at minimizing burden-shifting than might appear from the value of the imperfect agent. An imperfect agent may be able to ignore demands to shirk, and may be able to reject encroachment (apart from that useful for solving allocative problems), but the party organization operates through a vertical hierarchy; burden-shifting incentives still exist, although compensation may be engineered through the federal coffers.

The balance between the political party organizations at the local and national level must be just right: if the national party organization or the local party dominates the relationship, then the political safeguards will not resist transgressions uniformly. It may be that the equilibrium is forgiving: that the system tolerates a broad band of slight asymmetry between the levels, or that temporary imbalances can be recovered. But

---

[26] Consider the development of major public works projects in the United States. *Never get between a congressman and asphalt because you will get run over.* How did this reference to the importance of the highway spending bill to congressional members' reelection success become a Washington axiom? Pork is ordinarily cast as inefficient government spending, and its motivation is explainable generally by Weingast et al. (1981) (and see also Volden 2005), who provide the logic for the universalistic results over minimal winning coalitions; in translation, they help us to understand why in every highway bill there is something for every district due to the desire for political insurance provided by universalism. But originally great public works projects were a federalism issue, not just a budget issue, and public works projects were regularly vetoed. Madison and Hamilton split over their views on federal spending powers; Madison believed that public works projects were essentially local and should be funded and controlled locally. Although the New Deal is generally identified as the point of great expansion of federal powers, Elazar (1962) documents extensive cooperation between local, state, and federal government in the United States dating back to Reconstruction.

the opposite may just as well be true: it could be that small imbalances cause the system to tip irretrievably in one direction (see Diaz-Cayeros 2006). Political safeguards may not have the incentive or ability to self-correct.

Not all changes to the distribution of authority are plotted: forces outside the political system have implications for control that permeate the federal union. Chhibber and Kollman (1998, 2004) encourage us to think about the natural evolution in the party system, responding not to changes in the formal division of powers but instead to an issue's weight within it. In particular, as the importance of the fiscal jurisdiction controlled by the levels shifts (for exogenous reasons), the party system responds by adjusting the number of competitive parties at each level. To adapt, the party organization reorients itself, and perhaps permits a concentration of authority that ideally (from the point of view of federal robustness) it would not tolerate. Adaptation sanctioned by political safeguards is not always optimal.[27]

To understand why political safeguards may underperform, we need to look more closely at the way they work. Political safeguards depend on self-policing; a party must react to transgressions within its own ranks. But with a goal of electoral success, the party may be too forgiving of a well-liked transgression. When it does trigger, its punishment is limited. Cutting off support for a politician's campaign may effective against weak candidates or those in competitive elections, but there is little that the party can do to influence a strong candidate. Inefficient spending will be difficult to control (although it will be well distributed, perhaps reducing interregional conflict). Dependent on the political climate, other transgressions, such as ethics or rights violations, may be easier to call out when there is broad national consensus creating public empathy for the charge (so it is not politically costly), but Gibson and Mickey's work on enclaves demonstrate how unreliable this potential is.

---

[27] Volden (2005), among others, describes how electoral motivations can create inefficient fiscal policy and overcentralization. Political safeguards can also lead to too much decentralization. Federalism, when unbalanced, threatens individual rights. If rights policy is decentralized—a possibility in federalism—then the region's minorities may be discriminated against. A ripe condition for minority rights exploitation is a situation described by Gibson (2004) and Mickey (forthcoming) as an "authoritarian enclave"; a nondemocratic pocket within a democracy, tolerated by the national democratic government in exchange for the region's support in the national government's agenda. Political safeguards fail completely to guard against these opportunistic enclaves; in fact, it is the mutual dependence, the key mechanism of the political safeguard, that makes these enclaves possible.

In summary, the political safeguard overcomes the popular safeguard's information problem and has the potential to overcome inefficiencies and short-sightedness. It has much greater potential than popular safeguards to perceive and trigger in reaction to mild noncompliance. But it is not a fail-safe safeguard. It is inconsistent. It is sensitive to imbalance, which could compromise its ability to punish one level's transgressions. Political safeguards may trigger earlier and more frequently than popular, although not necessarily for the right reasons; the thresholds may not be set for efficiency concerns. Political safeguards cannot put federalism above tangible political priorities. Political safeguards are imperfect, unreliable, and should not be a federation's only protection.

4.4 JUDICIAL SAFEGUARDS

While the constitutional rules governing behavior are available as guidelines to any of the safeguards, the judiciary is charged directly with constitutional review of government action and therefore is best positioned to set its threshold according to the formal division of authority.[28] It also has handicaps, chiefly, its dependence on other institutions to punish and public suspicion that it does not represent the citizen's sense of the constitution.

---

[28] For example, under the U.S. Constitution, there are a variety of ways that the court may referee federalism. The boundaries on federal/state authority are stipulated by the enumeration of national powers in Article I, and limits on state action are stated explicitly in Article I, Section 10 and implied through the supremacy clause, the Commerce Clause, and the unifying clauses of Article IV: Full Faith and Credit, Privileges and Immunities, the Guarantee Clause, and the incorporating effect of the Reconstruction amendments. The court's willingness, or will, to use any of these means (or the equivalents) to intervene in the dynamics of federalism has fluctuated over time, and from country to country. The Guarantee Clause is an excellent example. Through it, the national government guarantees to its citizens that the governments of the states will remain republican democracies. Apart from justifying certain aspects of the national government's interventionist policies during the Reconstruction, the Guarantee Clause has not been relied upon in the United States, causing some legal scholars to argue that its usefulness has withered away. However, in other federations, most notably Argentina and India, the Guarantee Clause has been used frequently to justify national intervention in state government affairs. The efficiency gains of its use are not clear and its use remains controversial. The causes of these fluctuations are not yet well understood; the theory of judicial behavior is in its infancy, with a variety of theoretical paradigms, including legal, behavioral (ideological), and strategic. Of the three, the legal philosophy comes closest to the sincere idyll of the umpire.

Theory of Judicial Safeguards

The Court as Umpire. The chief problem of the last two safeguards, popular and political, was that each pursued private interests or those unrelated to federal robustness. The theory supporting judicial intervention in intergovernmental disputes is that it can be objective because its interests are not entangled in the dispute's resolution. (Ideally) it gets no votes, no campaign funds, no pork, and no extra power when it decides whether a government's action exceeds its constitutional capacity. Furthermore, unlike the other safeguards, its threshold is determined by a review of the constitution itself. So in many ways the judiciary overcomes some of the shortcomings of the other safeguards: it may be an umpire of federalism.

The ideal court-as-umpire is *disinterested*; literally, it has no personal stake in the dispute's outcome. It is removed from substantive considerations—it generally does not even incorporate distributional considerations into its decision making—and therefore can focus on ensuring the fairness of the decision-making process. As a monitor of process, it has two advantages: its deliberate observations and its ability to focus on a particular aspect of behavior.

The court may have a truer observation than other safeguards, not because of its impartiality, but instead because of the explicit *partiality* of the fact-finding. Recall that trigger mechanisms observe signals, with observations that depend on their institutional perspectives. If the signal is flawed or incomplete, then the safeguard's reaction could be imperfect. The court is never asked to make a snap judgment on an important decision. Years may pass between the first filing of a suit and the moment of the court's decision. The meanwhile is filled with the two sides, plaintiff and defendant, well-motivated to gather evidence to support their case. The end result is often a truckload of documents presenting interpretations and perceptions of a government's action. The court comes much closer to full information about an observation than any other safeguard.

The umpire can make an unpopular call; often, he has to. An illlustration is the publicly controversial U.S. Supreme Court case *United States v. Morrison*[29] striking Congress' Violence Against Women Act (VAWA). Criminal law is a policy area traditionally left to the states; the legislation made assault of women a federal offense, thereby creating a new jurisdiction for federal courts, and giving victims an alternative forum for trials.

---

[29] 529 U.S. 598 (2000).

Assault of women was already a crime in every state, and state courts were already engaged in hearing suits. The case appears complex because it is multidimensional: the outcome influenced both crime prevention and federalism. Suppose that people care about preventing violence against women, and they also care about federalism, but they accord the former a higher priority, probably much higher. The more politically salient issue is prevention of violence, and so legislators support the bill because it is politically impossible not to support it. The court takes a different perspective, regarding the bill not in terms of its efficacy in preventing violence against women, which it may do well, but instead on the second dimension, its effect on the balance of powers between the national and state governments. On this dimension, and this dimension alone, it bases its decision, and finds that the congressional action exceeds its constitutional boundaries; it is an act of encroachment.

It is possible that the public agrees fully with the court on the federalism dimension. But opinion, and politics generally, cannot pull apart dimensions. When the court has legitimacy as an objective umpire, it can make a call that is not really hard if the public could separate it from other issues in the case. In VAWA, suppose the court had followed the public's attention and had let the statute stand because of its value in protecting women. The national government might then seek to legitimize other acts of encroachment, perhaps some that are less beneficial, by the precedent in VAWA regarding federalism. As long as the judiciary is free of electoral or political influence, it can ward off extrapolations of politically guided decisions that permit further opportunism.

The Court as Focal Point Provider. The mystery—for positivists and normativists alike—is not figuring out the actions of the judges, but the purpose behind it, the role that judicial review plays. Judges declare constitutional meaning, but so does your average Jane when she says that it is her right to marry Jean. What does it mean for something to be "constitutional" and what is the importance of the court pronouncing its interpretation as opposed to any other institution, including the public?

In discussing the VAWA case I asserted that the court may have been fully in agreement with the public, despite appearances to the contrary. Numerous scholars have argued that the court is fairly deferential to public opinion (e.g., Dahl 1957, Funston 1975, Friedman 1993). This argument implies that the public has formed an opinion—reached a consensus—over what the distribution of powers are (or should become) and whether or not a statute is in accordance with it. But much more often the public has not formed an opinion or is divided. When the public is ambivalent the court may have a special status as a focal point provider, selecting among possible interpretations. Its role is to coordinate behavior.

A focal point provider may also be a revolutionary, uprooting a stagnant policy. Consider a world where 40% of the people believe that the government should never regulate what adults do in their bedrooms and 40% think that sodomy a perversity capable of destroying all decency in society and 20% do not know what they think either because the issue is complicated or they are conflicted or they just do not want to think about it. Suppose as well that an historical majority within one state supported legislation condemning the behavior, although the current population of the state looks more like the national distribution. Suppose the court strikes the law, finding the state legislation out of step with an evolved national standard of individual rights. No majority within the state exists to change existing antisodomy laws and no majority exists to override judicial nullification of the anti-sodomy laws and no matter how the court came down we could claim that it was in line or out of line with public opinion. If the public is of one mind, then the constraint on the judiciary is probably pretty binding (for a variety of hypothesized reasons). But when the public is divided, the judiciary has a lot of roaming room. And since by definition with the controversial issues public opinion is divided, it is exactly with controversial subjects that the judiciary may have the most effect. The court would appear most activist when the public is more divided, and in the areas that divide them.

By acting as a focal point provider, the court may be able to enlist the power of a more potent sanctioning force. For example, it may create consensus when the public or another safeguard was confused perhaps because it coordinates opinion or even because it acts as a catalyst for a public dialogue, and from that dialogue consensus is reached (Friedman 2005). In these cases, the court may act as a fire alarm, alerting another safeguard about an act of opportunism. A case of the court filling this role is developed in Section 7.3, a description of the Canadian Constitutional patriation.

Evaluation of Judicial Safeguards

The court can be an effective umpire and coordinator only if it is both better informed and truly disinterested. But as both the behavior school and the strategic school of judicial decision making point out, the court is not unbiased or disinterested; its judgments are not as removed from political influence as the umpire theory would have it.[30] In any federation, court assignments are a product of a political process. Be it via appointment or election, individuals are selected to *serve*. Political dependence often lingers after appointment. In the next three subsections, I consider each of these points: judicial independence in decision making, political bias in appointments, and enforcement capacity.

Enforcement Capacity. The judiciary has no punishment mechanism. It has no police, no military, no armed bandits. It also has no carrots to withhold. It has nothing to trade, no hungry constituents eager to buy another state's goods, no financial incentives to dole out. It does have an ability to promise leniency in the future, but this is of questionable efficacy and sure to damage the court's reputation with all parties in the future. For these reasons Hamilton described the court as the weakest of the three branches of government, and many scholars dismiss it today.

The chief limitation of judicial safeguards is a court's inability to punish. In the model, a safeguard needs both a threshold—implying capacity for review—and an ability to sanction should that threshold be crossed. The court does not have sufficient force to deter opportunism because it cannot penalize a government that crosses its line. It depends on other branches to execute any penalty.[31] Setting aside the bias implications of this arrangment, which I take up next, this dependence creates serious limitations on the court's apparent capacity. If it relies on the federal government to enforce, will it be able to rule negatively against the federal government? And if not, then it cannot have complete coverage of all types of transgressions: a federal union that relied primarily upon judicial safeguards that could not punish the federal government would be quickly overrun by federal encroachment.

Judicial Dependence. The judicial safeguard is weakened if it is dependent on other branches of government, but federalism may help the judiciary to achieve independence. The court is often viewed as dependent on

---

[30] See, for example, Segal and Spaeth (2002) and Epstein and Knight (1998).
[31] In fact, its effectiveness is so dependent on other branches that one might wonder why another branch would need to threaten the court with jurisdiction-stripping and other nastiness if it can just refuse to back up the court. That is, why would we even see any of these other costly punishments if the cheapest of all—inaction—can adequately render the court ineffective?

the national government—a "handmaiden of the executive," in Riker's (1964) words—a position that jeopardizes its ability to patrol national encroachment or its credibility in defining shirking.[32] The structural and political conditions that produce a dependent judiciary are not more likely in a federation than in a unitary state; in fact, federalism may alleviate these conditions, making an independent judiciary more likely in a federation.

First, the judiciary is more likely to be independent when alternative authorities are in competition with one another. In many federations, powers within the national government are separated, creating a need to coordinate the executive and legislature (often itself divided) before it can constrain the judiciary. Federations further divide power vertically, between federal and state governments: battles between them can protect the court.

Second, federalism may offer more opportunities for the court to acquire the legitimacy it needs to assert itself in controversial decisions. Legitimacy is a consequence of public beliefs, and experience feeds beliefs. With positive experiences in minor tests, the public grows confident in an institutional safeguard, entrusting it with more significant decisions. With no safeguard is this principle more true than with the judiciary. Federalism offers a perfect opportunity for many small tests, as the judiciary is asked to resolve disputes arising from the multiple governments. Higher numbers of states are a twofold benefit to the judiciary: first, it increases the number of potential disputes, and therefore small tests. Also, when the number of states is large no single state is as likely to perceive that it has been singled out for negative judgments. With experience, legitimacy grows. The judiciary can build the respect necessary to take on more controversial cases, perhaps even sufficient to allow it to reject the legislation of the national government.

I have just described the dependence of the judiciary on the other safeguards, a thesis developed and expanded through the remainder of the book. The thesis reverses the standard argument, proposing that judicial independence helps to explain federal stability. Judicial safeguards may not be an immediate product of constitutional design, but a by-product of its initial successful operation, where the court's ability to intercede grows as the federation persists.

---

[32] Bzdera (1993) provides empirical evidence of the centralizing tendency of federal high courts, and although bias is hard to document, the Canadian Supreme Court's independence has been questioned (see Section 5.3).

Time Constraint. Finally, Choper (1977) has argued that even if the court could patrol federalism, it should dedicate its finite resources to upholding rights and let the other safeguards (he cites particularly the political safeguards) maintain federalism. To this argument, one might have two quick counters: first, a balanced federalism is a method of pursuing rights, and a federation that becomes unbalanced threatens individual liberties, so even a court with a singular agenda might hear federalism cases because of their indirect effect on rights. Second, the political safeguards are not fail-safe protectors of rights: authoritarian enclaves are the starkest illustration of a general threat to rights posed by a politically-sustained federation.

Although some describe the Rehnquist Court's federalism doctrine as revolutionary, the U.S. Supreme Court has always patrolled one transgression important to federalism: interstate burden-shifting, and it has also showed a willingness to uphold the states' police powers (Eskridge and Ferejohn 1994, Rakove 1997). The shift has been in the extent that the federal government has been on the losing side. While legal scholars and political scientists have yet to explain the timing of this emergence, to dismiss the court as an incapable safeguard of federalism is to ignore two points raised by this analysis: first, federalism is about more than states' rights; all three edges of the triangle must be covered, and the court has always been active in patrolling burden-shifting. Second, its effectiveness is dependent on other safeguards, but that does not mean that other safeguards may substitute for it, functionally. What gives the court its bite? How do we translate these constitutional clauses from parchment barriers to real restraints? The court may declare state or national legislation to be unconstitutional, but its small capacity for punishment (generally restricted to reversal of the act) means that it is only capable of deterring minor opportunism. How can the constitution, as interpreted by the judiciary, prevent major acts of opportunism? While the judicial safeguard has certain advantages over popular and political safeguards, it also has weaknesses. It is incapable of single-handedly maintaining a robust federation but may be very useful when it works in combination with other safeguards, as subsequent chapters will argue.

4.5 AGAIN FITTING FEDERALISM'S COMPLEXITY

How does a constitution affect a federation's robustness? Madison's *Virginia Plan* was his proposal to remedy his observations of the union's flaws under the Articles of Confederation. The plan was not wholly accepted ... far from it. The proposed constitution that emerged from the constitutional debates contained many significant changes, the product of improvement and compromise. And it certainly was not immediately popular; ratification took two years and much persuasion. One cannot argue that the Constitution was more successful because Americans had more to gain from the union than under the Articles: although one might claim that there was a renewed sense of the necessity of union for defense, this was controversial; defenders of the Articles of Confederation pointed out that the American states had been victorious. And nothing really changed about the consequences of the union's failure: the strength of the British military force was better known, as well as the capacity of the American forces to defend themselves. Finally, the American commitment to anti-tyranny and general suspicion of state power was as alive as ever. It is difficult to make the case that the benefits of union, or cost of failure, is what has caused the American federation to be much more productive under the Constitution than under the Articles of Confederation.

Nevertheless, in the transformation from the bare-bones union of the Articles of Confederation to the intricately engineered Constitution, the union became much more robust. It did not eliminate opportunism: instead, it dealt with it far more effectively. In comparing the Articles of Confederation to the Constitution, a difference is immediately evident: the Constitution greatly expanded the procedural requirements for governmental action. It added institutional safeguards to protect the division of authority. In this chapter, I reviewed the basic building blocks that safeguard the distribution of authority. While intuitively each safeguard seems useful, no compelling argument has been made that any one is sufficient for federal robustness. Yet these safeguards seem critical to the success of the union. The Constitution did not change the purpose of the union, nor did it alter public attitude toward it. Instead, the Constitution introduced a complex set of safeguards that created an incentive environment of self-interested compliance.

The insufficiency of any one safeguard as a compliance-maintaining mechanism should not be surprising. Federalism is more complex than the typical compliance problem: the whole triangle of opportunism types (Figure 3.1) must be covered. At the same time, the safeguards available are not perfectly designed: they emerge from a political process, and may be flawed. Therefore, we should think of the safeguards as being incomplete, imperfect, and inefficient, and therefore an optimal system of safeguards must have *coverage*, *complementarity*, and *redundancy*.

The next three chapters develops a systems theory of safeguards, each dedicated to one of these topics. I introduce them here.

Coverage: Federalism has (at least) two types of actors (federal and state governments) and three methods of behaving opportunistically (federal encroachment on the states, interstate burden-shifting, and state shirking on its federal duties, all detailed in Chapter 3). Due to this dimensional complexity, the system of safeguards must provide complete *coverage*: the three types of opportunism must be resolved simultaneously. A system of safeguards cannot prevent burden-shifting and shirking, for example, and leave encroachment uncovered: to do so would be to tip the federation toward centralization, and likely to trigger a severe protest from the states. Some safeguards are equipped only to deal with one type of opportunism, or handle some more naturally than others. With the possible exception of popular safeguards, no single safeguarding mechanism is complete, in terms of its ability to cover all edges of the opportunism triangle. For example, dependence impairs a judiciary's ability to safeguard against national encroachment, and its objectivity in judging shirking would be suspect, but it may be perfectly adequate in safeguarding against interstate burden-shifting.

Complementarity: In Chapter 6, we will focus on the complementarity between safeguards of varying thresholds and sanctions. Safeguards may work together to boost one another's effectiveness. They are more than the sum of their parts; they make one another more effective. I describe the safeguards as either "mild" or "severe," where their name indicates the relative harshness of the punishment they inflict when engaged. They also differ in how frequently they are triggered: the mild safeguard triggers more frequently because it has less flexibility in its threshold, but the effect of the trigger is not as significant. The chapter will first show how these safeguards may work together, and when these safeguards may improve compliance and—a distinct effect—benefits. The argument is conditional: the safeguards may not achieve complementarity. The chapter demonstrates two variations on failure: first where the mild safeguard is not effective, and second where the severe safeguard is not sufficient.

Redundancy: While Chapter 6 focuses on combinations of safeguards to overcome the deficiency of incomplete coverage, in Chapter 7, I consider how safeguards are imperfect, and how they may fail to "fire." In this case, we are interested in the benefits of *redundancy*. We will consider how safeguards interact to fulfill contradictory functions, operating both as restraints and insurance. The chapter also suggests an explanation for the development of a federal culture.

4.6 MATHEMATICAL APPENDIX TO CHAPTER 4

In this appendix, I demonstrate how the targeted sanctioning capacity of the institutional safeguards alters the model from Chapter 3. We can compare institutional safeguards to intergovernmental retaliation. (This comparison is somewhat like asking would you prefer that bicycle brakes stop the front or the back wheel. The ideal system works on both wheels. Chapter 6 will combine institutional safeguards and intergovernmental retaliation to ask if the latter's efficacy is improved when the former is added to it.) The amount of punishment is decreased, but the amount of compliance may not be improved. Chapter 3's core result remains: opportunism is inherent to federalism. Even with more sophisticated safeguards, federal and state governments will transgress on federalism's boundaries.

In Chapter 3, I introduced a baseline of model of intergovernmental retaliation on the premise that governmental behavior is responsive to incentives. The trigger strategy employed by the governments set a threshold of tolerable behavior (as evidenced through some signal, such as union productivity), and should the signal exceed the threshold, the governments would react with a punishment of mutual retaliation. Intergovernmental punishments are an inefficient mechanism to induce compliance; although they can sustain some compliance, their effect is limited by outside options and by the cost to each government of retaliating, since more opportunism further reduces the productivity of the union.

Unlike the mutual retaliation of the baseline model in Chapter 3, this model targets punishment to affect the perpetrator only and costs the other governments nothing. In this formulation, if a player's signal exceeds the threshold then no other players pay a cost. In effect, the punishment is a fine that does not affect the utility of the other governments. This change creates a game in dominant strategies. It is still a strategic interaction, but each government's strategy is independent of the others, making the mathematics simpler to analyze. I show that none of the comparative statics change. As one would expect, the safeguard is a more efficient mechanism than mutual retaliation. However, the effect on the amount of compliance depends on the relative levels of punishment and the uncertainty in institutional safeguards versus intergovernmental retaliation. Differing monitoring capacities make the uncertainty vary between the two cases.

As in the model of intergovernmental retaliation, the single period utility for player i equals

$$u_i(x_1, x_2, \ldots, x_n) = \alpha \sum_{j=1}^{N} (1 - x_j) + x_i \qquad (4.1)$$

where $\alpha < 1$. As before, it pays to shirk while others comply. We can then write the value function for the repeated setting. The difference is that now the probability of punishment depends only on the government's own action. Therefore, θ depends only on x_i. Recall from the appendix to Chapter 3 that the signal $\omega = \theta + \epsilon$.

I first show that even with targeted punishment, full compliance would not be an equilibrium under some mild assumptions. Therefore, even with targeted punishment some slippage occurs.

$$V_i(x_1, x_2, \ldots, x_n) = \alpha \sum_{j=1}^{N} (1 - x_j) + x_i + \delta$$

$$[\Pr(\omega > T)(-Q) + V_i(x_1, x_2, \ldots, x_n)] \qquad (4.2)$$

Solving for V_i produces

$$V_i(x_1, x_2, \ldots, x_n) = \frac{\alpha \sum_{j=1}^{N}(1 - x_j) + x_i - \delta \Pr(\omega > T)(Q)}{1 - \delta} \qquad (4.3)$$

To solve for the first-order condition, I use the fact that $\Pr(x_i > T) = 1 - F(T - \theta(x_i))$. Taking the derivative of this new expression gives the marginal value of opportunism. As before, f is the density function associated with the probability distribution F.

$$\frac{1 - \alpha - \delta f(T - \theta(x_i))\theta'(x_i)Q}{1 - \delta} \qquad (4.4)$$

If full compliance were an equilibrium, then this expression would equal zero when $x_i = 0$. Given that small deviations are difficult to notice, we know that $\theta'(0) \sim 0$. Given that assumption, the above expression cannot equal zero at full compliance, so once again slippage occurs.

To derive comparative statics results, I now reconsider Model 1 from Chapter 3 but with targeted punishment.

Model 1, with Targeted Punishment: In Model 1, the error term is uniformly distributed between $-m$ and m. This implies that $f = \frac{1}{2m}$. Given that punishment is targeted, now $\theta(x_1, x_2, \ldots, x_n) = x_i^2$. This formulation implies that small degrees of opportunism will produce a very low signal to noise ratio: when x_i is near zero, x_i^2 is much smaller. The marginal value of opportunism can now be written as follows:

$$\frac{1 - \alpha - \delta \frac{1}{2m} 2x_i Q}{1 - \delta}$$

In equilibrium, the marginal value of opportunism will be exactly zero. Setting this expression equal to zero gives the symmetric equilibrium level of noncompliance:

$$x_i = \frac{m(1 - \alpha)}{\delta Q} \tag{4.5}$$

As before, noncompliance does not go to zero, no matter how high the discount factor. As long as $\alpha < 1$, opportunism is inherent. Slippage—noncompliance—is unavoidable. The comparative statics results are all the same as in the nontargeted case: the higher α, δ, and Q, the less slippage. Opportunism increases as the range of the noise (m) term increases.

Note that in equilibrium, each government's level of opportunism equals the *total* amount of opportunism from our previous model. This is an artifact of the assumptions about the signals. I will assume here that the structural safeguards are not better in monitoring a single government than they are in monitoring all of the governments as a unit, captured in the assumption that F was distributed between $-m$ and m in both cases. In the nontargeted punishment case, each government took into account the opportunism of the other governments, reducing the incentive to act opportunistically. Opportunism by others created an incentive not to be opportunistic.

However, overall, we might think of targeted punishment (institutional safeguards) as more effective than punishment that is not targeted (intergovernmental retaliation). If we make the baseline assumption that the targeted punishments are as effective at stopping slippage intergovernmental retaliation—if the amount of slippage is the same in the targeted punishment—then institutional safeguards create higher overall utility because the costs of punishment are lower. Only one person gets punished, not everyone.

In order for these results to hold, the safeguard must be able to punish as severely as intergovernmental retaliation, which is unlikely. Therefore, we can distinguish between the level of punishment under safeguards Q^S and the level under intergovernmental retaliation Q^R, and we can assume $Q^S \leq Q^R$. We can also assume a less noisy signal in the case of institutional safeguards. I define m^S, m^R, T^S, T^R similarly and assume $m^S \leq m^R$ and $T^S \leq T^R$.

Using Model 1, we derive the condition for institutional safeguards improving compliance. Let $x_i^S = \frac{m^S(1-\alpha)}{\delta Q^S}$ and $x_i^R = \frac{m^R(1-\alpha)}{N\delta Q^R}$ denote the amounts of opportunism under the two scenarios. Reducing, $x_i^S \leq x_i^R$ iff

$$\frac{m^S}{m^R} \leq \frac{Q^S}{NQ^R}$$

The monitoring improvement (reducing the error, m) must be significant to overcome the punishment capacity loss. In Chapter 6, I will combine these two mechanisms to generate conditions for compliance and utility improvement.

5

Coverage

Structural, political, judicial, and popular safeguards have their unique weaknesses and failings, but they do not operate in isolation. We know through the theory of separated powers that the safeguards contest one another beneficially: one safeguard, say, the judiciary, can check another, such as the political safeguard. Mutual antagonism is only a part of their intersecting influence. Safeguards also bolster one another's performance and stand in where others are weak. Federations are most successful when the safeguards complement and reinforce one another. I now begin to construct a systems theory of safeguards, where each is a unique component. In this chapter we will consider the *coverage* capacity of safeguards, the completeness of their ability to reduce each of the different forms of opportunism.

5.1 The Issue: Coverage as a Necessary Condition

To this point, I have described the challenge of a robust design as recasting incentives for the governments. Each has a natural temptation to deviate opportunistically from the division of authorities; without a shift in incentives, they would act on this temptation, and the resulting noncompliance reduces—perhaps destroys—the utility of the union. Therefore, it is necessary (although not sufficient) in the federation to minimize opportunism; federal design is a problem in compliance maintenance. I am not about to abandon this approach, but I do need to make it more nuanced.

The standard method for overcoming compliance problems is to alter the incentive structure by introducing sanctions, or negative consequences for noncompliance. All federal unions possess a natural sanction, the threat of intergovernmental retaliation. While effective in deterring significant transgressions, it cannot stop minor transgressions. A federation needs a remedy that does not ask the governments to sanction one another.

The public good provision literature is helpful, but we need to expand the literature's lessons to fit federalism's complexity. To frame a federation's challenge as a single production problem grossly simplifies what is instead an interconnected web of collective action problems. To argue that the complex interactions between member states, between the central government and the states, and among the institutions that mediate those interactions such as courts, party systems, bicameral legislatures, and constitutions can be explained by the same model that captures the grazing of sheep on a common field seems and is a stretch. In the classic commons problem (Hardin 1968), the village green is a common pasture for sheep-grazing. The size of the pasture can only support a set number of sheep. Collectively the villagers benefit from grazing limitations, but individually, each may reason that the likelihood of destroying the pasture from slipping in one extra sheep is small, but the return to the villager of an extra sheep is significant. Each is tempted to overgraze. A single monitoring mechanism is sufficient to overcome the commons problem.

Unlike the classic commons problem, a federation has different types of governments and different types of transgression, and each may require a different safeguard. Chapter 3 identified three types of transgressions: encroachment by the federal government on the states' authorities, shirking by the states on their responsibilities within the union, and burden-shifting by the states. These basic types are illustrated by Figure 3.1. A system of safeguards must cover all edges of the triangle.

If the safeguards fail to control opportunism along one edge, problems can develop along another. Consider the federation that effectively reduces shirking and burden-shifting but is not able to contain encroachment. The federation may become overcentralized as an unfettered national government takes advantage of the states; the constraints on the states may make it more difficult for them to defend themselves. The federation may be more unbalanced than it would be if no edge were covered. Likewise, an institutional structure that is unable to reduce the degree of shirking may become, in Riker's (1964) terminology, overperipheralized: the states will have great advantage over the national government, and the benefits of coordinated action will be reduced. Partial coverage is insufficient and perhaps even detrimental. A successful institutional remedy will be balanced, addressing all three types of opportunism. Later in the chapter, we will consider several illustrations of incomplete coverage (both in reality and in perception). For now, let me state the first necessary condition of federal institutional design: *Federalism's safeguards must fully cover the types of opportunism.*

5.2 THE COVERAGE CAPACITY OF SAFEGUARDS

The five types of safeguards that I have described have different jurisdictions and abilities. Most have gaps in their coverage capacity. Table 5.1 contains claims about the coverage capacity of each of these safeguards. This table is preliminary—it reflects the ideal types of each safeguard as portrayed most optimistically in Chapter 4. Further elaboration will come in the next two chapters.

It may be helpful to review briefly the five safeguards and their placement. Intergovernmental retaliation is available in all three transgression categories, but because it is difficult to fine-tune, prone to escalation, and, as Chapter 3 described, subject to inefficiencies when member governments have an attractive exit option, it is a poor resource for guarding

Table 5.1. *Preliminary Assessment of the Coverage Capacity of Each Safeguard*

Safeguard	Federal Action	State Action		Remarks
	Encroachment	Shirking	Burden-Shifting	
Intergovernmental retaliation	Y	Y	Y	Exit options may limit efficiency; unable to prevent low levels of noncompliance
Popular	Y	Y	N	Coordination problems; safeguard enhanced by competitive elections
Structural	Y	N	N	Fragments federal authority; incorporates state interests in federal decisions
Political	Y	Y	N	Must be an integrated party system
Judicial	Y	Y	Y	Must be law; cannot uphold convention

against mild or ambiguous acts of opportunism.[1] It is an excellent example of why we need to further refine the theory of safeguards, for a federal union relying exclusively on intergovernmental retaliation could be inefficient and unproductive. It is not meeting its potential.

Citizens too are safeguards; they may depose governments that do not suit them. Democracy facilitates citizen capacity to topple a government through the nonrevolutionary method of a contested election. The more competitive the democracy, the more likely that elected political figures heading governments will adhere to the boundaries of federalism—at least the boundaries that they believe the citizens notice. (More on that comment in Chapter 7.) Ideally, citizens will patrol both levels of government, watchful of encroachments of one on the powers of the other. Citizens cannot prevent burden-shifting; they are the primary motivation for it.

We now consider the three auxiliary safeguards. Structural safeguards are formal institutions, generally constitutional, such as separation of powers in the national government, a bicameral legislature, and formal state involvement in national decision making. The purpose of the structural safeguards is to constrain the national government from encroaching upon the states. Structural safeguards, by being written into the constitution, may be more reliable than other encroachment-limiting safeguards because we do not need to wait for them to emerge (as with the party system or the legitimacy of the judiciary) and they are not limited by informational gaps (as with popular safeguards): by writing them into the constitution they are less ambiguous. A reciprocal arrangement, where structural safeguards constrain the states, is extremely unusual. By definition, fragmentation is ineffective at the state level for federal problems (although it may serve other democratic purposes); no matter how you shuffle the aggregation of representation, it is not going to alter the net effect of state self-interest and essential disregard for the effect of its actions on other states. And incorporation of federal interests in state-level decision making is extremely unusual. The most notable exceptions are the interventions in India and Argentina

---

[1] For an approach related to this chapter, see de Figueiredo and Weingast (2005), who describe two "dilemmas" of federalism: preventing the states from taking advantage of one another (burden-shifting) and preventing the federal government from overawing the states (encroachment). Building from theory developed in Weingast (1997), they argue that the federal government must be strong enough to patrol relations between the states, but that the states must be collectively willing to punish the federal government in the case that it exceeds its authority. Both remedies are examples of intergovernmental retaliation.

and recent structural changes to the Russian federation, where the president may appoint regional viceroys to oversee state policy making. In general, in the pure type, structural safeguards do not affect state behavior.

Political safeguards, by contrast, are party systems, informal institutions that emerge as a consequence of formal institutions such as the electoral law. The party system's effect depends on its organization and character: a highly centralized party system will stifle state-initiated opportunism, while a decentralized party may reduce encroachment because the local concerns become vital to the electoral interests of central-level actors. However, neither one of these forms can produce a balanced federation; instead, a party system that is centralized or decentralized can upset the balance. Filippov et al. (2004) describe an *integrated* party system, where the levels of governments are rendered codependent by the common interests of the politicians within them. Chapter 4 reviewed their thesis, including the markers of an integrated party system. When a party system is ideally integrated, it smooths rivalries between the federal and state governments and so may inhibit encroachment and shirking. The political safeguards literature does emphasize the distributional benefits of the integrated party system; divisible public goods are spread broadly across the country, but this redistribution is engineered by the federal government. The theory is silent on how political safeguards might prevent burden-shifting's externality generation.

Last we turn to the judiciary. While the judiciary is a formally specified institution, its effect depends on the doctrine that the court develops from the tools given it within the constitution, its independence from other branches of government, and particularly on the willingness of other branches to enforce its judgments. Judicial safeguards evolve over the life span of the federation, and often doctrinal evolution and judicial legitimacy are path dependent. The appropriateness of judicial regulation of the distribution of powers within a federation has been debated, as reviewed in the evaluation of judicial safeguards in Chapter 4. Questions about its legitimacy in refereeing federalism disputes reduce its effectiveness. Although in the United States the Supreme Court has begun to limit the national government's encroachments, for the most part, the judiciary's best capacity is in regulating burden-shifting between state governments, since it is often viewed as beholden to the central government. In Riker's words, it is a "handmaiden" to the executive (1964:103). If the court is perceived to be biased in favor of the federal government, it not only will fail to halt encroachment but will also not be an acceptable forum for resolving shirking disputes, as states will reject the legitimacy of its intervention. In this manner, it may be an effective counter to burden-shifting but not shirking. The court is certainly not a complete solution to the federal problem of production. Nevertheless, to portray the ideal type, it does have the *potential* to safeguard all three types of opportunism.

We can use this preliminary characterization of the safeguards to make inferences about the robustness of particular federations. First, of the three types of opportunism, encroachment is covered by the most safeguards and burden-shifting the least. In federations without an active judiciary, burden-shifting between states will need to be countered with a more muscular assertion of intergovernmental retaliation, either from one state to another, banded together, or through the federal government. Second, the diversity in protection against encroachment might cause us to believe that it would be the least visible transgression type. While there is no good measure of the frequency of opportunism, the more common perception is that the federal government is *more* likely to overwhelm the states than the state to do significant harm to one another or to the federal government. Refinements in the next two chapters will help to explain this asymmetry. For now, we will turn to a few examples of federal experiences to illustrate the importance of overall coverage.

5.3 DEVELOPING AN INTUITION FOR COVERAGE

In this chapter and the next two, I will provide a series of examples to help to build an intuition for the design considerations. This chapter focuses on the importance of covering all three sides of the federalism triangle, of having safeguards that minimize or block all three types of transgressions. A part of the objective of these examples is to provide further experience with identifying safeguards—those that are written into the constitution as well as those that emerge—and getting a feel for their limitations. In this section we will consider the European Union, where safeguards emerged over time, Canada, where coverage was percieved to be inadequate, and the antebellum United States, where coverage withered.

The European Union

As a fledgling federation, the European Union is an excellent case for examining the importance of all three types of coverage. The federation

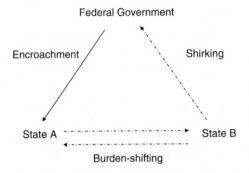

Figure 5.1. The Triangle of Federalism, Admitting Shirking and Burden-Shifting

emerged slowly from well-established sovereign states. As in the case of the American union, the member states were (and still are) highly suspicious of overcentralization and threats of encroachment on their authority. The extent of the EU's structural safeguards reflects this concern. Significant structural barriers protect against encroachment: the incorporation of member state interests in the Council, the supermajority decision-making process, and increasing fragmentation of EU decision-making (with the empowerment of the Parliament, as well as other procedural changes). Expansion has diversified the interests represented, making common agreement even more difficult, and further constraining the center through popular safeguards.

The main question for Europe's future is the adequacy of coverage against shirking and burden-shifting. If these transgressions are not sufficiently covered, future EU legislation would be rendered ineffective and the union imperiled. The concern is illlustrated in Figure 5.1, a modified version of the federal triangle. Coverage is not complete: encroachment is covered, but shirking and burden-shifting are left exposed. The consequence of this imbalance is a peripheralized federation that fails to realize the benefits of centralization. The federation will not perform as well as it could in the areas that require a unified policy.

Although structural safeguards cannot prevent shirking (see Table 5.1), every other safeguard type might. Intergovernmental retaliation is a safeguard of last resort; it is better if paired with another safeguard to fine-tune compliance.[2] Neither popular nor political safeguards against shirking

---

[2] Chapter 6 explores these complementarities.

are yet available in the European Union. A popular safeguard to prevent shirking requires citizen valuation of the union—generally through a common identity—sufficient that the people would reject their own member state's intransigence. At the founding of the European Union, citizens of the member states had just finished a war with one another; a common identity is only now developing, mainly within the younger generations (Hooghe and Marks 2001) and those involved in globalized businesses (Fligstein 2008). Political safeguards depend on party organization that spans levels of government, a phenomenon that has not happened to any significant extent in Europe. The remaining safeguard is the judiciary.

Legal scholars and political scientists write of the court being the engine that has quietly driven the European Union forward[3]; if so, it has done it by limiting the member states, not by encouraging encroachment. While one can make a compelling case that the European Court of Justice "constituted" Europe by transforming the treaties into a constitution,[4] we must be careful not to misinterpret the arguments. The court does not initiate legislation; it can only uphold legislation. The structural safeguards remain significant barriers to federal encroachment.

The court has encouraged the success of the European Union by upholding EU (federal) powers against member state shirking. In objecting to member state noncompliance, it clears the way for the central government (once its various components reach an agreement) to implement its policies successfully. Noncompliance reduces the productivity of the union. European Union legislation faces a high barrier, growing even higher as the fragmentation of central decision making grows as well as the diverse interests in an expanding union. When legislation passes the union may be confident that it enjoys broad support. The European Court of Justice has sustained that legislation.[5]

---

[3] See, for example, Burley and Mattli (1993) and Mattli and Slaughter (1995), but contrast the functionalist approach against an intergovernmental argument as in Moravscik (1991) or Garrett (1992, 1995) where the true engine is member state bargaining.

[4] See, for example, Weiler (1991) and Shapiro (1992).

[5] Previewing a theme that we will develop in Chapter 7, it is notable that the member states—and their citizens—have accepted this crackdown. While they may not share common interests, for the moment Europeans generally agree that the European Union is beneficial. Garrett's (1992, 1995) work on the European Union is consistent with this view, although expressed differently, as the outcome of intergovernmental strategizing.

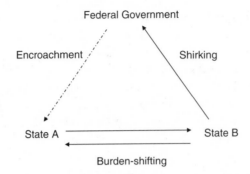

Figure 5.2. The Triangle of Federalism, Leaving Encroachment Exposed

The Rise of Provincial Nationalism in Canada

Canadians manage crisis by endurance; at least their patience with peren-
nial federal instability and constitutional uncertainty suggests as much.[6]
For the first 80 years of Canadian federation, the national government
and the provinces coexisted in a peace punctuated by occasional skir-
mishes, but without any sustained disharmony. In the middle part of the
last century, a provincial spirit awakened across the country, but first
and most thoroughly in Quebec.[7] The Quiet Revolution slowly stewed
federal–provincial acrimony as the francophone Quebecois increasingly
demanded greater autonomy to protect their unique culture. While the
last section detailed questionable coverage for shirking in the European
unification, Canada suffers from the reverse problem: provinces, especially Quebec, have frequently voiced the perception that Ottawa is
unconstrained, that it may encroach at will, in a scenario illustrated by
Figure 5.2.

In an effort to build Canadian national identity and appease Quebec's dissatisfaction, Prime Minister Trudeau patriated the Constitution in
1982, which since confederation (1867) had existed as an act of the British
Parliament. (Chapter 7 recounts the patriation saga.) Rather than squelch
provincial nationalism, constitutional patriation further embroiled the
country as Trudeau tacked on to the constitution a Charter of Rights
and Freedoms, an addition that several provinces feared would redistribute power in Ottawa's favor. Ottawa is now buried in the onslaught

---

[6] The patience of the Quebecois might have more to do with the difficulty of leaving
the union. See Dion (1996), Young (1994), and Clarke and Kornberg (1994).
[7] Other provinces agitating for devolution were British Columbia, Saskatchewan,
Alberta, and Newfoundland, all in search of greater control of natural resources.

of demands and claims from provinces and, increasingly, from organized political groups ranging from the aboriginal peoples to women. By far the most vocal and effective of the provinces complaining of the federal–provincial relationship is Quebec,[8] an exception in the federal–provincial standoff that this theory can help explain.

The Canadian case generates two questions in search of an explanation: first, what triggered the rise in federal–provincial antagonism? Second, how do we account for the dispute's asymmetry, where Quebec pushes federalism's boundaries while the national government has failed to realize its constitutional potential as a powerful central government, despite the fears of the provinces? In other words, if the federal government has nothing to stop it from encroaching, why does not Ottawa take advantage of this position? To emphasize the ethnic cleavage can only partially explain provincial nationalism: it cannot account for the timing of the movement (why were relations mostly harmonious for 80 years?) nor can it explain demands for decentralization in anglophone provinces. Likewise, to attribute the dissonance to divergent interests (economic or social) does not explain the coincidence in the timing between the ethnically-based movement in Quebec and the economically based movement out west. We can better explain the coincidence in these movements with a thesis based on a shift in the safeguards.

In most federations, the regions are effectively constrained from destructive burden-shifting by adjudication, but typically courts cannot convince the regions that they are independent enough from the central government to serve as an effective constraint on the central government's tendency to encroach. To stem central government abuse of its power, federations need structural handicaps to fragment authority at the central level, blocking the center from abusing its power. Canada's Westminster-model Parliament fuses the legislature and executive, and by tradition the Senate has been a rubber stamp: little fragmentation exists to check the national government. Political safeguards, too, are lacking: political parties in Canada are poorly integrated, with some parties holding different platforms at the provincial and federal levels, and sometimes openly dissenting with one another (Carty 1992, Filippov et al. 2004). However,

---

[8] To date, Quebec has held two referenda for secession (or sovereignty association, a complicated plan to let Quebec enjoy a formal place in the international community, but share its currency). The first, held in 1980, was defeated soundly, but the second, in 1995, narrowly missed a majority. In the meanwhile, two attempts to work out a constitutional compromise were rejected by the provincial legislatures (Meech Lake, reexamined in 1990) and by the voters themselves (Charlottetown, 1992).

for the first 80 years of Canadian federation, the provinces were protected from national encroachment by an unusual mechanism: the British Privy Council acted as the final court of appeals. Removed from any political sway, the Privy Council consistently reined in the national government's attempts to expand its powers to the satisfaction of the provinces.

Constitutional reform abolished appeals to the Privy Council in 1949. Some provinces challenged the move[9]; once the legal hurdles were cleared, anticolonial sentiments, as well as support for Ottawa's New Deal programs struck down by the Privy Council, made the transition politically feasible. By 1959, the last case worked its way through the system. The Supreme Court of Canada claimed status as the ultimate interpreter of the constitution, and with its new status came immediate accusations of judicial bias against the provinces[10] so unnerving that Chief Justice Bora Laskin dedicated a public address to a defense of the Supreme Court's integrity.[11] Criticism of the court continues to this day; in the Supreme Court consideration of a reference from the Canadian Attorney General regarding Quebec's right to secede unilaterally,[12] Quebec refused to recognize the court as a legitimate forum and withheld representation to plead its case.

The institutional shift can explain the timing of the rise in provincial sentiment: the provinces recognized that the straps constricting Ottawa's powers were cut loose as appeals to the Privy Council ended. Without constraint, the provinces feared an expansion in the national domain, and a consequent decline in their own independence. Their sole recourse has been to appeal to popular constraints by raising public suspicion of

---

[9] The national power to abolish appeals from the Supreme Court was clearly established in the constitution. Rather, Ontario (with British Columbia, New Brunswick, and Quebec) questioned the constitutionality of abolishing per saltum appeals (from provincial courts to the Privy Council, sidestepping the Supreme Court), arguing that as matters of provincial justice, the provinces had the authority to designate the ultimate appellate court. The Privy Council disagreed. See *A.-G. Ontario* v. *A.-G. Canada* (Reference re Abolition of Privy Council Appeals) [1947] A.C. 127.

[10] It is true that since the end of appeals to the London Privy Council, the Canadian Supreme Court has been more likely to rule provincial statutes unconstitutional than federal statutes. Hogg (1979) reports that from 1949 to 1979, the Supreme Court ruled 25 of 65 provincial statutes unconstitutional, but only four of the 37 federal statutes challenged in the same period. For a discussion of the charges see Cairns (1971), Laskin (1978), Vaughan (1986), and especially Hogg (1979) and Smithey (1996).

[11] The text of the speech is reprinted in Laskin (1978).

[12] Reference re Secession of Quebec (1998) 2 S.C.R. 217 (Canada).

Ottawa's greed for power, a tactic Quebec seems to have mastered, but played in other provinces as well.

Perhaps the popular safeguards are sufficient to maintain federalism in Canada, but popular safeguards are as finicky as the political safeguards. Just as a centralized or decentralized party system (as opposed to the integrated party system) can tip the federation toward undue transgressions, if citizens' conception of federalism deposits most authority with one level of government then the popular safeguard cannot prevent both shirking and encroachment. To function in both roles the citizens must develop a balanced allegiance, an identification with the *federation* rather than one particular government. When confidence in the auxiliary safeguard protections against encroachment has eroded (if only in perception), citizens may feel beleaguered by the federal government and react with a decentralized allegiance rather than the idealized balance. Popular safeguards, and the balanced identity required for them to safeguard both shirking and encroachment, are particularly unlikely in Quebec, where the Fleur-de-Lis flag rallies provincial nationalism. To extend fuller coverage in Canada and minimize damaging perceptions of bias, application of my coverage theory would recommend bolstering structural safeguards to minimize the potential for encroachment, most likely through constitutional change.[13] Effective fragmentation and incorporation of provincial interests may sufficiently free the Supreme Court from charges of bias that it may regain the objective status enjoyed by the Privy Council, reining in both encroachment and shirking, and minimizing threats of intergovernmental retaliation.

The Antebellum United States

The antebellum period in the United States has many similarities to the Canadian provincial struggle. The southern states' complaints leading up to the Civil War are analogous to the provincial dissatisfaction in Canada: in both cases, the subnational level believed that the federal government would discriminate against their preferred policies, making further centralization fearsome. Also, in both cases an institutional shift caused underlying tensions to surface. In Canada, a shift in safeguards

---

[13] Quebec has called for formal incorporation of provincial voice (at least its own) in federal governing institutions, and proposals for a Triple-E Senate (equal, elected, effective) remain a part of Canadian political debate.

appeared to enable federal encroachment, explaining provincial reaction. Was the shift of the same nature in the United States?

To address that question, we can start by examining the encroachment column in Table 5.1. Although all safeguards are theoretically capable of minimizing federal encroachment, not all were available at the time. Political safeguards did not exist, at least not in the idealized form of the integrated party system. Parties and party membership were fluid during this period.[14] Parties were capable of facilitating compromises, such as those engineered by Congressman Henry Clay in 1820 and 1850, but those bargains could only hold as long as the representational interests within the structural components remained fixed, which turns our attention to the structural safeguards. While the structural safeguards were not formally modified (in contrast with the Canadian case), increasing population in the northern states shifted control of the House of Representatives and executive in their direction. Once the balance rule in the Senate (matching admissions of free and slave states) was ended (not by the inevitable conclusion from population asymmetry, but prematurely by Justice Taney in *Dred Scott*[15]), the southern states lost a final toehold within the structural safeguards.[16] The institutional shift in the United States was not a formal alteration of the procedures for resolving disputes, as in Canada; it was the end of a political compromise.

The loss of effective structural safeguards may not have been an issue had the electorate been of one mind about the boundaries of federal authority, but they were not. For many enfranchised citizens of the South, slavery was an element of property rights. Any federal attempt to eliminate that right would be an act of encroachment. As Foner (1970) describes it, northerners slowly congealed to a common position (in our language, a threshold), even if held for different reasons. Abolitionists opposed slavery on moral grounds. With the western lands made more attractive to laborers squeezed by the arrival of low-wage-demanding immigrants, white northern labor could be persuaded to oppose slavery's expansion as well, out of concern for labor competition in the territories. The

---

[14] For example, Henry Clay was a presidential candidate five times under three different party labels, running as Democratic-Republican (1824), National Republican (1832), and Whig (1840, 1844, 1848).

[15] *Dred Scott* v. *Sanford* 60 U.S. 393 (1857), holding that property rights (including claims to slaves) do not cease as citizens cross state lines; additionally arguing that Congress could not bar slavery in the territories, effectively ending the Missouri Compromise of 1850.

[16] For a full analysis, see Weingast (1996, 1998).

emergence of a consensus (over the threshold) in the North polarized the electorate.

The southern insistence on slavery in the new territories deserves investigation. Although some southern arguments claimed that slavery's expansion was necessary to remain profitable, the greater fear was the threat to slavery within the existing slave states (Foner 1970). Republicans promised to leave slavery alone in the existing slave states in exchange for the territories, and future admitted states, being free soil. Many southerners feared that in accepting this compromise, they implicitly would have conceded that the institution of slavery was flawed. If the rationale behind the northern consensus was itself crystallized around individual rights rather than property rights or economic interests, then the North could rally support in the federal government for an intervention against slavery in the South. The Republican promise to leave slavery alone was not credible in the long run; it was sustained only by the threat of intergovernmental retaliation. It opened up the potential for federal intervention, perhaps justified by the Guarantee Clause.[17]

Whether federal intervention would be an act of encroachment or intergovernmental retaliation to combat shirking (when no other remedies were available) depends entirely on one's perspective. Remember, transgressions are in the eye of the beholder, as each safeguard defines its own threshold of tolerated behavior. If the electoral consensus shifted in the North, it could justify federal aggression; in the South, equivalent electoral consensus justified southern secession; the former is intergovernmental retaliation, the latter is costly union exit. Enfranchised southerners could frame the end of the sectional balance as a failure of federalism's institutions to stop encroachment. Northerners could frame it differently; the safeguards did not fail when the sectional balance ended. Instead, southern interests were artificially protected through the balance rule, which was merely a method of permitting the persistence of shirking in the South; it was a toleration of an *authoritarian enclave*, to return to the language of Gibson and Mickey from Chapter 4. It was not surprising that the southern states seceded, nor was it surprising that the North refused the secession. It was consistent with the ideology and economic

---

[17] Article IV, Section 4 of the U.S. Constitution is known as the Guarantee Clause:

The United States shall guarantee to every state in this union a republican form of government, and shall protect each of them against invasion; and on application of the legislature, or of the executive (when the legislature cannot be convened) against domestic violence.

interests of each electorate, the South running from perceived uninhibited encroachment and the North attempting to end shirking. Chapter 7 further develops the importance of perception in defining a transgression.

5.4 DISCUSSION

Meeting the criteria defining a federation is not sufficient for the union to function well, or even be federal in practice. It fails to work well when its safeguards do not manage opportunism. In the robust federation, all three types of transgressions—encroachment, shirking, and burden-shifting—are covered. Covering just one or two types of transgressions is not enough: examples from Canada and the antebellum United States demonstrated how incomplete coverage unbalances a federal system. Incomplete coverage by may even exacerbate asymmetries if it constrains a government's ability to defend itself through intergovernmental retaliation.

No single safeguard can efficiently cover all three transgression types; complete coverage is provided by a network of safeguards. To gain further insight into the interdependence of the safeguards, the next two chapters focus on the safeguard system along single edges of the federalism triangle, examining the safeguards' varying effectiveness and imperfections.

6

Complementarity

Safeguards may be too weak or too strong to counter transgressions effectively. A flyswatter cannot pound a nail, and a hammer is more likely to damage a surface than squash the fly flitting from it. Safeguards do not have infinitely flexible sanctions: the judiciary has a light touch, while intergovernmental retaliation quickly becomes unwieldy and is best reserved for major transgressions. This chapter continues to develop the systems theory of safeguards by exploring how the punishment capacity of safeguards complement one another.

6.1 THE ISSUE: INEFFICIENT SAFEGUARDS

"After an unequivocal experience of the inefficiency of the subsisting federal government, you are called upon to deliberate on a new Constitution for the United States of America." With these words, Alexander Hamilton opened the editorials which became the *Federalist*. His one-word diagnosis of the Articles of confederation's flaw was *inefficiency*, exactly the word that any modern political economist would choose. In order for any safeguard—structural, popular, political, or judicial—to deter transgressions, it establishes a threshold that when crossed, triggers a punishment. With pencil and paper, it is possible to derive the efficient threshold and punishment combination. The sanctioning mechanism in place under the Articles of Confederation was not efficient in this sense; the expectations of behavior, in terms of state compliance, were not consistent with the incentives provided by intergovernmental retaliation. Instead, the Articles generated much lower levels of compliance than hoped because the only safeguard, intergovernmental retaliation, could not punish effectively.

The founders kept using a word that might seem curious: energy. They wanted an *energetic* government. When they used this word, they did not mean an overextended government, like the modern dual-career two-child-plus-dog family. This is a life that requires energy. The governmental equivalent, where the government involves itself in an increasing range of social and economic dimensions, was the opposite of what the founders had in mind. Instead, their craving for a government with energy echoes the modern call for a simpler life: limited government focused on defined tasks, effective because its authorities would be respected by the states. An energetic government required an improved system of safeguards to preserve its authority. It required the creation of institutional safeguards that could complement intergovernmental retaliation.

A safeguard's effectiveness depends on its judgment and the severity of its punishment. To visualize the effect of a trigger mechanism—a safeguard—on governmental behavior, Chapter 3 introduced an illustration that captured the implicit calculus of a government in the face of strategic incentives. That figure is duplicated here for convenience as Figure 6.1. The horizontal axis represents the extent of the transgression; at the far left, the government does not transgress, and movement to the right increases the severity of the deviance from the constitutional rules. The safeguard's threshold—when crossed, it triggers punishment—is marked on the illustration at T. Because observations can be misleading (known as imperfect monitoring), there is a chance that actions taken to the left of the threshold will appear to be to the right. (The reverse is also true: sometimes unacceptable transgressions will appear to be tolerable.) The dotted line graphs the likelihood that an action appears to exceed the threshold, triggering punishment.

With this line we can see the anticipated reaction frequency of the safeguard, but not its full effect. For that, we also need to gauge the effect of punishment on the perceived transgressor. On the illustration this

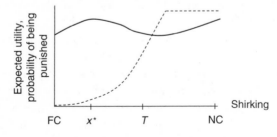

Figure 6.1. Intergovernmental Retaliation Generates Inherent Opportunism (Duplicated)

effect is captured by the solid line, marked as the transgressor's expected utility curve. Moving from left to right, the curve rises initially as the government benefits from its transgression, but as the likelihood of triggering the sanction increases, and therefore so does the probability of being punished, expected utility peaks, then decreases. It rises again when punishment is certain, implying that a government would not stop with moderate transgression, but instead transgress to the fullest extent possible. (Think of it like having a last meal before facing the firing squad: why not enjoy this moment when the future is grim?) Under most circumstances, with imperfect monitoring full compliance is unsustainable. The question for the federation is the following: are the safeguards able to induce sufficient compliance, and are potential benefits of the federation great enough, that partial compliance is preferable to dissolution? Formally, the calculation compares the peak at x^*—the benefit of union membership tolerating some noncompliance—and the benefit from full noncompliance, or (off the illustration, but included in the analysis about exit options), the expected benefits from exiting the union.[1]

Setting aside the complications of the observation (discussed in the next chapter), the placement of the threshold and the punishment capacity together determine the safeguard's effect on behavior. It follows from intuition (confirmed by the math in the appendix) that the weaker the punishment, the more frequently the safeguard must sanction. If the punishment changes, the threshold must change as well.

For example, suppose that the maximum penalty that a court can assign is reduced by law. A change to the court's punishment capacity does not appear to be related to where the court draws the line on legal behavior, and so there is no immediate connection between the constraint on its punishment capacity and its threshold or probability of punishing. But governments will transgress more. In Figure 6.2, the safeguard punishes with the same probability (the threshold is the same) but with less force. The threshold and punishment are not well-matched, and the dotted line represents the decline in behavioral modification—compliance declines from x^* to x'^*—because the court can no longer punish as severely. If the court is to have the same effect, it must become less tolerant, moving its threshold to the left.

---

[1] As improbable as it may seem, both academics and government agencies made calculations of exactly this sort during the debates and public dialogue leading to Quebec's secession referendum of 1995. For a sense of the debate, including estimated costs, see Young (1994) and Vaillancourt (1998).

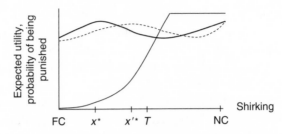

Figure 6.2. Behavioral Response to a Weakened Safeguard

Construction of a safeguard is a delicate balancing act: the union is more attractive when governments comply, but sanctions, necessary to sustain compliance, make the union less attractive. For the union to be feasible (incentive-compatible), the safeguards must be carefully rigged. If a safeguard is easily triggered, it cannot have a severe potential punishment. On the other hand, for safeguards that trigger infrequently, mild punishments are ineffective (as in Figure 6.2).

The threshold/punishment pairings allow us to elaborate on our preliminary classification of the safeguards by categorizing them by the severity and frequency of their punishment. Although the range of a safeguard's sensitivity as well as severity of its punishment both lay along a continuum, and it is a fine art to place a safeguard along those ranges, suppose, for purposes of discussion, that we can agree on the following rough categorization: let safeguards that have mild effects—a legal judgment, a political loss—be classified as "mild," while those that could destroy the union are "severe." Therefore we would agree that as deterrents, political or judicial safeguards would be mild, while a civil war or attempted secession would be severe. Notice that the sensitivity of the safeguard is negatively correlated with its punishment effect. We would expect to see mild institutions triggering more frequently, or for smaller acts of shirking, while severe institutions would trigger infrequently. The mild and the severe safeguards complement one another. Pairing mild and severe safeguards for each transgression type may provide more efficient coverage than if any one worked alone.

Creating complementary safeguards has an observable effect on behavior. Suppose a union is sustained by intergovernmental retaliation alone, as in Chapter 3. It has severe consequences and therefore triggers infrequently, with a threshold at T. Complementing it with a mild safeguard that triggers more frequently (a threshold at t) alters the expected utility curve so that it resembles a roller coaster (See Figure 6.3). We can

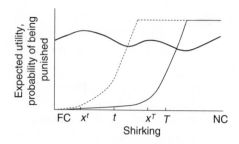

Figure 6.3. Complementary Safeguards

analyze this figure in the same way as Figure 6.1. Utility peaks at x^t— the government will not fully respect the boundaries on its authority, but will engage in some minor opportunism. If a government transgresses more, its expected benefit declines until t, at which point it starts to rise again, since the smaller penalty is already being paid. As the transgression becomes more flagrant, utility again increases until x^T, when intergovernmental retaliation becomes more likely. In this particular example, the equilibrium degree of shirking is x^t.

Two observations are worth noting. First, *without adjusting the first safeguard, the addition of a second, milder safeguard can only increase compliance.* Adding a mild safeguard—as long as the more severe remains fixed—will deter minor transgressions. Second, *without adjusting the first safeguard, the addition of a second, milder safeguard may increase utility.* Informally, in the illustration, whether the mild safeguard makes the federal union more beneficial to its member governments depends on whether the first "hill" is bigger than the second. With two safeguards, each with its own trigger mechanism, there are two distinct probability curves. Together, these safeguards improve the efficiency of the union: the mild safeguard sustains compliance at higher levels, and minimizes the frequency of intergovernmental retaliation, while the continuation of the threat of a battle between governments—the severe safeguard—dampens the temptation of larger transgressions.

The utility and compliance improvements offered by the second, mild safeguard provides the opportunity to reduce the likelihood of triggering the severe mechanism by shifting its threshold to the right. But adjustments must be made with caution. If the severe safeguard were adjusted with the addition of the mild safeguard (by increasing its tolerance or reducing its punishment force), then utility and compliance may *decrease* with the change to the safeguard. Later in this chapter, we will examine two forms of insufficient complementarity: (1) an overly mild safeguard and (2) an overly weakened severe safeguard. In a third category, punishments that are too severe case an immediate dissolution of the union.

When safeguards complement one another, each is able assume a different role. Chapter 5 explored a form of complementarity: safeguards could be combined to improve coverage of the three transgression types. Even when focused on one transgression type, a single safeguard may not be adequate; its punishment capacity may be too strong or too weak, an inappropriate and ineffective match to the extent of the transgression. Through complementarity the system is transformed from ineffective to strong. Pairing complementary safeguards may boost federal performance.

6.2 THE COMPLEMENTARY COVERAGE CAPACITY OF SAFEGUARDS

We are now prepared to develop our classification of the safeguards according to their ability to inflict punishment. Table 5.1 offered an initial sorting of the safeguards according to their potential (under ideal conditions) to influence behavior in the three broad types of opportunism. Table 6.1 further refines the classification, distinguishing the safeguards by their capacity to punish as well as by transgression type. The classification is a rough scale of effect: mild sanctions are marked □, variable sanctions are ❑, and a severe sanction is ■. Where the safeguard has no coverage capacity, the area is left blank.

■ *The Severe Type: Intergovernmental Retaliation.* Intergovernmental retaliation is a safeguard with potentially disastrous effects. It is a state's declaration of secession or federal dissolution of state governments. It can lead to civil war. While one might hope that it could be restrained to a simple tit-for-tat of opportunistic sparring, at best it is a crude device, and always biased. One government's misinterpretations of another government's actions could cause tensions and aggressions to escalate. It is a serious safeguard. It is best not to involve intergovernmental retaliation for the mundane matters of minor transgressions, but preferably to reserve it for significant transgressions.

The ratings I have assigned to each safeguard consider its potential in isolation. When intergovernmental retaliation is the only safeguard available, it is inevitably a severe sanctioning mechanism. When it is reinforced by other safeguards it may have potential to span a wider range of punishment force. For example, in the United States the federal

Table 6.1. *Refined Assessment of the Coverage Capacity of Each Safeguard, Considering Sanctioning Capacity*

| | Federal Action | State Action | | |
| | | | Burden- | |
Safeguard	Encroachment	Shirking	Shifting	Remarks
Intergovernmental retaliation	■	■	■	Exit options may limit efficiency; unable to prevent low levels of noncompliance
Popular	❏	❏		Coordination problems; safeguard enhanced by competitive elections
Structural	□			Fragments federal authority; incorporates state interests in federal decisions
Political	□	□		Must be an integrated party system
Judicial	□	□	□	Must be law; cannot uphold convention

government withholds funds to induce state compliance, for example, with highway funds, education, and pollution control. This limited intergovernmental retaliation is both tolerated and kept in check by other safeguards, particularly popular safeguards. Whether it is tolerated at efficient levels is controversial. I will raise the federal spending powers again in Section 7.3.

□ *The Mild Types: Auxiliary Safeguards.* The auxiliary safeguards, structural, political, and judicial, have relatively mild effects, particularly when compared to intergovernmental retaliation. A party may expel a politician or a bicameral legislature may stall legislation. However personally disappointing these punishments are, they are not on the order of a civil war.

❏ *The Variable Type: Citizen Control.* Between the safeguards with severe consequences and the mild types lies citizen control. The effect of popular safeguards may be mild, voicing displeasure or failing to reelect a particular candidate. The punishment grows as citizen discontent grows: rather than one or two isolated candidates failing, whole slates, even parties may suffer. At the extreme, and very rarely, there is the potential for revolution. In democracies, the citizens can be the gateway for more severe retaliation; secession attempts and government overthrows depend on citizen support.

6.3 THE INSUFFICIENT MILD SAFEGUARD

Adding safeguards is not always effective. Mild safeguards may be too mild. If so, governments may choose to ignore it, accepting its penalty.

Figure 6.4 graphs the outcome from the addition of an overly mild institution. The dotted line represents the probability of triggering the mild institution. In this graph, the safeguards do not complement one another well. The government's induced action is at x^T, well to the right of the mild safeguard's threshold. The mild safeguard was an insufficient deterrant; the government prefers to accept the mild safeguard's punishment, perhaps even with certainty, trading off a mild sanction against the gains from a more flagrant transgression.

Safeguards may also be too mild because they trigger too infrequently given the small disincentive they can mete out. Recall that the safeguard's effectiveness is a product of both punishment force and threshold. If the threshold is too tolerant (t may be set too high), the safeguard will not be able to deter the lure of moderate opportunism. The threat of triggering the severe safeguard may maintain partial compliance, but in these cases, while a mild institution is present, it has little or no effect on compliance.

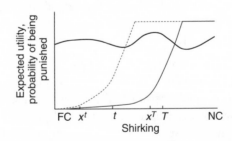

Figure 6.4. Insufficient Mild Safeguard

Subnational Fiscal Responsibility

To illustrate the effect of the mild safeguard, we will examine several cases of a single phenomenon: subnational debt. In federations, state governments have spending authority, an independence that introduces the possibility that the state's spending will exceed its revenue capacity. It can borrow to support its spending, but as a member of a federation another option is available: it may ask for a federal bailout. State fiscal irresponsibility can inhibit federal prosperity[2] and as such is a transgression that should be minimized. To use our framework, we need first to diagnose the form of opportunism and then examine how safeguards may alter the states' incentives.

Is state fiscal irresponsibility a case of shirking or burden-shifting? Setting aside the potential for graft, we can assume that the state expenditures finance public policy, not the private accounts of corrupt leaders. When states burden-shift they often produce externalities, where one state's policies affect the citizens of another state. When a state overspends, some spillover effects may be negative, but they may also be beneficial for citizens in other states. Deficit financing is a legitimate strategy for economic growth; if the risk pays off, then other states may benefit from the strength of their neighbor directly as well as indirectly, through the positive effect on the federal union. The potential for fiscal collapse is worrying, but even failures may have positive direct effects for neighboring states, as individuals, firms, and capital may relocate to more thriving regional economies. The case to treat subnational debt as burden-shifting is weak.

Independent governments bear full responsibility for their fiscal decisions, giving them an incentive to exercise caution before engaging in fiscally risky strategies including overspending. Membership in a federation has a potential to distort the state governments' risk assessment because the risk of fiscal failure could be cushioned through a federal safety net, including the potential for bailout. Framed as such, state fiscal irresponsibility is shirking. The hard budget constraint, where the federal government refuses to bail out a state in budget crisis, is a remedy that recreates the incentive of the independent government by forcing the state to bear full responsibility for its fiscal decisions. The hard budget constraint requires two conditions to work. First, the federal government needs to be able to commit credibly to a policy of no bailout.

---

[2] See Section 2.2 for a discussion of Weingast's market-preserving federalism argument and the importance of fiscal responsibility for federal economic growth.

Second, because the state might still borrow to finance its overspending, the state's incentives to engage in risky policy should be changed through a sanctioning threat from a safeguard.

What safeguard might prevent this opportunistic behavior? The state's worst-case scenario is that its transgression causes the federation to disband. The more the state values union membership over independence, the more that the severe safeguard of intergovernmental retaliation (through a secession threat or complete rupture) deters major shirking. But at the same time, the fear of failure makes it more likely that the federal government will bail out a failing state, especially if that state is important to the union's economy—a California or Ontario. Consistent with the theory of Chapter 3, mild shirking is tolerated, and the federation underperforms. A mild safeguard is needed to improve compliance further. If there is a law, the judiciary might uphold it. But as we will see, political and popular safeguards are more active (and perhaps more effective) than the judiciary.

We can first consider political safeguards. Recall Filippov et al.'s (2004) argument from Chapter 4: an integrated party system frees the local politician from the opportunistic demands of her constituency by refocusing attention on the party's overall welfare. The integrated party system may make legislators at all levels more attentive to the nation's fiscal health. Rodden measures the integrated party by vertical co-partisanship (same party at federal and state executive) and Senate co-partisanship (same party of upper house and federal executive). Evaluating data from 12 federations over 18 years, both measures are positively and significantly correlated with a surplus of the combined national–provincial budgets (Rodden 2006:129–32). The aggregate data indicate the effect of partisan coordination and interdependence to control shirking; when absent, state spending may increase.

Rodden's case studies further highlight the effectiveness of an integrated party system in minimizing state fiscal shirking. A particularly large state (or collection of states) might exploit its economic size, betting that the union believes that it is too important for the national economy to be allowed to fail. Highlighting the importance of what he calls electoral externalities, where the electorate boosts the importance of the party, Rodden analyzes Germany and Brazil in detail; in both, voters expected federal aid for fiscally troubled states. In the German case, overspending was limited by a strict harmonization scheme and an interdependent party system; in Brazil, the federal government had much discretion about how and when to distribute funds. Political deals could be struck with subnational leaders from small, overrepresented states. The insufficient mild safeguard in Brazil periodically leads to state overspending.

The importance of the political safeguards is corroborated by Parikh and Weingast (2003) in a study of fiscal deficits in India. They hypothesize that a centralized party system (supported as well by the threat of President's rule) prevented state fiscal shirking. (Recalling our theory, a centralized party system has an asymmetrical effect: it may minimize shirking but will abet federal encroachment.) The waning of the centralized party system is correlated with an increase in fiscal deficits.

A good contrast is the case of Argentina, where the party system is decentralized. No mild political safeguard exists to manage state shirking, and federal discretionary funds are subject to political manipulation. The thrifty province is not rewarded (Jones et al. 2000, Nicolini et al. 2000). To constrain provincial fiscal shirking, the federal government may formally intervene (Dillinger and Webb 1999). During an intervention, the federal executive (with the approval of the national legislature, if it is in session) dismisses the provincial governor, replacing him with a federal manager. The provincial legislature and judiciary may be dismissed as well. Such aggressive tactics are rare: of those countries with federal practices, only India and Argentina have employed the intervention in the past generation.

The intervention is a great example of targeted intergovernmental retaliation, but it is not necessarily as severe as it seems. It is invoked most often for political corruption at the provincial level or for mishandling of finances. In India, the intervention (President's rule) has been a deterrent. But in Argentina, the effect is less clear. Although it has been used as frequently, and its severity is just as considerable—in terms of institutional effect—it does not always carry a harsh negative consequence. First, often a federal manager brings access to federal revenues to restore fiscal balance in the intervened province. Second, once fiscal order is restored, the voters elect whomever they please, regardless of federal preferences. Very often, voters reelect the same politicians who were deposed during the intervention. The people have blunted the blow of intergovernmental retaliation, reducing the punishment capacity of the federal government. A safeguard that could be severe in theory is rendered mild, and even somewhat ineffective. The intervention fails to prevent provincial fiscal shirking. Provincial overspending contributed to Argentina's fiscal crisis at the end of the last decade, and the root problem of shirking remains to be solved.[3]

We see from the Argentine example that a third safeguard, the people, is unreliable. In Argentina, the electorate undermines the force of the federal government's retaliatory action; if the state government is popular, fiscal shirking is *more* likely. But in other cases, the popular safeguards have been effective controls on fiscal responsibility. In Chapter 4, I described the preference and informational problems that inhibit the citizens' role as a safeguard. First, they are unlikely to agree, and second, even if they do, they may not know that one another share the same position or observe the behavior in the same way. However, the budget is relatively easy to monitor,[4] which helps to overcome informational problems. The budget is often fully reported. Deficit is easily distinguishable from surplus. Finally, zero deficit is focal, improving the likelihood of public coordination on a threshold. Should citizens choose to insist on it, they can enforce it.

The citizens are the primary enforcement of the hard budget constraint in the United States. In 2003, as the recession deepened the budget deficits in the states, calls were heard from statehouses and editorial pages and even some Senators for the national government to bail out the states from their fiscal crisis. Early that year, California Democratic Governor Gray Davis announced a significant budget deficit, and called for a combination of spending reductions and tax increases, just as Republican Governor Pete Wilson did in the early 1990s, during California's previous fiscal crisis. But one of the conditions of Proposition 13, passed in 1978, was to require a 2/3 majority in the state legislature before any tax increase could be approved. The Republicans controlled the legislature and refused to approve the tax increase. Voters cried fiscal incompetence. Not content to wait until the next election to vote out Gray Davis, they supported a recall, and replaced Davis midterm with political neophyte Arnold Schwarznegger.

Although the extent of the California electorate's reaction was severe, the sentiment was not unusual. In 49 of the 50 states, the state governments are required to balance their budgets (Vermont is the exception), and most are banned from borrowing to cover expenses. The strictness of

---

[3] For a complete analysis of the institutional determinants of the Argentine fiscal federalism, see Jones et al. (2000), Tommasi et al. (2001), and Spiller and Tommasi (2007).

[4] Monitoring subnational budgets is not completely straightforward, with complications including significant intergovernmental transfers, countercyclical spending requirements, and fund accounting.

the requirement varies from state to state—some allow carryovers, budget revisions, or short-term financing—and there is evidence that states are more likely to have a surplus, the more strict the rule (Inman 2001, 2002). Interestingly, however, these requirements often have no enforcement mechanism. That is, in reading the constitutional clause or statute, no penalty is identified should the budget not be balanced.[5] No legal remedy exists in most cases. Nonetheless, when questioned, government aides in 22 states reported the existence of some enforcement mechanism, often citing the law itself (Snell 2004). In the language of our theory, the law stipulates a threshold, but no punishment. The primary enforcement mechanism is the public expectation that the budget be balanced. Even in states that allow debt, borrowing is hardly the same routine matter as at the federal level. It becomes a matter of public discussion, suppressing its use. When a balanced budget is expected, popular safeguards are effective motivators of fiscal responsibility.[6]

Viewed in aggregate, these accounts demonstrate the importance of the mild safeguard while holding fixed in the background an effective severe safeguard. The mild safeguard is a way to fine-tune the federation's performance by increasing compliance from that sustained by the crude severe safeguard; when the safeguards complement one another, the federation performs better. While the relevant mild safeguards vary—political safeguards, popular safeguards, and a mild form of targeted intergovernmental retaliation—they perform identical functions: to alter the subnational government's incentive structure to induce higher rates of compliance. Not one of these economies failed (although Argentina came very close in 2000) but their performance varies across countries as well as within, in correlation with the efficacy of the mild safeguard.

6.4 THE INSUFFICIENT SEVERE SAFEGUARD

While mild safeguards may improve compliance, they are only effective when a sufficient severe safeguard is also present. Without it the system of safeguards fails to prevent significant transgressions. Figure 6.5 illustrates the concept of an insufficient severe safeguard. While the mild safeguard

[5] There are some exceptions: some, including Minnesota and North Carolina, impose mandatory budget cuts midyear if a deficit is projected. Alabama punishes the treasurer with a $5,000 fine and two years in jail, as well as impeachment (Snell 2004).

[6] For empirical evidence, see Peltzman (1992) and Lowery et al. (1998).

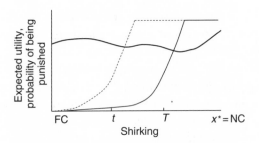

Figure 6.5. Insufficient Severe Safeguard

manages to shape incentives to a small degree, the severe safeguard fails completely to motivate the governments. Moving to the right along the horizontal axis, notice the relatively high expected utility in the interval $0 < x_i \leq t$; the mild safeguard is deterring moderate shirking, and governments anticipate fairly high benefits from relatively high degrees of compliance. Moving farther right, where transgressions have higher immediate rewards, the mild safeguard is too harmless to be an effective deterrent. The severe safeguard is needed to complement the mild and to provide complete coverage of the noncompliance space. But in Figure 6.5, we see that in the interval $t < x_i \leq T$ the severe safeguard hardly manages to display any effect. Expected utility is maximized in the inverval $x_i > T$, specifically, at full noncompliance. Compliance is unsustainable, which for federations likely means that no union is possible.

Figure 6.5 displays the fundamental importance of an effective severe safeguard. If the mild safeguard, such as a court, were acting alone, it could not sustain high levels of compliance. A mild mechanism works by punishing frequently, but because it punishes frequently, its punishment must be small. Minor transgressions do not offer enough short-term benefit to overcome the cost of the mild safeguard's sanction, but a more significant transgression may be a net benefit. With such a weak punishment, as a player becomes highly likely to trigger the punishment regime through its noncompliance, it might as well deviate fully. Alone, the mild safeguard can only ward off small transgressions, a contribution too small to sustain any union. Its usefulness only becomes evident when paired with a severe safeguard that prevents major deviations.

This claim demonstrates the importance of a fear of failure. In Riker's (1964) theory, a necessary condition for federalism was a significant external threat. This threat would propel one state to want to expand its territory to increase its defensive resources, and if it could not do so by force, it would invite a second state to join it in federation. This same fear of a common enemy would motivate the second state to accept the first's offer to federate. Thus, federations are born, and sustained, of fear: of the three basic motivations to federation, military security generally is the top priority. It is important to note that the fear of an external threat is not itself an institutional mechanism. It creates the value of the world outside of the federation; the more potent the external threat, the greater the disincentive of action that could cause the union to fall apart. A particularly fearsome external threat may make a low-productivity federation relatively more attractive.

It follows that if fear of failure helps to sustain a federation, then an attractive outside option hurts the union's long-term potential. As long as the federation performs well and governments are not punished, the federation is more beneficial than a slightly less attractive outside option.[7] But at the start of a punishment period, a government's expected benefit is lower, and may be less than the value of its exit option. It may choose to exit the federation rather than suffer the consequences of intergovernmental retaliation, however brief. Knowing that a government may make this choice, the intergovernmental retaliation is not as severe as it might have otherwise been, and therefore it cannot sustain the same high levels of compliance. Overall productivity of the federation drops.

Of course if the outside option is attractive, rather than fearsome, the sanctioning threat of the severe safeguard is muted and the union likely will not transpire. But troubling are the unions that could be mutually beneficial—superior to independence—but do not happen because they cannot be sustained: compliance requires punishment, and if the punishment is triggered, the outside option may look better than staying in the union and accepting the punishment. In these cases when the exit option's value is slightly worse than federation, the exit option may be disruptive; intergovernmental retaliation needs support to boost the net benefit of union to a level where exit options no longer seem attractive. The European Union serves as an example.

The European Union

As the above analysis argues, while federations may limp along with inadequate mild safeguards, it cannot survive without a sanctioning force

---

[7] For a formal proof of these claims, see Bednar (2007a).

severe enough to deter major transgressions. Severe safeguards are rendered impotent by credible exit options. Therefore, most "examples" of insufficient severe safeguards are phantoms: they are federations that never happened. The European Union violates this general rule; despite a relatively mild trigger threat among the member governments, the union flourishes, with a trend of minimal noncompliance.[8] The health of the European Union is puzzling because of the apparent insufficiency of its severe safeguard of intergovernmental retaliation. Member states maintain a claim on their sovereignty, so a threat to quit the union is credible. The ability to impose a high penalty, necessary to induce high levels of compliance, is limited by the value of the alternative; members would prefer to leave than to continue within the union, accepting the high punishment. The robustness of the European Union, despite significant exit options that limit the severe punishment capacity, begs explanation.

One particularly devastating aspect of the intergovernmental retaliation is that it is difficult to target; punishing others harms oneself, whereas the mild safeguards are targeted and relatively costless to implement. In the European Union, one of the mild safeguards, the judiciary, has been modified in a manner that makes it more effective at deterring more significant transgressions. Unlike most constitutional courts, the European Court of Justice (ECJ) can inflict relatively severe penalties on governments for violating European law. The union is freed from being as dependent on intergovernmental retaliation to induce compliance.

As an example of persistent shirking and accelerating penalties, consider the ECJ's judgment against France for its fishermen's violation of the EU law protecting immature fish to promote fishing stock sustainability. The ECJ initially ruled against France in 1991, and at the time requested that France step up its inspections of fishing ports to ensure compliance. France persisted in its defiance, despite repeated negative judgments. Ordinarily, a negative judgment from the ECJ carries the same penalty as in the United States: the state government is asked to stop its violating action (or inaction) and come into immediate compliance. The ECJ has a sanctioning power usually unavailable to higher courts: for continued governmental violations, it may impose

---

[8] Goldstein calls member state noncompliance "remarkably rare" when compared to other new federations (2001:135, 150).

a fine. In 2005 it imposed a penalty of EUR 20 million, with an additional EUR 57.8 million each subsequent 6 months of noncompliance.[9] In a written statement issued at the time of the decision, the court explicitly described the penalty as a warning for other member states who might be tempted to protect local interests by shirking on EU law.[10]

High penalties cannot be imposed frequently: consistent with our theory, the threshold must shift to a more tolerant position if the mild safeguard is going to mimic a more severe safeguard. But the result of giving teeth to a mild safeguard is that it will be able to deter more significant transgressions, making it more effective for a larger share of the noncompliance space. The net effect on other member states is positive: with one member state now induced to comply when otherwise it may have transgressed, the productivity of the union is higher. The value of the union is elevated, making the exit option appear less attractive. It will consequently boost the effectiveness of the intergovernmental retaliation.

The European Union has a second modification that causes it to break from the standard federalism mold: à la carte membership. In some limited circumstances, member states may opt in (or out) of specified domains. When a member state does not benefit from one dimension of the union, it can decline membership within that aspect of the union, but still participate in others. The British and Danish have opted out of the common currency, for example. The net effect is that the member state's benefit from its (partial) membership is higher. Again, in a case like the European Union when the exit options are feasible, any relative boost to the value of the union for a member state will make exit less enticing. It is possible that the overall union may suffer because some members have opted out of some aspects, but perhaps not: if those member states were forced to join the union fully, they may be tempted to behave opportunistically more often and to a greater extent. Successful federations are studies of feasibility; sometimes a distribution of authority that differs from one member state to the next is best for all.

---

[9] To put the fine in perspective, the fishing industry is worth approximately EUR 1.37 billion annually to France.

[10] It must be noted that the ECJ continues to suffer from the same inherent weakness as most other courts: should a member state refuse to pay the penalty, it is not clear what authority would have enforced the judgment. The ECJ remains beholden to another source for its rulings to have full effect. Generally this is an executive, but it may also be political legitimacy, sustained by popular support.

6.5 DISCUSSION

The chapter began by asking how the U.S. Constitution transformed a tenuous union into one that has proven successful. Phrased more generally, we may ask: why would the addition of relatively mild safeguards be effective in inducing compliance, in overcoming the inefficient by-product of rivalry, and in making a federation robust? An answer provided by this chapter is that they cannot do it alone.

The natural illustration of the failure of mild safeguards is the case where they do not exist at all. In the United States, under the Articles of confederation, no mild safeguard existed to motivate the states to respect one another or to resist the temptation to shirk on the Congressional requests. Burden-shifting and shirking were countermotivated only by intergovernmental retaliation—the fear that the union would fracture leaving the states separately vulnerable. With intergovernmental retaliation as its only safeguard, the union could sustain only limited productive capacity. Publius yearned for a "firm Union" (*Federalist* 9) made possible through an "energetic" government with "vigor" (*Federalist* 1). The Constitution brought mild safeguards and the union became more productive and more secure. Although Publius did not make this connection directly, the mild safeguards, when effective, provide "energy"; they fine-tune the federation's performance by inducing higher levels of compliance than can be sustained merely by fear of disbanding the union or by internal threats. The threat of an internal trade war—even a civil war—is the most severe punishment available. Against this backdrop, the threat of a political defeat seems tame, and a court's judgment is kitten's claws. Yet the establishment of mild safeguards was essential in the transformation from the Articles of Confederation to the Constitution, and no federation today is established without attempting to include them.

In this chapter, I made the following points:

1. Complementary safeguards can improve compliance over a single one, but not universally. In particular, as long as the original severe safeguard is not adjusted, it will never decrease compliance.
2. Complementary safeguards can make the union more attractive to its members.
3. If the mild safeguard's threshold is raised to too high a standard, it can fail to increase compliance.
4. When a mild safeguard is added, the severe safeguard may be set to trigger less frequently, for an increase in the benefits of the federation. However, the combination of safeguards must be adjusted with one

another's capacities in mind, or the design may backfire, reducing overall compliance levels.

5. Mild safeguards should not be studied in isolation: to understand their effect, one must know how they complement more severe safeguards.

6. Attractive exit options limit the effectiveness of the severe safeguard; mild safeguards may be transformed into moderate to improve compliance, boosting the value of the union above the exit option.

This analysis suggests that the institutional framework that supports a federation is not only complex, but its components are interrelated, are *interdependent*. Calculation of each safeguard's efficacy, let alone capturing its effect empirically, requires a systems approach, where each safeguard is evaluated within the fuller institutional context. In the next chapter, we will look even more closely at interdependence. By acknowledging the imperfections of each safeguard, we find how they support one another so the sanctioning system can approach an ideal despite the flaws of each component.

6.6 Mathematical Appendix to Chapter 6

A Model of Complementary Safeguards

We return to the model development. Suppose that a second safeguard can target punishments and gets an independent signal but that it can only levy minor fines. For convenience, I work with Model 1 introduced in the appendix to Chapter 3, altered to fit targeted punishments (institutional safeguards) in the appendix to Chapter 4.

What I do now is add a second trigger mechanism, with its own threshold and own punishment. It follows that if the second safeguard's punishment is minor, it must be punishing much more frequently to have any effect and so the second threshold is lower than the first. Here, I assume that the signal $\omega_2 = x_i^2 + \epsilon$, where ϵ is a random variable that is uniform in $[-m_2, m_2]$. I will denote the threshold as t and the punishment as q. I assume that the more severe safeguard has a threshold T and a targeted punishment Q. My choice of upper and lower case letters captures the fact that $t < T$ and $q < Q$.

A first way to see the effects of the second safeguard is to plot the value as a function of the amount of opportunism. See Figure 6.3 within the chapter's main text, at page 151, and read the graph from left to right, along the transgression axis. Initially, the benefits of shirking increase as a government transgresses, but peaks and then declines as the first safeguard's sanction takes effect. Continuing to the right, at some point the probability of being punished by the mild safeguard approaches one and once again (provided T is much larger than t) the government can benefit from opportunism. Eventually the severe safeguard's force creates a second peak.

Given this intuition, we can write the value function V_i as a piecewise function:

$$V_i(x_1, x_2, \ldots, x_n)$$
$$= \frac{\alpha \sum_{j=1}^{N}(1 - x_j) + x_1 - \delta(\Pr(\omega_2 > t)(q) + \Pr(\omega > T)(Q))}{1 - \delta}$$

for $x_i^2 < t + m_2$,

$$V_i(x_1, x_2, \ldots, x_n) = \frac{\alpha \sum_{j=1}^{N}(1 - x_j) + x_1 - \delta(q + \Pr(\omega > T)(Q))}{1 - \delta}$$

for $t + m_2 < x_i^2 < T + m$, and

$$V_i(x_1, x_2, \ldots, x_n) = \frac{\alpha \sum_{j=1}^{N}(1 - x_j) + x_1 - \delta(q + Q)}{1 - \delta}$$

for $T + m < x_i^2$.

Since both punishments are targeted, this is also a dominant strategy game. The interesting case is the one in which the government chooses $x_i^2 < t + m_2$. Otherwise, the state is punished with certainty by the weaker safeguard, and the government's problem is the same as in the single safeguard model except that it now pays a cost q for violating the new safeguard. In the range where $x_i^2 < t + m_2$, the first-order condition is

$$\frac{1 - \alpha - \delta \left(\frac{1}{2m_2} 2x_i q + \frac{1}{2m} 2x_i Q \right)}{1 - \delta}$$

This implies

$$x_i^{*2} = \frac{(1 - \alpha)}{\delta \left(\frac{Q}{m} + \frac{q}{m_2} \right)}$$

Recall that the equilibrium level of shirking in the single safeguard case was

$$x_i^* = \frac{(1 - \alpha)}{\delta \frac{Q}{m}}$$

Comparing these two expressions establishes that without any adjustment to the first safeguard, the addition of a second, milder safeguard can only increase compliance. Whether or not it increases utility depends on some conditions which I now derive.

The introduction of the second safeguard has three effects. First, as I just showed, it increases compliance. This increase in compliance also decreases the probability that the second, larger safeguard has to be used. This increases utility as the probability of targeted punishment falls. However, the second safeguard might punish opportunism. If so, this reduces governmental utility.

The precise details are less important than the intuition. Let Δx_i denote the increase in x_i due to the introduction of the new safeguard.

$$\Delta x_i = \frac{(1-\alpha)}{\delta\left(\frac{Q}{m} + \frac{q}{m_2}\right)} - \frac{(1-\alpha)}{\delta\frac{Q}{m}}$$

Let ΔP_1 equal the *change* (due to a change in the threshold) in the probability that the first safeguard punishes government i and let P_2 be the probability that the second safeguard punishes. The change in the value function ΔV_i equals the following expression:

$$\frac{\alpha N \Delta x_i + (1-\alpha)\Delta x_i + \Delta P_1 Q - P_2 q}{1 - \delta}$$

If this expression exceeds zero, then adding a second safeguard increases utility. We can simplify the above expression into the *complementarity condition*. If this condition is satisfied, then the second safeguard increases utility.

$$(\alpha(N-1) + 1)\Delta x_i + \Delta P_1 Q - P_2 q > 0$$

I make the following observation: *the punishment from the additional safeguard could always be set to zero, therefore the optimal set of two safeguards cannot give lower utility than the optimal single safeguard.* In general, two safeguards (properly chosen) will be better than one.

In Figure 6.3, with two safeguards, each with its own trigger mechanism, there are two distinct probability curves. Together, these safeguards improve the efficiency of the union: the mild safeguard sustains compliance at higher levels, and minimizes the frequency of punishment regimes that are triggered, while the continuation of the punishment regime threat—the severe safeguard—dampens the utility gained from higher levels of cheating, and so prevents large deviations.

We may now consider how one might design the optimal mild trigger, for example, the judiciary. Assume that the severe safeguard is fixed and adequate. That is, it is sufficient to sustain some degree of compliance, although not full compliance. For a given T, Q combination, as well as an α, it is possible to consider the optimal placement of the court's trigger threshold and the amount that it fines. This calculation will be highly dependent on the functional form assumed in the model.

The safeguard has "bite" when its punishment probability curve is steep (see Figure 6.3): in this range, small changes to the amount of transgression have large effects on the probability of punishment. Safeguards are efficiently complementary when their probability of punishment curves cover as much of the compliance space as possible. This observation has important implications for the optimal design of institutions. When the complementarity condition is not met, the addition of the mild safeguard fails to improve utility or compliance. If the severe safeguard was adjusted with the addition of the mild safeguard (by raising T or reducing Q), then utility and compliance may *decrease* with the change to the safeguard. The chapter's main text describes the two forms of insufficient complementarity: (1) an overly mild safeguard and (2) an overly weakened severe safeguard.

7

Redundancy

Our final concern with a federation's safeguards is their *imperfection*. When safeguards make mistakes, they levy their sanctions too frequently, or not frequently enough. If they systematically fail to react, then the federation becomes vulnerable to opportunism. On the other hand, a safeguard might punish too frequently. While punishment will occur in every federation,[1] if the safeguard punishes too frequently, frustration with the system mounts, as membership in the union becomes less attractive than an outside option of independence. Under either circumstance—sanctions that come too frequently or not frequently enough—the federation is jeopardized.

Referring to the baseline model of safeguards in Chapter 4, a safeguard's imperfection has two sources: an observation (the signal, ω), which is the safeguard's impression of reality, and a threshold (T), its "trigger point," when the safeguard will levy its sanction. Imperfections arise because safeguards are not necessarily designed efficiently. Safeguards are often political creatures, or established for other purposes, or have interests of their own and reasons for acting that are peripheral to solving a federation's compliance problem. Tangential goals motivate the safeguard to trigger when it does; formally, its threshold is not necessarily set efficiently. It is also likely that what is optimal may change over time, converting an early efficiency into a flaw.

If the only concern were that a safeguard would fail to react, then the solution could be captured by two words: add safeguards. But the former problem has not evaporated. Safeguards sting; if they trigger too frequently, or inaccurately, then they flip from being incentives to

---

[1] In equilibria derived in Chapters 3 and 4, punishment occurs even when no one deviates (beyond the tolerated level of noncompliance).

dis-incentives, reducing both the extent of compliance and the benefits of union. Simply adding more safeguards will not improve the system.

In addition to extraneous punishment, multiple safeguards limit the federation's ability to adapt. This third problem is known generally as a status quo bias. When decision makers have conflicting opinions about the direction of change, policy stagnates. It is well established that as the number of veto players increases, policy is more stable. The downside of stability is that the system cannot adjust when circumstances demand it. Tsebelis (2002) associates policy stability with several undesirable outcomes including government and regime instability[2]; this certainly does not seem to be a prescription for federal robustness. Fernandez and Rodrik (1991) argue that utility-enhancing institutional reform is often resisted because of the uncertainty associated with how the new system will distribute benefits. This uncertainty can only be resolved through experience. Rather than enabling experimentation, safeguards can exacerbate the tendency identified by Fernandez and Rodrik. A federal system of safeguards that works too well may stifle the very system it is designed to protect.

Alas it would seem that we have a trio of contradictory concerns: safeguards that fail to fire, safeguards that fire too frequently, and safeguards that create a status quo bias. Redundancy is a powerful sword that cuts two ways. How can a system of safeguards reconcile these problems? In this chapter we take up this design riddle.

7.1 THE ISSUE: IMPERFECT SAFEGUARDS

To this point in the book I have characterized the safeguards as impersonal, disinterested trigger mechanisms, but a safeguard's decisions are made by humans, with our politics and misjudgment. In order for any safeguard—structural, political, judicial, popular, or intergovernmental— to deter transgressions of federalism's boundaries, it must establish a threshold that when crossed, triggers a punishment. But someone must have an incentive to pull that trigger. On paper it is possible to derive the efficient threshold and punishment combination which balances the degree of compliance against the probability of a punishment. But real safeguards are not simple if–then rules. Rather than being the passionless, detached referees of theory, the safeguards are composed of *people* with ambitions, idiosyncrasies, and weaknesses. The real people behind the triggers may set thresholds and punishments for private reasons, or may

---

[2] See also the discussion in Persson and Tabellini (2003:27–9).

have perspectives that cause them to interpret (and react to) observations differently. Real people may pull the mechanism away from optimality.[3]

Threshold Inefficiencies

The sole source of inefficiency that we examined in the last chapter was a safeguard's punishment capacity. An insufficient punishment could be supplemented by a complementary mechanism; together the safeguards would more closely approximate efficiency. In some cases the complementary safeguard failed, as in Figure 6.4, where the mild institution was ineffective, and ignored. While Chapter 6 focused on the punishment as the source of these deficiencies, the safeguard's trigger could also be at fault. The threat capacity of a trigger mechanism is a combination of the punishment and its frequency: a weak punishment can be invigorated through a lower threshold, with more frequent punishment. In Figure 6.4, it is easy to see that a small shift in the mild institution may cause a lumpy shift in behavior, as equilibrium levels of shirking shift from approaching full compliance, to that sustainable by the severe trigger alone. The disutility of a punishment cannot be calculated without both the threshold and the severity of the punishment, since the threshold indicates the likelihood of the punishment.

Safeguards can be trigger-happy or overly tolerant for as many reasons as there are safeguards. For example, political safeguards are derived from parties. The party's motivation is clear: get its candidates elected. Individual politicians within the party want to be reelected, or elected to higher office, or to be offered an economically secure position after they leave office. Structural safeguards suffer from the same vulnerabilities. None of these goals necessarily puts politicians in a position of wanting to patrol the federation when punishing may clash with their own self-interest or their party-based collective interest. Even the courts, reading the same law, are inconsistent safeguards. Justices' decisions are influenced by strategic, behavioral, historical, or legal reasons, all which point in multiple directions.[4] The justices' application of these reasons to their interpretation of law can change as justices move on or off the court, or as their own thinking evolves. In sum, if the safeguards have inconsistent threshold settings,

---

[3] Or toward it. Human intervention often softens the rigidity of a flawed mechanism.
[4] Not even historical methods of setting a threshold—determining at what point law implies a negative consequence—are deterministic. See Rakove (1996) for a compelling argument about the multiplicity of constitutional interpretations that can be supported from a careful reconstruction of the American founding.

or generally set them for reasons only indirectly related to federal performance, then the safeguard may be inefficient, and even ineffective. This imperfection inherent to all safeguards is a design challenge I address in this chapter.

Diverse Observations

We can begin by thinking about how a safeguard's makeup opens opportunities for perceptual differences. A trigger is composed of two variables: the information received by the mechanism (the observation, ω) and its rule of tolerance (the threshold, T, that when crossed causes the trigger to fire). Modeling convention flows from analytical convenience: typically one assumes that the signal—the observation—is common to all. That is, we assume that all safeguards process the observation in the same way, categorizing it identically. But just as witnesses to a crime differ in what they remember of events, safeguards have different perspectives, causing each one to focus on different facts, or interpretations to diverge.

Signals are not singular bits of information: they have multiple attributes exhibited across multiple dimensions. Any particular signal may not convey the complete set of attributes. When this distortion is random, it creates inference problems as I described in Chapter 3, when motivating stochastic error. In interviewing eyewitnesses, one expects certain features of a crime scene to stick in the memories of all witnesses—the amount of blood, the speed and direction of the escaping car—but other details to be remembered differently or not at all—how many shots were fired, even the sequence of events. We would not necessarily expect any pattern or predictability to the distribution in reported observations, but they would differ from one another.

With imperfect mechanisms, systematic flaws may be connected to the monitoring capacities of the safeguarding agent. It is possible that an agent's perception may be influenced by characteristics particular to the agent; one witness noticed the quality of the perpetrator's coat, having tried a similar one at the store; another recognized the shout to the accomplice, unintelligible to others, because her grandmother spoke the same dialect at home. Valuable information connecting a suspect to the crime may come from only one witness, and, importantly, could only be provided by that particular witness.[5]

---

[5] The theory of diversity of perspectives and interpretations is developed in Hong and Page (2004) and Page (2007); see Hong and Page (2005) for a model of signal subjectivity.

Likewise a federal safeguard may only "notice" certain attributes. The subset of attributes that a safeguard considers is its interpretation of the event. Interpretations are closely tied to a safeguard's (or the agent directing that safeguard) set of past experiences. This bias creates imperfection in the safeguard's response. Politicians, the soul of the political safeguards, tend to notice what their constituents bring to their attention, or focus on the elements of policies that are most likely to influence votes. Voters, en masse, may be surprisingly good at making informed choices when issues are salient to them (Lupia and McCubbins 1998, Hutchings 2003), but much policy never hits their radar. For other safeguards, signal perception can be independent of interests. The court is an excellent example. Any case has many attributes. A judge's legal training can cause her to focus her attention on a particular subset, perhaps weighing 5 of the case's 10 attributes more heavily. A different judge, trained at a different law school, may look at three of the same attributes and two distinct ones.[6] The perceptive biases of safeguards are often attributable to each one's function and composition.

Finally, safeguards will diverge in the way that they map their observation into a decision about what happened. Kornhauser (1992) and Cameron and Kornhauser (2005), in theory applied to judicial decision making, describe legal reasoning as the application of a legal rule that partitions a multidimensional case space; the method of partitioning the space will ultimately reduce the case's vector of attributes into a simple binary set of guilt or innocence. It is not the same as setting a threshold: instead, it is a method of locating the observation on one side or the other of the threshold. For example, everyone may agree that murder, causing the death of another, is illegal and punishable, but is physician-assisted suicide murder? The threshold may be commonly held even as the observation is subject to interpretation. Page (2007) describes the same process generally as a predictive model: a mapping of facts, as encoded by an agent, into a judgment or an inference about the truth.

To sum up, signals can be distorted in three ways: agents may observe different aspects of the signal, sometimes in a manner that is not random

---

[6] Notice that this diversity in judgment is different from error correction where appeals improve the judiciary's accuracy because it provides a second look (Shavell 1995), but instead considers diverse interpretations of the same facts, as Daughety and Reinganum (2000) justify the appellate process. Strict rules of evidence remove the discretion that can lead to observational bias (and therefore judgment inconsistency), particularly in legal domains with significant consequences for the convicted (Schauer 1991).

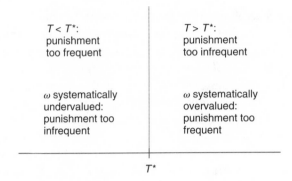

Figure 7.1. Effect of Imperfect Safeguards on Punishment Frequency

but instead a function of the agent (an encoding or interpretation); agents may have different perceptions of what the dimensions mean; and agents may have different decision rules or mental models that cause them to process the signal differently, arriving at a different judgment about reality, and therefore perhaps even disagreeing about which side of the threshold the signal falls.

Figure 7.1 illustrates the problem of imperfect thresholds and biased or inconsistent signals. These flaws—in the way the threshold is set and in the consistency of the perceived signal—are observationally difficult to disentangle but analytically distinct, and in fact have contradictory influences on the federation's robustness. While a theoretical optimum may be derived relative to the punishment capacity, here indicated at T^*, if a safeguard's threshold is consistently more demanding than optimal (to the left of T^*) it punishes too frequently; if it is less demanding, it is overly tolerant, allowing too much opportunism without punishment. The safeguard could also be flawed in its perception of action (ω): if it consistently perceives a government's action to be tolerable (to the left of the threshold) then it will be overly permissive, even if its threshold is set appropriately. Finally, the safeguard may also systematically overvalue the perceived extent of a transgression—perhaps due to bias against the government—and punish too frequently. These imperfections are likely in any safeguard. Is it possible to design a *system* of safeguards that overcomes the imperfections of its components?

7.2 Overcoming—and Embracing—Imperfection

Institutional imperfection immediately generates a trio of problems, with a fourth following consequentially. Calibration of punishment frequency is a delicate balancing act: the safeguards can (1) fail to punish or (2) punish too frequently; either one can upset the federation. Orthogonally (and somewhat maddeningly) even if a sweet spot is found, the system must not be locked permanently on the original distribution of authority. (3) The system needs to be able to dislodge itself from the stagnation of the status quo when circumstances recommend it, and the better the system maintains the current distribution of authority, the less it is able to adjust. This last problem leads inevitably to a fourth: (4) the system needs a method for accepting beneficial changes while rejecting those that are detrimental to the federation, which must include a metric to gauge societal benefit. These problems resonate throughout the social sciences generally; we see them especially in the collective action and organizational design literatures, as both are concerned with system reliability. In this section, I draw insights from these related fields to complete the principles of federal safeguard system design.

Problem #1: *Solving the Failure to Punish*

The literature on system reliability captures the first part of our puzzle very well. Bucking the conventional wisdom favoring governmental streamlining and equating redundancy with waste, Bendor (1985), studying Bay Area mass transportation, argued convincingly that it is the system *without* redundancy that is poorly designed. A system without redundancy depends on every component to function perfectly. If any component fails, the system fails. The old adage "a chain is only as strong as its weakest link" may have inspired a cult game show but it is defeatist advice for organizational design. Instead, Von Neumann (1956), Landau (1969), Bendor (1985), and Ostrom (1999) all embrace inherent human fallibility: it is impossible to eliminate error, but it is possible to design an organization to overcome internal flaws, to minimize the consequences of the failure of any one component. Von Neumann and Bendor's concern is a failure in functionality, a failure to react. When the problem is information failure, parallel information processing is beneficial (Simon 1969, Cohen 1981). Ostrom's (e.g., 1990, 1999, 2005) research on successful management of common pool resources engages both information and reaction concerns.[7]

---

[7] Ting (2003) embeds the redundancy problem within a principal-agent problem, finding that redundant agents benefit principals when the agents' preferences are distant from the principal's but redundancy is harmful when the preferences are close.

Asks Landau, "Can we ... build an organization that is more reliable than any of its parts?" (1969:350) The recommendation is straightforward: introduce redundancy when failure is possible. Successful parallel systems have two characteristics: (1) redundant components should have fully overlapping functionality and (2) as much as possible, they should have uncorrelated vulnerabilities. That is, while their capacity should overlap, they should fail for different reasons. Note that the components need not be identically designed; actually, it is their *diversity* that makes them useful as insurance, because the redundant component can only be useful if it does not fail when the first does. The advantages of redundancy are easy to compute: if one component has an estimated failure rate of 10%, then two, operating in tandem but with independent sources of error, would have only a 1% chance of failure.

But what of reliability's endurance? Momentary reliability is an oxymoron. Reliability implies that a system functions now and will continue to function in the future when circumstances are different, perhaps unpredictably so. A reliable system adapts to changing circumstances. It innovates.

Part of what makes a system healthy and adaptive is the element that cannot be planned: the adjustments that will emerge through experience. Landau (1969:347–50) praises redundancy for increasing the potential for innovation. Landau cites Von Neumann to suggest that redundancy not only improves reliability, but also enhances adaptability.

Self-organizing systems exhibit a degree of reliability that is so far superior to anything we can build as to prompt theorists to suggest 'that the richly redundant networks of biological organisms must have capabilities beyond anything our theories can yet explain.' In Von Neumann's phrasing, they 'contain the necessary adjustments to diagnose errors as they occur, to readjust the organism so as to minimize the effects of errors, and finally to correct or to block permanently the faulty component.' Error refers here to malfunction, and Von Neumann states that there is now little doubt that they are 'able to operate even when malfunctions set in ... [while] their subsequent tendency is to remove them.' (Landau 1969:350).

Therefore, what we are looking for, to quote Ostrom (1999), is a parallel *adaptive* system. Ostrom expanded Bendor's phrase "parallel systems" to emphasize the organic nature of her social systems, as opposed to the physical architecture of Bendor's transportation systems; she also wanted to emphasize the evolution and flexibility of the system. While in a social system like federalism we are not dealing with Von Neumann's biological organisms, much of how a social system evolves is unplanned by the designers, even as the mutations occur within the framework established at the founding. While one hopes that the initial design is well thought out, a complex environment introduces challenges and needs unforeseeable to the social system's planners. As with Von Neumann, Landau, Bendor, and Ostrom, we are interested in a system that maintains its functional capacity despite a changing environment. To be robust, it must be adaptive—what North (1990:80) calls *adaptive efficiency*—a point I will return to below.

The system reliability literature has provided excellent advice on solving the problem of safeguards that fail to react: construct redundancies. It has even given hints about solving the third problem of adaptation, escaping the status quo's gravitational force. But the systems design literature offers no help for dealing with the safeguard that triggers too easily, punishing too often.

Problem #2: Tempering Frequent Punishment

Punishing the innocent is a significant concern of any system of justice, and avoiding it must be a priority for safeguard system design. With flawed safeguards, redundancy—the prescription from system reliability—exacerbates the potential of injuring innocents. If one safeguard resists triggering (correctly) but the other punishes, the damage is done. In the movies, if two women misunderstand a man's remark thinking that he has said something rude, the fact that one resists the temptation to slap him across the cheek does not make up for the drink the other one threw in his face. He is still wet, even after the misunderstanding is cleared up.

Federal safeguard system design has a familiar cognate in statistics: the trade-off between the risks of making a Type I and Type II error. With the Type I error, or false positive, the null hypothesis is rejected incorrectly, while the Type II error, or false negative, fails to reject the null hypothesis when it should. As opposed to the reliability problem posed above, where the concern is that a component will fail to act—the Type II error—it is the opposite issue that statistics views as more problematic: rejecting a conventional hypothesis incorrectly.

Statistical theory informs us that for any fixed sample size, Type I error and Type II error risks are offsetting: reducing the risk of one increases the risk of the other. The prescription is again straightforward. Consider the Type I problem first. Set the critical value (the threshold) based on an acceptable failure rate. To augment the *power* of the test (its ability to avoid Type II errors, false negatives), increase the sample size.

Translating the false positive to the federal context, the consequence of a safeguard failure that causes it to trigger a punishment too often could be huge if the safeguard triggers intergovernmental retaliation, including retaliatory opportunism and even withdrawal from the union. So from statistics we learn that these problems compete with one another, and if convicting the innocent is more loathsome than undue leniency, then we should solve that problem first. So much for the reliability lessons above; it seems that adding safeguards will only augment the problem by making punishment more certain. We cannot have it both ways. Or can we?

The system reliability literature offered only one conception of redundancy: as *insurance*. A second form of redundancy will help to solve the problem of overly frequent punishment. If a safeguard punishes too frequently, one problem may be that its perception of its signal is flawed in one of the ways described in Section 7.1. If this is the case, then a second safeguard, with an independently drawn signal, could improve the efficiency of the system's reaction. Here the second signal (or safeguard) is not insurance but *confirmation*. By creating a higher bar before a punishment is triggered, the confirmation structure solves our second problem of overly frequent punishment.

For illustration, recall the Green and Porter world of oil cartels, a model described in Chapter 3. In their analysis, the unique signal is the price of oil: if the price drops, oil producers take it as a suggestion that supply has increased because one cartel member has defected from the agreement to constrain production. Green and Porter did not consider the possibility of two signals, but they could have. For example, a second signal could come from input pricing. If independent truckers and tankers suddenly demand a higher price for transporting oil, it could be due to a higher demand for their services, also a signal that could indicate a deviation. Or, conversely, if the output price of oil drops, but the input price remains steady, then cartel members may be more confident that the price hit a demand shock and no mutual punishment is needed.

The theory of the second signal is related to the results in Sah and Stiglitz (1985, 1986), who compare two organizational forms, what they dub a *hierarchy* and a *polyarchy*. In a polyarchy, a project is accepted if one (of two) agents accepts it. Both must reject it for it to be rejected. In a hierarchy, two agents are necessary to approve a project, and therefore only one is sufficient to reject it.[8] Their model can be translated to

---

[8] It is tempting to draw parallels between the names for these organizational forms and federalism's *federation* or *unitary system*, but within this section I interested in the relationship between the safeguards, not between the governments.

federalism as follows: consider their "project" to be an action taken by a member government, and the polyarchy and hierarchy to be characteristics of a system of safeguards. The hierarchy echos the reliability literature. It is a redundant system of safeguards, with one backing up the other (insurance); punishment is inflicted if either one of the safeguards is triggered. Likewise, equivalent to the polyarchy is a second form of redundancy; this time, two safeguards must be triggered before the punishment is levied. In this sense, the redundancy is confirmatory.[9]

The hierarchy, as insurance, commits more Type I errors: it builds in a level of conservatism that rejects more good projects than the polyarchy. The danger of the polyarchy, requiring confirmation to reject, is that it accepts more bad projects, thereby committing more Type II errors through its relative leniency. Preference for one type of organizational structure over another would depend on the relative utility of making a Type I versus a Type II error. In Sah and Stiglitz, this calculation is based on the relative prevalence of good projects to bad projects, as well as the relative loss from bad projects compared to the gain from good projects. As with statistical theory, Sah and Stiglitz's theory of polyarchy

---

[9] Adapting the model from Chapter 4, incorporating the Sah and Stiglitz approach, might look as follows. Consider an additional institution that does nothing more than provide a second look—an additional measure on the signal. Now, if $x_i^2 + \epsilon > T$, rather than immediately triggering a punishing sanction, let a second institution get its own independently drawn signal. Let the two signals be ω_1 and ω_2. Note that since the second signal is drawn from the same distribution (i.e., is a result of the same action), its mean and variance are identical. Remember that in equilibrium no one deviates from the common behavior (usually some degree of partial compliance), therefore all signals less than the threshold are due to stochastic error. In equilibrium, it was unlikely before that $\omega > T$; now, the punishment is not triggered unless both ω_1 AND ω_2 exceed the threshold. Adding an institution in this way, by requiring a "second look," means that fewer punishments will be triggered. The punishment regime is best thought of as a compliance-maintenance regime; that is, as long as the incentives are adequate, in equilibrium no one deviates and the punishment is triggered by random environmental noise. When we reduce the frequency of the punishment, the equilibrium behavior induced may be higher, since each player gains more from being in a cooperative state. Therefore a second, identical, complementary institution works on the first two goals, maximizing cooperation and minimizing the cost of enforcement. This is the most common application of redundancy: reduction of the Type I error.

On the other hand, if the concern instead is about the likelihood of a Type II error, that the institution might not trigger frequently enough, one might introduce a second signal and trigger a punishment if ω_1 OR ω_2 exceed the threshold. The frequency of punishment increases. This might be a good solution in the cases where a more severe punishment is not available or the threshold cannot be moved to a more efficient position.

and hierarchies urges us to weigh the cost of punishing the innocent against the cost of undue leniency.

While this theory gave us more aid in defining how to avoid over-punishment, it did not directly provide a method for eliminating both problems. However, the theory was limited by the simplicity of the problem space: review of undifferentiated projects by undifferentiated agents. We have not yet exploited the analytically beneficial complexity of federalism. To resolve both the first and second problem simultaneously—that is, to find that sweet spot in punishment frequency—I am going to employ two aspects of federalism: first, multiple trigger mechanisms means that individual safeguards can punish more or less frequently than the others; second, transgressions are not binary—comply ver-rus do not comply—but instead can assume any degree of severity. Both aspects should be familiar at this point in the book: I intro-duced the breadth of the transgression space in Chapter 3 and multiple safeguards in Chapter 4 and have used both consistently throughout the analysis.

With varying levels of noncompliance as well as safeguards that are quite distinct from one another, there is no reason why a federal system could not encourage different relationships between the safeguards, where some confirm while others act as insurance. In medicine, confirmation is known as the second opinion. If a doctor says your cholesterol would be lower if you lost weight and exercised more, the recommendation is only beneficial, and you would be wasting your time to seek another doctor's advice. But when treatment for a diagnosis is itself potentially injurious, such as invasive surgery or a long-term course of prescription drugs, patients regularly seek a second and even third opinion, wisely. When the downside of incorrect punishment is high, as with intergov-ernmental retaliation, we would want to have a redundant safeguard as confirmation, to double-check the observation. We can follow this logic to make the following prescription about federal system design: encourage the insurance structure to dominate for low levels of transgression and the confirmation to dominate when apparent transgression—and therefore the severity of punishment—are high.

In the second half of this chapter, I develop a theory of the public's role as signal confirmation. In a democracy, it both tempers intergovernmental retaliation and makes its threat credible, which I illustrate with an example from Canadian constitutional history. But first we need to solve the third problem: overcoming stagnation.

Problem #3: *Adapting the Distribution of Authority*

We are still left with the problem of how to ensure successful adaptation. Just as Type I and Type II errors involve a trade-off, so it would seem that improving the reliability (reducing Type II errors) of the system of safeguards naturally reduces the adaptability of the federation: strict compliance means no experimentation. There is no straightforward way to eliminate this problem without softening up on perceived opportunism.

Our interest in robustness is akin to North's (1990:80–2) concept of *adaptive efficiency*. Like our transformation from redistribution to production, to understand why an economy performs well over time, North suggests that analyses shift from the lens of allocative efficiency and Pareto optimization to adaptive efficiency, and a focus on how rules affect the evolution of the economy. Adaptive efficiency is also concerned with "the willingness of a society to acquire knowledge and learning, to induce innovation, to undertake risk and creative activity of all sorts, as well as to resolve problems and bottlenecks of the society through time" (1990:80). Institutions affect the incentives to innovate, to explore the environment in search of novel solutions.

March (1991) describes the trade-off between exploration and exploitation in organizational learning about a multidimensional reality space. In his model, learning is bidirectional. In any given time period, with some probability the organization adapts its beliefs along a dimension of reality if its belief differs from that held by a preponderance of its members. It uses these beliefs to develop the organizational code, a set of rules and procedures. Likewise, with some probability individuals are in turn socialized into the organization, adopting its beliefs and conforming to its prescribed practices. Individuals who conform their behavior to the code with high probability are called "fast learners," while those that have a low probability of conforming are "slow learners." Which type of learner is better for the organization?

The organizational code is a set of practices meant to maximize the organization's productivity given the aggregated knowledge of its individuals. The organization can choose to *exploit* current knowledge by rewarding compliance with its code, essentially by retaining fast learners (conformers). This method has intuitive appeal until one remembers that the environment changes, and if the individuals have conformed to the organizational code, they stop sampling the environment.

The organization has no other way to learn than through its members, and so it fails to adapt to new circumstances. Alternatively, it could employ slow learners, who continue to *explore* the environment. By bucking the organizational code they do not take advantage of all that the organization has learned, but there is some chance that in resistance they teach the organization something valuable that helps it to adapt. "The fraction of slow learners [those who socialize slowly, most resistant to adopting the organization's code] is a significant factor in organizational learning" (March 1991:77). Nonconformists improve the organization's performance.

To apply March's theory to federalism, let us treat the distribution of authority as the organizational code. A system of safeguards is faced with the choice between adhering to the distribution of authority as currently understood versus tolerating deviance. Deviations are a form of experimentation and can help the federation's members to learn more about the current state of the environment and therefore how to (and when to) adapt the distribution of authority to improve the federation's performance.

The conflicting belief, as evidenced through the opportunism of one or two member governments, is unlikely to cause the whole federation to change course. But with some probability the safeguard will revise its beliefs about what is tolerable when governments drift from the status quo, and that drift generates benefits. This updating, this learning about the environment and therefore the best response to behaviors, is only possible if governments are allowed to explore. Opportunism must be possible.

The reliability literature fingered competition as a source of redundancy. Competition creates redundancy because of organizations competing for jurisdiction. In Bendor (1985) it was the unplanned redundancies, evolved out of competition between organizations, that led to more reliable transportation. The Bay Area commute has redundancies in the system that emerged out of a political, competitive process; BART (local light rail), was centrally planned, with engineering priorities to streamline the design, and does not even have parallel tracks. Landau's (1969) intuition was that redundancy—in overlapping functionality—leads to innovation. When components have redundant functions, or functional overlap, then when one fails and another "takes over," it innovates, and the organism adapts. Putting these two together, we see that competition between safeguards can help beneficial redundancy to flourish. Reading between Landau's lines, we can infer that if the safeguards are different, they may have different approaches, which will translate into different tolerances for observed opportunism.

I owe a note of sympathy to the reader: to this point, opportunism has been cast as the story's villain. But we see from March that some nonconformity is the source of learning about a changing environment. Without this experimentation, the federation cannot adapt and will not remain robust.

As an illustration, consider the case of Iowa's regulation of the length of truck trailers. Iowa set a maximum trailer length that was lower than that commonly used by interstate trucking agencies. In 1981, the Supreme Court struck down Iowa's regulatory legislation,[10] affirming lower court decisions that it was unconstitutional because it burdened interstate commerce. Iowa defended its regulation with an argument that the reduced trailer length was safer. What if it had been able to show that the regulation reduced the number of fatal accidents? Then its shirking would have taught the rest of the union something about the state of the world, about the connection between actions and outcomes. (And if all states simultaneously adopted the same regulation, or (ideally) if haulers did so voluntarily, then the regulation would not be held unconstitutional. It was its variance from standard practice, not the regulatory content itself, that made the regulation unacceptable to the court.)

Although opportunism can be useful, we need not embrace it unconditionally. We can qualify our enthusiasm for it in three ways:

1. Experimentation should be limited to minor deviation from constitutional practice.
2. Experimentation, as an act of mild opportunism, should still be subjected to the same standards, including the potential of punishment.
3. Accepted changes to the distribution of authority should be in the best interest of the union as a whole.

Experimentation should not put the union at risk.[11] First, flagrant acts of opportunism are likely to trigger a severe reaction like intergovernmental retaliation; their potential benefit as learning exercises are swamped by the destructive cost to the union. Second, to prevent any member government from taking advantage of this need for experimentation, the policy of punishing mild opportunism should not change. Finally, we need a

---

[10] *Kassel v. Consolidated Freightways Corporation of Delaware*, 450 U.S. 662 [1981]. Note that Indiana and Illinois have lower maximum operating truck weights than Iowa or Michigan: is this a case of burden-shifting?

[11] Axelrod and Cohen (2000) have developed a set of conditions for beneficial diversity.

theory of how opportunism/innovation leads to beneficial changes in the intergovernmental relationship.

Downs and Rocke's terrifically titled book *Optimal Imperfection* (1995) presents the case that a system of safeguards that seems too mild may actually be beneficial. Governments often are uncertain about future domestic demands, and therefore hesitate to commit to treaties that they think they might have to (temporarily) break in the future. With low punishments, governments can deviate when necessary to appease domestic audiences, and return to compliance when interests suit. We see the value of this repeated in the federation: I have called structural, political, and judicial safeguards *mild* because their potential punishments are not as severe as the harshest potential from popular safeguards and intergovernmental retaliation: revolution and domestic war. Governments can transgress in small ways at small cost when they have short-term supplementary benefits from opportunism. Returning to the truck trailer regulation, Iowa must have known that its legislation had a good chance of being struck down, but the negative consequence of the judgment was minimal. Between enactment and the Supreme Court's judgment it was able to reduce the traffic on the interstate highways, and although it was unable to show a broader benefit (in terms of improved safety), without this experimentation we would not have evidence to the contrary.

There is a second sense in which federations are optimally imperfect. Under the conditions I have specified in this book, full compliance cannot be sustained (Bednar 2006). Opportunism is built into the system as a normal part of federalism's operation. These ordinary transgressions are minor deviations; significant deviations are rare. It is as if federalism could not help but heed March's advice; nonconformists are automatically incorporated into the union. By being incapable of enforcing perfect compliance, governments can experiment around the edges of the distribution of authority at little cost, and the system as a whole may learn from what they find.

For example, consider California's antipollution measures, including requiring catalytic converters on new cars sold within the state, and more recently, a quota of low- and zero-emission vehicle sales. Automakers cannot afford to avoid the regulations by pulling out of the state's market, and production technologies limit their capacity to build a separate line of cars for California alone. Therefore California is in effect regulating national auto sales. The pecuniary externalities imposed by California have both diffuse and concentrated incidence: the changes raise the cost to purchase a new vehicle, and when prices rise, demand lessens, so the effect is felt doubly in states with an economic dependence on auto production, like Michigan. Legal challenges are mounting, but unlike the truck regulation case, it is not clear that they will prevail.[12] And political and popular safeguards are showing no signs of intervening: to the contrary, several northeastern states have suggested that they will soon follow California's lead. As some automakers begin to make adjustments, California's experimentation will help us to better understand two variables: first, what is the effect of reduced emissions, even locally, on a global environmental problem? And second, what is the real cost of the new technology? The externalities generated by California's regulation are indisputable. But a system that tolerates mild opportunism may end up learning more about the environment than one that shuts down all noncompliance.[13]

This plan of distributing the function of safeguards within the system prompts two questions. First, our plan seems to contradict what we thought we understood about design. That is, we believed that for mild opportunism, redundant safeguards would be useful, as insurance. But to minimize the likelihood of punishing the innocent, we proposed a confirming redundancy for severe punishments. Would not this built-in conservatism make major acts of opportunism even more likely? Second, these insights are useful, but now we need a better sense of adaptation. How do we have confidence that the alterations are in the common interest?

Problem #4: Identifying Socially Beneficial Adjustments

The questions concluding the previous paragraph are aspects of our fourth problem: identifying and accepting beneficial transformations to the distribution of authority while rejecting detrimental manipulations. Benefits should accrue to society generally. Notions of the "general good" or "public will" are abstract; if they are to be transformed to concrete public policy, citizens should have ultimate influence. It is time to unpack further the popular safeguard to understand better its weakness and potential. To do so I will enlist an enigmatic concept: culture.

---

[12] California is required to seek permission from the EPA to impose stricter regulations than the national standards. Until 2007, this step has been pro forma; every petition for exemption has been granted. At the time of writing the EPA has denied California's bid to require higher vehicle fuel standards, but California is preparing a legal challenge. Interestingly, many other states are siding with California in support of its petition.

[13] But recalling Georgia's banishment practice, not all opportunism has potential learning externalities.

Culture haunts the federalism literature.[14] The federalism literature repeatedly, persistently, refers not only to the existence of a federal culture, but also its *necessity* if a federal union is to endure. Upon inspection (sometimes you have to read carefully), virtually all great theorists of federalism employ it. Although Tocqueville admired the United States federation, he argued that imitation would be "impracticable" without the American culture of federalism (1959:248). Elazar (1987:78) writes: "In many respects, the viability of the federal system is directly related to the degree to which federalism has been internalized culturally ...." Even more explicit is Maddox's (1941:1124) testament to the power of a common myth: "Unifying forces of a spiritual, emotional, or ideological character not only contribute to the formation of union but give it sustenance and vigor in its struggle for survival." Riker (1964:111) writes that political safeguards are the immediate source of federalism's maintenance, but "standing behind these institutions is the popular sentiment of loyalty to (different levels of) government," which is "the fundamental feature of the maintenance of the bargain." Fear cannot sustain a federation in the long run: a common identity provides a continuing basis for union.

My goal is to build an analytical apparatus around the intuitive insights offered by the federalism scholars. To do so, we must look more closely at how culture enters into their logic.

1. The word federalism derives from the Latin *foedus*, or covenant, as Daniel Elazar points out. It defines (and is defined by) a relationship between citizens, a commitment to a fraternal union of mutual respect combining shared rule and self-rule. Federalism is much more than an organizational form; it is a "process as much as structure" (1987:67). In order for federalism to be successful, the people must practice a sharing of authority as well as respect of one another's ability to rule oneself.

2. V. Ostrom describes a "pattern of order" (1991); like Elazar, it is covenanting with one another, a promise to behave in a mutually understood manner when confronting new problems (1991:57). Common manners, customs, habits of thought, and cognition

---

[14] In the interest of full disclosure, I admit that as a student of positive analysis, I have done my best for a decade now to ignore these arguments. Culture is worse than a fuzzy concept: it is slippery. But it is also a siren that lures because understanding it appears to have enormous payoff. I am now engaged in a parallel project with Scott Page to model cultural evolution and its effect on institutional performance. See Bednar and Page (2007), and more information on our Web sites.

combine to form a body politic that is capable of action. With a common culture, citizens have a sense of responsibility for governing themselves: it is the opposite of "the government governs" (1991:247). "Federalism is not just a form of government; it is a method for solving problems, a way of life" (1991:247).

3. In Riker's 1964 federalism thesis, crucial to the success of the American federation has been the citizen identification with both of their governments: state and federal. The slow transference in citizen loyalty from the states to the national government, spurred by mobility of labor and capital, of leaders, of the development of the military and the rise of patriotism, all contribute to the development of a national identity, so that progressively, over the course of American history, citizens identify themselves not as Hoosiers or Virginians but instead as *Americans* (1964:103–10).

4. In terms of laying out the mechanics of a cultural argument, the most specific body of work is from Barry Weingast (1995, 1997, de Figueiredo and Weingast 2005). Citizens (of the several states) must cooperate to resist any transgression by the central government.

> Another subtler way to think about a transgression is to disassociate it from the target. For many citizens, the importance of a transgression lies in its nature, regardless of who is the target. This view of transgressions implies that citizens have a duty to challenge the sovereign when the latter attempts a transgression, regardless of the target. (1995:14).

A necessary condition for mutual defense is that "all citizens hold the same views about transgression and citizen duty .... [T]hey agree on a set of actions that trigger their reaction" (1997:251). Resonant with Elazar and Ostrom, the social transformation that Weingast describes is the emergence of a culture, a covenant between the people to defend each one's right to rule oneself. While Weingast limits the function of the citizens to a check on tyranny and overcentralization, otherwise he takes the Elazar argument one step farther: culture does not immediately translate into governmental self-restraint, but instead, it becomes a trigger mechanism. It coordinates the punishment capacity of the people, establishing the credibility of their threat to punish a government that oversteps its bounds.

Consider the role that culture plays in each of these arguments: it unifies the people and enables them to act. A federal culture permits people to judge governmental action—both state and federal—as right or wrong within the federation, and—crucially—gives them the confidence that others think the same way and will also act accordingly. It is not a constraint; it does not prevent governments from acting in a particular way, but instead, it enables the popular safeguard to become effective. It coordinates the people so they may effectively assume control over their federation. Popular safeguards are rendered potent by culture.

Understanding better how culture influences behavior, and particularly its importance in making popular safeguards effective, provokes two immediate concerns: what is the right cultural condition and where does it come from? We will consider the questions in order.

If we approach the first question functionally, as this book does generally, we need to determine what the federal culture would look like to make the citizens most effective in balancing their federation. Ideally, the culture that develops is not one of allegiance to one level of government over the other. Instead, and crucially, it is a valuation of the federation itself. Citizen loyalty at the provincial level may prevent federal encroachment, as Madison argued, but will not prevent state-level shirking. Development of a national identity, as Riker (among others) argues is natural, may minimize squabbles, but probably not, given the fight over pork that we have seen within the U.S. Congress.[15] Despite Hamilton and Madison's reference to the public's natural attachment to their state in *Federalist* 25, 45, and 46 (they were trying to convince skeptical crowds that they need not fear tyranny, and this was a convenient argument), they could not have been arguing for a *blind* attachment: citizens must patrol *both* levels of government. Far from being immune to concerns of tyranny, they believed that a vibrant federation, where both levels of government heed their constitutional limitations, would prevent tyranny.[16] "The Federal and State Governments are in fact but different

---

[15] A federal culture does not imply identical goals: instead it is a common identity created by common valuation of the federation as mutually beneficial for pursuing social and private goals. To the extent that identity is connected exclusively to the state governments, safeguards are less likely to coordinate successfuly. It may be for this reason that Riker wrote about the shift in citizen identity (loyalty, in his words) from the state to the federal government as being the ultimate necessary condition for the maintenance of federalism. However, as others have pointed out (e.g., Weiler 2001), federalism, when it lasts, has a tendency to centralize. It may be this problem of transfer of loyalty, of identification with the center, that causes safeguards to "go soft" on the central government. Citizens need a lively dedication to their *federation*, not to the federal government.

[16] Hamilton makes this argument in *Federalist* 31, and Madison in 45 and 51. Disintegration through state shirking is more likely than consolidation (and tyranny), writes Madison in *Federalist* 45, and he mentions the importance of "ligaments" that bind together the states and federal governments. In *Federalist* 46 and 51, we

agents and trustees of the people, instituted with different powers, and designated for different purposes" (*Federalist* 46).[17] If citizens can detach sentiments for one government from its feelings for the other they may develop a more general attachment to federalism, rather than to any one government. This is the culture that preserves liberty and order. It is the development of Ostrom's federal practice, of Elazar's covenant.

We can now turn to the second question: how does the federal culture emerge? Cultural science is not sufficiently advanced to provide a fully satisfying answer, one which would provide the necessary and sufficient conditions for culture's emergence. But we can dissect the problem further, and in that dissection, understand the process that converts the public into popular safeguards. Identifying the mechanics is the first step toward a theory about the conditions that encourage a federal culture to develop. Several issues hinder the public's capacity to serve as a safeguard; as these issues are identified, they can be minimized, encouraging the popular safeguards to flourish.

The constitution provides a guide to acceptable behavior; its focality coordinates citizens.[18] In the language of this model, to the extent that citizens agree with the proposed interpretation, it provides a common threshold. But this consensus does not come easily. Quite obviously, "the public" is not a singular entity but a composition of individuals. Embedded within the public are diverse preferences, diverse observations, and

get a better sense of these ligaments. Madison cites citizen control—balancing the exercise of power against the constitution, as Hamilton described in 31—because these levels of government are but two instruments to serve the public.

[17] Despite the long-run inefficiency, governments at each level often court citizens as if citizen allegiance were zero-sum. Pettys (2003) calls it "federalism's forgotten marketplace." Below I discuss the Canadian Constitutional patriation, but an element of it is immediately relevant. One great student of Canadian federalism, Donald Smiley, was very critical of the national government's patriation strategy, which seemed based on the premise that the federal government is in a competition with the provinces for citizen attachment. He cites survey research by Elkins and Simeon that citizens do not feel compelled to choose between their governments.

[C]itizens generally see no need to 'choose sides'—to renounce either their federal and provincial loyalties and identities," and go on to suggest, "We have urged that political leaders weigh carefully any actions or policies which might lead people to feel that a choice as being forced on them—a dilemma posed in terms of 'he who is not for me is against me.' We believe firmly that no such final choice is necessary or desirable (Smiley 1983:83–4, quoting Elkins and Simeon 1980:308).

Ideally, citizens will not be encouraged to choose between governments; policies will not be written or framed in ways that vie for voter allegiance.

[18] See Hardin (1989).

diverse information. The number of individuals who must be coordinated set popular safeguards apart from any other safeguard type: its implementation is a problem of mass action. Two elements must be coordinated to make the popular safeguard effective: the threshold (defining what a broad consensus of the public will and will not tolerate) and the signal (a common perception of the government's action). In order for the public to be an effective safeguard, they need to know that others have also perceived a transgression and will rise up to oppose it. The likelihood of public consensus rises with the flagrancy of the transgression.

We can simplify the representation of this problem by considering four stages: (I) where there is no public agreement; (II) where there is general agreement that problems need to be solved, albeit perhaps no agreement on the solution; (III) where there is general agreement on how to solve the problem, but this general agreement is not commonly known (formally, no common knowledge); and (IV) cases where the public agrees with both the problem and the solution and this general concurrence is publicly known. Only in this fourth stage is there sufficient consensus to trigger popular safeguards.[19] These stages correspond to the consolidation of a public opinion, evolving from no consensus, through stages where preferences and information are congealed sequentially, until there is sufficient consensus—and sufficient information about that consensus—to trigger the public.

Popular safeguards—made possible through a consensus one might call federal culture—are a means to preventing socially harmful adjustments. It is a negative method for achieving socially beneficial adjustments because of the way these safeguards work, triggering in reaction against unacceptable governmental activity. Popular safeguards are activated when public interests and perceptions converge, a potential made more likely as deviance increases. For the most part, ordinary disputes of federalism's boundaries will not trigger the popular safeguards, even if it gains public attention; with minor transgressions, public convergence is unlikely and "auxiliary precautions" (*Federalist* 51) are needed. Popular safeguards are the medium for accepting significant changes to the distribution of authority; the fact that it is difficult for the people to coordinate their behavior offers some hope (although not fail-safe) that accepted changes will be in the public interest. Over time, through experience with their federation, the public acquires a sense of what is appropriate and

---

[19] While the electorate—as majority of participants—may act earlier, this may not be the same as a consensus, minimizing the potential effect.

becomes willing to defend it.[20] Development of a federal culture, where popular safeguards may be activated, transforms the federal state into a federal nation.

Putting It Together: The Theory of Redundant Safeguards

The emergence of the federal culture—the creation of popular safeguard's potential—is the fiber that connects the system of safeguards to create a robust federation. Multiple mild safeguards interact—sometimes competitively—to monitor and sanction minor transgressions, under the public's eye. The severe intergovernmental retaliation is held in reserve for significant transgressions. Holding it back, and serving as intermediary, are the popular safeguards, playing the role of confirming signals before allowing the severe safeguard to be triggered. The imperfection of the system admits experimentation; the complexity of it serves as a filter for socially beneficial adjustments.

Figure 7.2 illustrates the system of federal safeguards, highlighting the critical role played by the popular safeguards. The system's structure is organized by the variance in transgression; different components are activated as the opportunism becomes increasingly noncompliant. First, in Stage I, there is general tolerance for low-level opportunism. Mindful of the lessons from March, perfect conformity is not desirable. For minor acts, public disagreement takes hold and there is little opportunity for common signal cueing even if the public had a common preference. This is a realm of dispute, assuredly, but it is also a realm of invention: Innovation is driven by the interaction of citizens with different goals and perspectives. The disagreement that results from these differences can lead to new proposals.[21] Too much of a common identity can be dangerous for a federation in the long run.

In Stages II and III, we see the value of Madison's "auxiliary precautions." Where preference coherence is impossible, it may still be possible to sustain agreement and respect for the system of institutional

---

[20] See Friedman (1997) arguing that Americans do not value federalism because we do not know what really is at stake.

[21] Cohen writes: "organizational decision-making performance when there are conflicting subgoals may be better than it would be if all subunits evaluated alternatives in terms of a single organizational goal." Errors are minimized or contained, while innovation may occur because you shake free from the status quo bias: "fewer alternatives look as good to participants as current policy" (1984:446). For the benefits of different perspectives, see Page (2007).

	Stage I	Stage II	Stage III	Stage IV	Stage V
Structural, Political, Judicial Safeguards	Inactive	Active	Active	Active	Active
Popular Safeguards	Inactive	Inactive; Consensus on Procedures	Latent; Consensus on Threshold	Active; Consensus on Signal	Active
Inter governmental Retaliation	Inactive	Inactive	Inactive	Poised	Active

Increasing transgression ⎯⎯⎯⎯⎯⎯⎯⎯⎯⎯→

Figure 7.2. The System of Safeguards

safeguards—structural, political, and judicial—to manage opportunism and uphold compliance within the federation. This procedural consensus is represented in Stage II: the public has no consensus over constitutional interpretation but they agree on a common method for resolving disputes: to entrust the remedy to the procedures instigated by the constitution, embodied in the structural, judicial, and political safeguards. In the absence of public consensus on what behavior constitutes opportunism, let alone a common judgment about a particular action, the electorate may at least agree on a common procedure to resolve disputes. Even when citizens have widely diverse preferences they can agree on the institutional mechanics to choose the appropriate reaction to manage intergovernmental relations. The electorate agrees to abdicate the safeguarding of federalism to other institutional sources. Initial skepticism may lessen over time if the institutional and quasi-institutional safeguards—structural, political, and judicial—prove themselves to be suitably intersecting so that biases are overcome in the long run.[22] By letting mechanistic reactions by institutional safeguards resolve ambiguous charges of opportunism, much that could become conflictual in a federation is swept under the public

---

[22] In essence, this is Knight and Johnson's (1994) critique of deliberative democracy: if the public is asked to express itself, rather than learning from one another, divisions in society may be further entrenched.

radar or easily dismissable as "politics as usual," relieving the public of wrestling with the issues themselves.

Stage III differs from II in its potential: here there exists a common sense of what might constitute appropriate behavior, a common popular threshold. However, it is not sufficient for citizens to have a common threshold if there is no agreement on the interpretation of the signal, or a lack of confidence that others perceive an action in the same way. Schofield (1985:218–9) captures the problem:

> The fundamental theoretical problem underlying the question of cooperation is the manner by which individuals attain knowledge of each others preferences and likely behavior. Moreover, the problem is one of common knowledge, since each individual, i, is required not only to have information about others preferences, but also to know that the others have knowledge about i's own preferences and strategies. ... It seems to me that this problem is the heart of any analysis of community, convention, and cooperation.

People's perceptions about the way others think affect their own political action (Anderson 1991, Mutz 1998, Chwe 2001). Citizens get information about one another's perceptions from a variety of sources, including polling data, sequential primaries, and even public education, but it is possible to cue mass perception through more indirect sources, including rituals (Chwe 2001)—patriotic national holidays are especially relevant—and even newspaper headlines (Anderson 1991). Anonymous, mass expressions of political preference act on an individual, influencing her own expressed attitude by giving her confidence that her perceptions are socially shared. A common culture may do more than coordinate tolerated behavior; it may cohere the signal space, reducing an individual's uncertainty about how others perceived what they saw, thereby enabling her to act knowing that she will not do so alone.[23] Therefore it is not until Stage IV that the public will become effective as a safeguard of federalism, when the noncompliance becomes so egregious that sufficient numbers of citizens are confident that others perceive the action in the same way.

Returning to Stage III it is easy to see a second, vital role for the auxiliary safeguards. These safeguards are active in this realm, but they are the only ones to be reliably (subject to the caveats of imperfection) active. Their effects are generally too mild to deter the more significant acts of opportunism that begin to be presented in this realm. The slumbering

---

[23] Complete conformity is both unrealistic and undesirable. Diversity in perception is essential to robustness because of informational uncertainty. The cost of that diversity may be a slight shift upward in the threshold triggering citizen action.

public is a more formidable force, but their potential lies latent, absent the coordination necessary to trigger them. Herein is the secondary role of the auxiliary safeguards: to provide a debate stage, where ideas are batted about (formally, about the appropriate threshold or even interpretations of events). As information builds about a growing consensus, these mild safeguards may cohere the public and spread word of the consensus, to establish common knowledge—shared public confidence—that the tolerable line has been crossed. Therefore, with the aid of another safeguard, the public may be activated in Stage III. Two examples in the next section provide intuition.

Stages II, III, and IV illustrate the mediating influence of the popular safeguards. Recall the earlier expressed concern about intergovernmental retaliation: it has the potential to escalate dramatically. It is the instance of a Type I error, where we wanted a confirming signal before the safeguard could be triggered. A robust federation will reserve it for extreme cases of opportunism. In democracies, intergovernmental retaliation requires substantial public support. As I have repeatedly stressed, popular accountability is fickle, not in the efficacy of its punishment, but in its ability to coordinate to punish. This is not a single median voter deciding; popular assent requires solving a significant coordination problem: agreement on a threshold—where to draw the line on tolerable behavior—as well as agreement on what transpired, that is, the observation. And mere *agreement* is not sufficient: it must approach common knowledge. All (or enough) must agree on the threshold and signal and be confident that everyone else knows that everyone knows. The informational requirement to trigger the popular safeguard, and then to credibly threaten intergovernmental retaliation, is high. Democratic states may provide just this transformation in the safeguard system, from a quick trigger but mild punishment at the low ends of noncompliance, but a slow-reacting, thoughtful response to extreme opportunism. The extent that democracies engage the citizens to be involved in the regulation of their government may explain why democratic federations, more so than their nondemocratic counterparts, appear to be more robust, as well as more likely to present themselves as federal in practice.

But democracy—even a thriving one—is not *sufficient* to temper intergovernmental retaliation. The danger of citizen attachment to one level of government over the other is now more apparent. If allegiance is vested in a single government, as opposed to the federal union, then the difficulty in achieving consensus over transgressions is lessened. If citizens identify primarily or exclusively with their province or with the federal government, then actions by the other level will be more quickly perceived as a transgression. Citizens may be quick to react—or, more devastatingly—be quick to sanction intergovernmental retaliation. Rather than being reserved for severe Stage V transgressions, intergovernmental retaliation may be activated as soon as Stage II, or perhaps even in response to sanctions inflicted by one of the auxiliary safeguards. Given the potential of intergovernmental retaliation to escalate, early—and therefore more frequent—triggering is highly undesirable. Paradoxically, the muddled judgment that is a byproduct of a identification with the *federation*, rather than any particular level of government, slows the severe response. Democracy, when paired with a federal culture, provides the finely tuned system of safeguards that leads to robustness.

7.3 Developing an Intuition for Redundancy

The theory in the last section is nuanced so in this section I present three brief illustrations. I start with a short description of a general shift in the U.S. Supreme Court's willingness to rein in the U.S. Congress to underscore the interplay between judicial and political safeguards and then follow with two short analyses of specific moments in time, the Republican resistance to the Alien and Sedition Acts in 1798 and Canadian Constitutional Patriation in 1980–1982.

Rethinking the Court's Role as Safeguard

The judiciary is generally regarded as a competent patrol of burden-shifting, but frequently is suspected of being entangled in the interests of the federal government, calling into question its ability to safeguard the union against federal encroachment and perhaps also shirking, which requires the court to take a position about the appropriate scope of national authority to determine if the state has infringed upon it.[24] The judiciary's usefulness as a safeguard depends heavily on other institutional safeguards: its independence is a function of structural safeguards that leave it free to intervene without fear of retribution, but at the same time to be effective its decisions will be backed by executive force, if necessary.

[24] Quebec has long suspected the Canadian Supreme Court of being biased toward Ottawa to such an extent that in the 1998 hearings regarding the constitutionality of unilateral secession, the Quebec government refused to send an official representative to argue its case. Cairns (1971) overviews the charges of bias in Canada.

The idealized court is independent, detached from politics. This detachment implies that its threshold is set with regard to procedure rather than outcome.[25] However, this narrowing of perspective does not eliminate interpretive bias from the judiciary, and in its complex organization one finds a system designed with the principles of redundancy in mind. One method of minimizing judicial inconsistency where it matters most—on important cases with broad influence or severe consequences—is to reduce the potential of any one judge to introduce a deviant interpretation. As Schauer (1991) points out, legal rules help to remove the discretion that can lead to inconsistent adjudication; when consequences are greater, the rules governing admissible evidence, and how to evaluate it, are more stringent. Judicial hierarchy is another method of reducing the negative effects of imperfection while capturing its positive effects. In general, as a dispute progresses up the appellate chain the number of judges sitting on the bench increases. In the United States, a trial judge determines the law, but is often aided in judgment by a jury of 12 who are charged with hearing evidence and collectively determining the position of the signal. Jury nullification, used rarely, is an act of the jury setting the threshold as well. Federal appeals are argued before banks of three and the Supreme Court rarely hears cases with fewer than its full bench of nine. Such redundancy in signal interpretation and threshold determination tips a hat to the subjectivity of both.

Many courts, including the U.S. and Canadian Supreme Courts, openly acknowledge differences in judgments that emerge even among a group as homogeneous as nine people united by an unusual affection for the Constitution. The size of the majority is often a strong indicator of the ruling's sticking power. Dissenting opinions are valuable indications that even specialists may disagree over the law or the facts or both. In Supreme Court decisions, the holding's legal significance is revealed through the content of the decision; only upon reading the decision carefully may one come to understand the verdict. The written decision frames the case, essentially laying out the location of both threshold and signal, and justifying both through a coherent perspective. Given our interest in the creation of a robust federation, it is worth noting one influential high court that does not publish dissenting opinions: the European Court of Justice.[26] Dissents

---

[25] See Ely (1980) for an engaging and important exposition of this theory of judicial review.

[26] The U.S. Supreme Court has also had significant periods where no dissents were written.

reveal doubts and underscore fissures: in emerging unions the imposed singularity in legal interpretation might help a legal culture to congeal. The court's influence on federal culture, and in particular its effect on public sentiment, is an affair I return to in the Canadian Patriation example. The court also deserves reexamination in its role within the redundancy of the auxiliary safeguards. In the remainder of this subsection, we will consider its interaction with the political and structural safeguards.

The reexamination is prompted by the perception-shaking decisions of the Rehnquist Court, particularly (for this book) regarding federalism. After a few fits and starts where the court clearly was moving but its direction remained unclear,[27] the court set its course with the 1992 *New York* decision.[28] The Low-Level Radioactive Waste Policy Amendments Act of 1985 officially sanctioned an interstate accord to solve the vexing problem of disposal of radioactive waste (produced by hospitals and military sites). The court struck the provision within the Act requiring a state to take title of the radioactive waste in the event that no disposal site was found. For a revolution in judicial oversight of congressional power, these are pretty innocent origins: yes, Congress was the loser, and technically a state the winner, but the decision was justified with eyes focused on the people. First, the court pointed out that Congress's regulatory power was limited to individuals, not the states. Congress could provide incentives (more on that in a bit) but could not *coerce*. The problem with coercion, the justices explained, is that it reduced the efficacy of electoral accountability as a check on governmental power:

[W]here the Federal Government directs the States to regulate, it may be state officials who will bear the brunt of public disapproval, while the federal officials who devised the regulatory program may remain insulated from the electoral ramifications of their decision. Accountability is thus diminished when, due to federal coercion, elected state officials cannot regulate in accordance with the views of the local electorate in matters not pre-empted by federal regulation.

The federal government's insulation presumably derives from an informational problem: dissatisfied citizens punish their state officials, unaware that the state was only following the federal government's orders. The court's intervention was needed to make it possible for the people to control their federation.

[27] My first publication on federalism (actually, my first publication full stop) was an attempt to make sense of the court's "unsteady path" in its federalism interventions (Bednar and Eskridge 1995).

[28] *New York* v. *United States*, 488 U.S. 1041 (1992).

From there the court rolled up its sleeves and got to work. Or so some have characterized it, complaining that the court became interventionist when it should defer federalism questions to the political process. But the political safeguards proved that they can fail. Although the political party system may be ideally organized to free the politician from unquestioning constituent service, this is not always sufficient to ensure that its reactions are efficient or optimal in policing federal or state governments' adherence to the distribution of authority. It is against the nature of the political safeguards to engage in an activity that is politically unpopular on all fronts.

The *New York* decision proved not to be a swerve on an unsteady path, but a decision to take one road where two diverged, for knowing how precedent causes way to lead on to way, the *Lopez* decision clearly established the Court's direction, soon after affirmed by the Violence Against Women Act (VAWA) holding (discussed in Chapter 4).[29] In the first case, the court struck a congressional act banning possession of firearms near schools and the second made assault of women a federal crime. Both statutes were justified based on the federal government's responsibility to regulate interstate commerce, an argument that the Court did not credit.[30] Structural (through state incorporation), political, and popular safeguards all failed for identical reasons: it is politically untenable to stake out a position against bills with titles like "The Gun-Free School Zone Act" or "Violence Against Women Act." How could any elected official be *for* violence against women or guns in schools?

I do not want to get caught up in judging the court's judgments: my interest is in their departure from the congressional argument, which passed litmus tests from the structural safeguards and political safeguards. These cases are useful for highlighting two roles of the judiciary in establishing effective redundancy. First, it is likely that any safeguard directly influenced by public horror will uphold any attempt to relieve it, any broader perspective being eliminated by the evening news. Therefore in these types of cases (not in all), a safeguard's thresholds may be systematically set too high, punishing too infrequently. The Court could look beyond the images of a 12th grader carrying a .38 and five bullets to school or the distressed face of the VAWA plaintiff, pointing a finger at

---

[29] *United States* v. *Lopez*, 514 U.S. 549 (1995); *United States* v. *Morrison*, 529 U.S. 598 (2000).

[30] The federal government also lodged a Fourteenth Amendment justification of VAWA which was also dismissed.

two fellow students who raped her. It set its threshold based not on political expedience but instead on a constitutional frame, and considered the signal not to be the particular case at hand but instead the larger question of legal implications. As the Court wrote in *Lopez* and again cited itself in the VAWA decision:

> Congress could regulate any activity that it found was related to the economic productivity of individual citizens: family law (including marriage, divorce, and child custody), for example. Under the[se] theories ..., it is difficult to perceive any limitation on federal power, even in areas such as criminal law enforcement or education where States historically have been sovereign. Thus, if we were to accept the Government's arguments, we are hard pressed to posit any activity by an individual that Congress is without power to regulate.

If we accept the long chain of this-leads-to-that argument used by Congress to justify the Acts, then in principle Congress is free to assume complete control over criminal law or many other domains of state authority.

Ordinarily political or structural safeguards are sufficient to patrol non-compliance (Kramer 2000) and judicial intervention is not needed (see Figure 7.3). In fact it is possible, as in Case A, that the threshold for the political or structural safeguards ($T_{s/p}$) is more sensitive than the judiciary's threshold T_j. Even if the thresholds are perfectly aligned, sequentially the political and structural safeguards are *ex ante* defenses, so under ordinary circumstances the judiciary would not be triggered. But the structural and political safeguards are influenced by the "Do Something!" public reaction to specific events that can cause them to shift their threshold outward to tolerate governmental action that they would not normally accept, as in Case B. When this happens the judiciary is the first

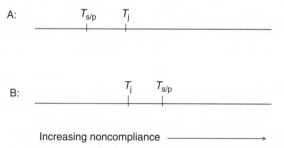

Figure 7.3. Varying Structural or Political Safeguards Threshold Affects Judicial "Activism"

safeguard triggered. Its intervention can appear to be activism when its consistent threshold is exposed by the political or structural safeguards' inconsistency.[31]

The first principle of insurance redundancy was error independence: the court satisfies this criterion to the extent that it is able to free itself from fads in popular opinion. A second principle was related to the inherent ambiguity of knowing what has occurred, or its implications. With informational ambiguity it is useful to have multiple signals, multiple perspectives on any observed behavior. The court views evidence differently from political and structural safeguards. Justice Breyer's dissent in VAWA argues that it is difficult to establish bright line rules to determine tests of economic activity. Given the ambiguity, he argues that Congress is the best judge. In direct contrast to Breyer's dissent, when appropriate rules are not clear—or, more explicitly here, it is hard to determine where a case falls relative to the rule—then multiple points of information are useful. If the judiciary's decision is based upon a fault in its perception of the observation, then remedies are available. Although difficult to overturn in the short run, a judicial decision is not the end of the story. The judicial act may crystallize public opinion (Friedman 1993), making a constitutional amendment possible, as we will see below. Working within the realm of Stage II (Figure 7.2), the judiciary may be an effective insurance when political safeguards are bound to fail, and may be effective confirming devices before precedents are established that lead to significant shifts in the distribution of authority.

Whether or not one agrees with the thrust of the U.S. Supreme Court's new federalism doctrine, it has altered perceptions about judicial capacity to safeguard federal encroachment. However, the Court is capable of its own inconsistencies. Given its justification for intervention in the commerce clause cases, it is baffling that it has left regulation of congressional spending powers virtually untouched. In 1987, the Supreme Court upheld the federal government's use of its spending powers to affect state choices in *South Dakota* v. *Dole*,[32] where the federal government required states

---

[31] The Rehnquist Court's federalism doctrine does seem to be a shift that cannot be explained by mere exposure. However, congressional activity may have adapted to the consistent lack of sanction from political or structural safeguards whose individuals within them find the opportunism politically rewarding. This potential calls to mind Peterson's (1995) legislative theory of the adaptation of federalism, where the distribution of authority shifts not due to overall efficiency but due to political expediency.

[32] 483 U.S. 203 (1987).

to raise the minimum drinking age or it would withhold 10% federal highway money. The Court decided that the federal government's goal was to promote "the general welfare"; since then, the national government has increasingly relied upon its use of spending powers to assert its will in state government spending. The U.S. states, which must balance their budgets yearly, depend heavily on federal transfers, and do not have much wiggle room to refuse money even if it comes with strings attached. In the United States, conditional spending has become an increasingly important source of federal influence on state policies.[33]

The problem with conditions on spending is the mess it makes of popular accountability.[34] Spending power trangressions are generally not severe enough to be classified as Stage IV (Figure 7.2) where the public could be counted upon to reject them. Instead, many fall in Stage II or III, where the mild safeguards have failed but popular safeguards have not yet overcome the informational requirements to be triggered. In the *New York* decision, the Supreme Court objected to the take title provision because it gave Congress power over the states and rendered popular control virtually impossible. In the same decision, the Court praised Congress' use of its spending powers to create incentives for action because a power relationship has not been created: states can always refuse the federal money. If they choose to conform their policies to receive the money, they do so by choice. To illustrate how power eliminates choices, Moe (2005) suggests a mugger who holds his victim at gunpoint, shouting "Your money or your life!" True, the victim has a choice, but the one she wanted most, to keep her money and her life, has been eliminated by the mugger. The same is true for the state: it is forced to abandon its policy sovereignty or lose money that it often needs desperately.[35] With conditional spending, the

---

[33] In a study of the use of spending powers in a number of federations, Watts (1999) calculates that in the United States, 29.6% of national transfers to the states were conditional, compared to 21.6% in Australia—the other federation with broad spending powers—and 12.3% in Switzerland and less than 1% in Canada.

[34] The work of Halberstam implies an important, and hopeful, remedy: under certain conditions, shared spending powers, what he terms "vertical federalism" may *empower* state governments against a central government's encroachments. In Germany, the European Union, and Switzerland, budgetary decision making is shared, forcing the center to consider the interests of the states. See Halberstam (2006).

[35] The tie between power and money is sufficiently tight that at least one federalism scholar has identified control over revenues as the only measure of power that matters. See Diaz-Cayeros' (2006) study of fiscal centralization in Latin America.

state is compelled to act, and voters may not understand that the federal government was pulling the strings.[36]

Resisting the Alien and Sedition Acts

The Alien and Sedition Acts were passed by the Federalist Congress in the summer of 1798 when war with France appeared likely. As affronts to individual rights, not the federal distribution of power, one might think that these acts would have remained outside of our interest in the American story of federalism, but Thomas Jefferson and James Madison enlisted federalism's safeguards to confront them.[37] Jefferson and Madison watched the structural safeguards erode through the first half of the year, and placed their faith in the public:

> For public opinion alone can now save us from the rash measures of our hot-heated Executive; it being evident from some late votes of the House of Reps. ... that a majority there as well as in the Senate are ready to go as far as the controul of their Constituents will permit.[38]

Electoral control might be significant if the people could form a coherent judgment. But as this chapter has repeatedly stressed, forming a common judgment (both in the forms of thresholds and signals) in a large diverse body is no mean feat, even for politicians as skilled as Jefferson and Madison.

As the summer neared, the insufficiency of popular response seemed increasingly likely. Madison points to information deficiencies as the key problem in activating the people:

> The management of foreign relations appears to be the most susceptible of abuse, of all the trusts committed to a Government, because they can be concealed or disclosed, or disclosed in such parts & at such times as will best suit particular views; and because the body of the people are less capable of judging & are more under the influences of prejudices, on that branch of their affairs, than of any other. Perhaps it is a universal truth that the loss of liberty at home is to be charged to provisions agst. danger real or pretended from abroad.[39]

---

[36] Many legal scholars have raised this alarm. See McCoy and Friedman (1988), Somin (2002), and Baker and Berman (2003).

[37] More generally, federalism and individual rights are intertwined, with one bolstering the other, and with consonant fates. See the discussion on liberty in Chapter 2.

[38] James Madison to Thomas Jefferson, Letter dated February 18, 1798, in Madison (1999:584).

[39] James Madison to Thomas Jefferson, Letter dated May 13, 1798, in Madison (1999:588).

Thus it appeared that the public, at least in sufficient numbers, could be persuaded to set their threshold higher, to tolerate more infringements on their personal liberties if their president claimed that it was necessary to protect themselves against an invading nation. At a minimum citizens could be convinced that others condoned the encroachment, so that they would not act to defeat the measure.

In this setting, Jefferson and Madison quietly penned resolutions condemning the acts, Jefferson's slipped to a friend in the Kentucky legislature, and Madison's fed to the Virginia house. The Resolutions described the U.S. Constitution as a compact between the states and the federal government, with the Constitution delegating certain specified authorities to the federal government, but (as the Tenth Amendment declares), reserving to the states, or to the people, any residual powers.[40] The Sedition Acts extended federal authority beyond that delegated to it. In Madison's version of the resolutions, he begins by expressing the "warm attachment" that Virginia has to the constitution and the union; out of affection and commitment to it, the states were "duty bound" to resist the federal encroachment.

Almost immediately—in a letter to Thomas Jefferson dated just one week after the Virginia Resolution was read in Richmond—Madison expressed some doubt about their method.

Have you ever considered thoroughly the distinction between the power of the *State*, & that of the *the Legislature*, on questions relating to the federal pact. On the supposition that the former is clearly the ultimate Judge of infractions, it does not follow that the latter is the legitimate organ especially as a Convention was the organ by which the Compact was made. This was a reason of great weight for using general expressions that would leave to other States a choice of all the modes possible of concurring in the substance, and would shield the Genl. Assembly agst. the charge of Usurpation in the very act of protesting agst the usurpations of Congress."[41]

Madison's concern was that by conscripting the state legislature, the resolutions judging the federal act could be construed as themselves an act of shirking. Perhaps this is why he stopped short of recommending that

---

[40] In Madison's report on the Alien and Sedition acts, a reexamination of the Virginia Resolution, he emphasizes the fact that federal powers are derived from the Constitution, to which the states are parties, rather than from the states themselves. See Madison (1999:608–62), especially 609–10.

[41] James Madison to Thomas Jefferson, Letter dated December 29, 1798, in Madison (1999:592).

the act be considered null and void (unlike Jefferson's Kentucky Resolutions), and why later he condemned South Carolina's nullification as misconstruing his intent. He did not want to trigger intergovernmental retaliation.

If nullification was not his intention, what was the value of the resolution? Surely Madison hoped to stir enough opposition to force a repeal of the legislation. The resolution becomes an informational device, declaring what behaviors were admissible. In so doing they broadcast a threshold as well as a judgment of the signal—the Virginia Resolution pointedly declaimed the Congressional acts "unconstitutional"—in a widely publicized manner, divorcing the issue from party politics. The decomposition of the union into insoluble states can help to foster consensus. When one state declares their views of the signal and threshold, other states can build from it.[42] By reframing the issue as states' (and therefore, individual) rights rather than defense, the citizens might be prompted to act. Public dissent did grow steadily, and the acts became a major factor in Jefferson's victory over Adams in 1800.

Canadian Constitutional Patriation

Although Madison and Jefferson did not appeal to the courts to resolve their dispute, in later years Madison described the potential of the judiciary to regulate jurisdictional conflict between the federal and state governments. Enlightened, impartial jurists make

decisions at once indicating & influencing the sense of their Constituents, and founded on united interpretations of constitutional points ....[43]

The phrase is remarkable for identifying two elements of our analysis: the threshold held by the public as well as identifying to the public that the threshold had been crossed. The judiciary's declaration of law is a *reflection* of public consensus, but at the same time the judiciary *influences*

---

[42] We can see the same effect in the current state lawsuits challenging the federal Environmental Protection Agency's policies. Rather than writing resolutions, more than a dozen states have taken their challenge to court. The suits are widely publicized, and although the states may prevail in court, they already have awakened public awareness of federal actions that citizens might have otherwise overlooked (Rabe 2004).

[43] James Madison to Spencer Roane, Letter dated June 29, 1821, in Madison (1999:779) [Written in the context of describing a hope for eventual consensus between state and federal jurists as state courts become staffed by "abler Judges"]. In general, see Rakove (2002) for Madison's philosophy of judicial review.

the public by establishing a common perception through its determination of whether or not an act crosses the threshold.

Canadian Patriation offers an excellent opportunity to see how the trigger mechanism is broken into the three components of punishment, threshold, and signal, and how the safeguards interact. In particular, it will help us to see better how popular safeguards may be activated by the judiciary.

Since the country's founding in 1867, the Canadian constitution was an act of the British Parliament, even bearing a title identifying it as such: *The British North America Act*. Increasing Canadian nationalism spurred calls for the constitution's "patriation," and in March 1980, after a short period in opposition, Prime Minister Pierre Trudeau returned to office promising a constitution that was more reflective of the Canadian needs and independence. He was also facing significant dissatisfaction in Quebec, where a referendum was scheduled in May to consider secession. Trudeau promised to include Quebec's concerns in the constitutional revisions, and the referendum was decisively defeated, with 60% voting no. In September of that year, Trudeau called the provincial premiers to Ottawa to discuss constitutional reforms. After a week of meetings, the parties could not come to an agreement, and the first ministers' conference disbanded. Almost immediately, on October 2, Trudeau announced that he would move forward with his own plan, which he dubbed "The People's Plan," despite significant provincial objections. Of the 10 provinces, only Ontario and New Brunswick supported the prime minister.

The threat of intergovernmental retaliation was real. Not only had the Quebec leadership exhibited a willingness to employ the threat of secession a mere few months earlier, but Premier Lévesque could now build a compelling argument of federal betrayal to bolster the secessionist case. And the oil-rich western provinces had their own significant dissatisfaction with Ottawa because of price controls and revenue disputes.

In addition to simmering threats of intergovernmental retaliation, structural, political, and judicial safeguards were also triggered. Although the Canadian national legislature includes no specific incorporation of provincial interests (unlike upper houses based on subnational unit representation), the opposition Progressive Conservative party threatened a filibuster within the House of Commons to stop unilateral (that is, without provincial consent) patriation. A second structural safeguard peculiar to Canada had also been activated: the British House of Commons, who needed to approve the constitutional reform, engaged in serious discussion about the appropriateness of the federal government's unilateral action, even forming a commission to study the question of provincial consent.[44] Political safeguards were activated: the Canadian political party system, particularly Trudeau's Liberal Party, was (and remains) significantly decentralized, with provincial and federal members of the same party often espousing opposite views. In particular, Claude Ryan, of the Quebec Liberal Party, opposed Trudeau's constitutional plans, favoring a more decentralized Canada. Despite this multifaceted opposition expressed through a variety of safeguards, Trudeau pressed forward.

In the meanwhile, three separate provincial challenges to the prime minister's action were raised in provincial courts, with the Canadian Supreme Court agreeing to resolve the divided opinions. It was asked three questions: (1) does the prime minister's proposed constitutional revisions significantly alter federal–provincial authorities? (2) is there a tradition that any constitutional change that significantly alters the distribution of authority receive provincial consent? (3) is this tradition constitutional? On September 28, 1981, the Court announced its decision.[45] To the first question, it said yes, the constitutional reform changes the distribution of power. And to the second, it said yes, there is a norm established that when such a shift in power occurs, the provinces are consulted. But as to the third, they answered less definitively: the Court held that the norm was a *convention*, not constitutional law, and therefore it could not be sustained judicially.

With no apparent negative consequence, the prime minister's path seemed cleared to move toward adoption. Instead, he compromised.[46] Why did he compromise at this point? He had already been threatened

---

[44] The Kershaw Committee's report recommended that the British Parliament should not accept any resolution emerging from the Canadian Parliament without a "proper degree of provincial consensus" (Sheppard and Valpy 1982:187).

[45] The decision is deeply fragmented.

[46] Trudeau was traveling in southeast Asia when the Court's decision was announced, so Ottawa's immediate reaction came from the Justice Minister, Jean Chrétien, who said that he believed that the prime minister would proceed with his plan. But after a night's sleep, Trudeau softened. In a press conference the morning after the Court's decision, Trudeau said:

> ... the federal Parliament has the legal authority to ask Westminster to enact the constitutional measure ... though there is in Canada a political convention or practice that such a request not be made without the agreement of the provincial governments. I understand that the Supreme Court ducked the question of how many provincial governments should agree. We are, therefore, in the same situation we were in before the matter went to the Supreme Court. ...

with a variety of punishments from structural, political, and intergovernmental safeguards. Why retreat because of the judiciary, when the judiciary admitted it could not stop him?

We can consider the events within the context of the model. The structural and political safeguards had tried and failed to stop Trudeau, and the judicial safeguard had declared its own impotence. With respect to Figure 7.2, we know that the perceived transgression surpassed Stage II as the mild safeguards were triggered and failed to stop the federal government's action. On the other hand, the public had not risen en masse to challenge Trudeau during the year of public debate, and no province, including Quebec, had staged a secession attempt, perhaps bearing in mind the significant defeat of Quebec's previous attempt. Therefore the transgression does not appear to be as severe as Stage V, or even Stage IV. It fell in Stage III, out of reach of the coercive powers of the mild safeguards, but without sufficient public information about the federal government's act of encroachment meant to coordinate public response. Stage III is the zone where the mild safeguards can assume their coordinating role, and this is exactly what the court did.

The court announced its perception of the signal, the observed behavior. The decision reads:

The two Houses of the Canadian Parliament claim the power unilaterally to effect an amendment to the B.N.A. Act which they desire, including the curtailment of provincial legislative powers. This strikes at the basis of the whole federal system. It asserts a right by one party of the Canadian governmental system to curtail, without agreement, the powers of the other part ([1981] 1 R.C.S. 753:847–48).

The court's declaration is a stoically phrased lightning bolt: Trudeau's intended reforms cut to the core of Canadian federalism, fundamentally changing the distribution of authority.

In responding to the second question, the Court identified the threshold: "The exercise of such a power has no support in constitutional convention. ...[I]t is the proper function of this Court, in its role of protecting and preserving the Canadian Constitution, to declare that no such

But in response to a reporter's question he said, "I have not ruled out absolutely the possibility of listening to what the provinces have to say" (Sheppard and Valpy 1982:246).

I have had to simplify the events. For a more complete recounting of the patriation, read either McWhinney (1982) or Shepard and Valpy (1982). Both come as close to page-turners as political science books get. Also worth consulting is Banting and Simeon (1983), an edited volume with excellent scholarly articles.

power exists" ([1981] 1 R.C.S. 753:848). Normally, traditionally, by *convention* such a significant revision requires provincial consent. Again came the Court's charge, cloaked in mundane writing: it was a reform "unconstitutional in the conventional sense" ([1981] 1 R.C.S. 753:909). The Court declared that although Trudeau was not violating any laws, he was violating the national customs, the federal practice.

Conventions, although not law, are part of a constitution. They are designed to ensure that the "legal framework of the Constitution will be operated in accordance with the prevailing constitutional values or principles of the period" ([1981] 1 R.C.S. 753:880). The decision contains an extended dissection of law and convention, which the Court summarizes as: "constitutional conventions plus constitutional law equal the total Constitution of the country" ([1981] 1 R.C.S. 753:883–84). Therefore, conventions must be upheld with equal gravity as law.

Finally, it also declared its own punishment capacity, or, more accurately, lack thereof: it would not punish the prime minister for this transgression because it could not. Nevertheless, the federal government was violating the Canadian federal compact. After reminding the public[47] that if it had been a matter of law, the court could have sanctioned, it told them that conventions are sustained through different safeguards:

It is because the sanctions of convention rest with institutions of government other than courts, such as the Governor General or the Lieutenant-Governor, or the Houses of Parliament, or with public opinion and, ultimately, *with the electorate* that it is generally said that they are political ([1981] 1 R.C.S. 753:882–83, italics mine).

The Court could not have issued more clear instructions to the voters without appearing partisan.

The Court's charge had the potential to galvanize the public in ways that the political arguments and federal–provincial bickering could not. While when surveyed the public indicated support for constitutional reform, Trudeau was going against Canadian federal practice. The determination was not new; the charge that the norm existed had been bantered around for over a year in the press. But recall that the popular safeguard has to overcome a diversity problem (common agreement) as well as the

---

[47] The decision was awaited anxiously. It was the first Supreme Court decision to be televised, and Sheppard and Valpy report that 2,000 copies of the decision were printed—10 times the usual run—which were distributed "mostly to a mob of journalists, lawyers and spectators, struggling ten deep in a courthouse corridor" (1982:240).

information problem necessary for collective action (did we all see the same thing?). The Court's declaration provided the common knowledge of both signal and threshold that the public needed to have confidence that everyone else saw it in the same way (as well as a little nudging about punishment).[48] With the common threshold and common perception of the signal, the public threat of punishment became very real. With public dissatisfaction, the specter of intergovernmental retaliation returned. Not only was Trudeau's personal stature at risk through the electoral mechanism, but the electorate's accord could serve as the confirming go-ahead that the provinces would need to reconsider secession. A politician as skilled as Trudeau, the man who winked as cameras filmed him pirouetting behind the Queen, would understand immediately the implications of the Court's declaration in a way that Justice Minister Chrétien did not: to proceed unilaterally would violate the essence of Canadian federalism, of the public understanding of the relationship between the goverments. With the Court's announcement, Trudeau understood that the public knew it, and knew that he knew it.[49]

While not one of the five safeguards (structural, political, popular, judicial, and intergovernmental) was sufficient on its own, as a redundant system, the safeguards were effective in resisting unilateral federal opportunism.

7.4 DISCUSSION

As Landau (1969) celebrates, the U.S. federal system is filled with redundancies, a characteristic true of most federations. What is the use of having multiple safeguards, and particularly, how might they overcome the flaws of one another? Madison recognized our potential for poor judgment; we would continue to behave as error-prone humans when we entered the ballot booth or sat in the legislature. Rather than trying to cover up the

---

[48] The Court explicitly rejected having any "parental role" ([1981] 1 R.C.S. 753:775) in creating a convention. Perhaps they did not start it, but they were invaluable in sustaining it.

[49] In his memoirs, Trudeau wrote that he responded to the decision "on two levels":

As a lawyer, a teacher of constitutional law, and a former minister of justice, I felt that if the court said what we were doing was legal, we should go ahead and do it. But as a politician, I wondered whether the public would understand our decision, or whether they would think I was being reckless. It might seem that we were defying the judgment of the court by simply proceeding with what a majority had said was contrary to convention (1993:316).

influence of human imperfection on governing institutions (or give up, as some would have liked, and establish an aristrocracy), Madison enlisted our flaws, turning destructive forces into social support. While his theory suggested the benefits of competition for oversight, we can extend the principles to cover imperfection of the safeguards. Imperfection has hidden benefits: with a closer examination of imperfection, we are able to understand how a system might simultaneously ensure compliance and encourage innovation.

In this chapter, I have extended the baseline model written in Chapter 4 to consider the effect of adding additional safeguard to overcome the individual safeguard's problems with imperfection. Of equal concern is two distinct problems: safeguards may fail to "fire" or they may fire too frequently. We are also interested in tolerating some small degree of noncompliance to encourage innovation, perhaps at some small cost to the nonconformist. Echoing the themes of the past two chapters, the lesson of this chapter has been the same: safeguards can fail, and so multiple safeguards can improve the federation's robustness. However, with this chapter we see that redundancy as a solution to imperfection is not as straightforward as increasing the number of safeguards.

In particular, the design of the federal system of safeguards is very different from other problems of redundant system design, where the components are not tangled in disagreement (although, recalling Bendor, they may be in competition with one another), but rather share a common goal. In federalism the safeguards may be deeply divided on basic constitutional issues or the conception of the union. Furthermore, they may perceive actions differently, both in the basic observation as well as in how they frame it—what meaning they ascribe to it. Finally, apart from the judiciary, the safeguards rarely have federalism on their minds when they act. (When voting, have you ever thought: "I'm doing this for the federal union"?)

This model of federalism admits that the safeguards disagree about what constitutes compliance, but in this chapter, these disagreements may be useful. Mild transgressions are difficult to diagnose, and therefore are controversial. One safeguard may tolerate it while another is triggered. In our theory of redundancy, this disagreement is unproblematic and perhaps even useful. Not only does the imperfection of the safeguards open up a window for exploration, but when multiple safeguards view actions from different angles, all agents learn more about a complex environment.

In a robust federation, there is one sense in which the safeguards agree: they tolerate one another. Toleration of the institution is not the same as agreeing with the decision one makes; to the contrary, safeguards may try to reverse one another's work. But they do not try to topple the existence of one another. They agree on the procedure for resolving disputes. The same cannot be said for inefficient federations.

The lessons of the chapter are:

1. When the cost of punishment is high (relative to the cost of mistakenly not punishing), redundancy should be used as *confirmation*, to confirm the signal before triggering the punishment.
2. When the cost of punishment is low, redundancy should be used as *insurance*, to ensure that some punishment is triggered.
3. Either type of redundancy, confirmation or insurance, is most effective when paired safeguards have uncorrelated errors—they fail for distinct reasons.
4. Adjustment is desirable, which requires exploration, or a search for new alternatives. Therefore, some imperfection in the mildly punishing safeguards is beneficial.
5. The popular safeguard is distinct from the mild, quick-reacting auxiliary safeguards (structural, political, judicial) and intergovernmental retaliation with its potentially serious consequences. It can serve as a bridge between the two types. Competitive democracy is not sufficient in itself to realize the full benefits of popular safeguards; instead, the development of a federal culture, with a common conception of the relationship between the governments, will give citizens the fullest capacity to temper the reaction of the other safeguards.

The institutional system will most consistently resist opportunism when there is redundancy in each function, and the institutions covering that function do not fail for the same reasons. Redundant institutional functions, motivated independently, better—more consistently—prevent opportunism, improving performance. Therefore, the optimal system of safeguards will vary in its reaction across the space of opportunism, with more severe, but cautious, safeguards reacting to egregious acts, while minor opportunism is regulated by the quick-reacting but mild-punishing auxiliary safeguards (structural, political, and judicial). The electorate is a powerful punisher in its own right, and even more powerful as a means to release intergovernmental retaliation. It is unlikely to be any real force at low levels of opportunism, where acts can be justified politically (and are often quite appealing to constituents; even nonconstituents resign themselves to accepting it as a part of politics). But as the severity of the noncompliance grows, if a federal culture has developed, then citizen preferences and interpretations cohere into a common threshold. Establishment of the common knowledge about the signal is a crucial step in activating public concern. One can think of this as a double-duck test: first, we identify what it means to be a duck, and then we determine if the object before us is a duck. When the electorate agrees on both aspects of the double-duck test, they can react.

The rule of law requires credible sanctions for transgressions. An intuitive concern is with the sufficiency of the threat to deter opportunism, as was the focus of Chapter 6. The focus of this chapter is different: it is concerned with the system's consistency. Cohen (1981) describes the potential for optimization with parallel processing:

> If the essential problem of organizational adaptation is coping successfully with the complexity of the environment, and if we believe the individuals in the organization are generally not capable of solving its whole problem alone, this property of generating powerful performance from interactions of weak components will have to be present for high quality adaptation to occur.

Even in this case, where the only concern is reliability, Cohen does not promise a first-best solution. With the complicated problem space described in this chapter, it is even more true that there is no guarantee that an optimizing dynamic will emerge.[50] One useful ingredient—a federal culture—cannot be designed, but must emerge (although its emergence is facilitated by confidence in the other safeguards). Optimality may not be reached. But with the design considerations offered here, we can encourage it.

---

[50] See discussion in Ostrom (1999:526–7).

8

Tying the Gordian Knot

James Madison's writings motivate most of the analysis in this book, so naturally I turn to him as I conclude my argument. In June of 1821, Madison's friend Spencer Roane, a judge on the Virginia Supreme Court of Appeals, wrote for guidance on disputes in the way federal and state courts interpreted the constitution. Madison wrote the following passage in his reply:

The Gordian Knot of the Constitution seems to lie in the problem of collision between the federal & State powers, especially as eventually exercised by their respective Tribunals. If the knot cannot be untied by the text of the Constitution it ought not, certainly, to be cut by any Political Alexander.[1]

A Gordian Knot is an intricate problem, insoluble in its own terms. As the Greek myth goes, in order to win the prophesized rule of Asia, Alexander cut through the knot rather than untie it. Alexander's brash brandishing of the sword may have cemented his reputation for boldness, but it also revealed his readiness to violate the terms of a problem. He did not untie the knot: he eliminated it for his own ends. This sort of opportunistic reinterpretation is exactly what a federation needs to guard against.

A constitution may divide authority between states and the federal government, but written rules do not eliminate the essential problem of federalism: how to prevent rivalry between governments from spoiling a union's potential. The distribution of authority as laid out by the constitution is inevitably ambiguous. The lack of clear boundaries tempts opportunistic interpretation of them. If the state and federal governments clash, one solution might be to let the most powerful government interpret

---

[1] James Madison to Spencer Roane, Letter dated June 29, 1821, in Madison (1999:777).

the constitution to serve its own interests—the federation's equivalent of an Alexander. The federal system would then be used to channel benefits to the powerful rather than to encourage socially productive behavior. In order to achieve social goals—the federal bargain struck at the founding—the enumeration of powers is only the *beginning* of constituting a federation: it is also necessary to work out a procedure to resolve disputes and make prudent adjustments.

In championing fragmented authority—separation of powers—James Madison revealed a deeper genius: an innate understanding that the right combination of institutions could harness self-interest for the collective good. The *Federalist* focuses attention on common goals: although written as editorials in a New York newspaper, the papers do not discuss how much the citizens of New York would gain, either particularly or relative to other states. Instead, the papers emphasize the greater military security, the economic advantages, and the improved practice of democracy that the institutions birthed by the constitution would generate. And more than anything else, the *Federalist* proclaims confidence that the safeguards will incite governments to follow the rules.

Any federation's success hinges on widespread confidence in its safeguards. The rules that regulate the states and federal governments, that limit the extent of their authority, are at times costly to obey. For a union to endure, its members need a sense that their investment, in sacrifice of political sovereignty and at times immediate economic gain, will pay off. Each government also needs to believe that other governments will be similarly inspired to make sacrifices. The ability and commitment of the safeguards to uphold the boundaries of authority must be beyond question.

The federal constitution also needs to include a way to adapt the rules to fit changing circumstances. While amendment procedures are a part of most constitutions, generally they have such a high bar for success—requiring tremendous public and institutional consensus—that they limit the federation's ability to experiment and learn. Successful federations balance exploration with exploitation. The state and federal governments choose between adhering to the constitutional code (exploiting) and deviating from it to experiment with new policy (exploring). Too much exploitation and the federation stagnates; too much exploration and the federation falls vulnerable to counterproductive opportunism. The constitutional challenge is to engineer a system that minimizes transgressions and yet allows the experimentation necessary for adaptation.

Finally, constitutional design needs to leave illusions of precision behind because the components of a constitutional system are inevitably flawed. Safeguards are staffed by real people who can make mistakes. Safeguards may punish when they should not, or fail to punish when they should. Small mistakes should not bring down a union. Just as Madison embraced human self-interest, modern constitutionalists should bear in mind safeguard fallibility. The system needs to be able to recover from its own imperfections.

These constitutional desiderata—compliance, adaptation, and resilience—prompt us to reconsider the Gordian Knot, and in particular, a neglected aspect: how such a knot was tied. No individual was able to unravel it. With federalism, no single force—whether constitutionally derived or tyrannical—should be able to dictate the boundaries of federal and state authority or force other governments to work for it. Each government should remain relevant. With a well-functioning system, major violations are punished, upholding compliance; minor transgressions, when allowed, promote exploration of the policy space and adaptation of the rules; and the multiple safeguards, each judging governmental actions independently, means that the system is not vulnerable to the failings of one component. A robust system encompasses all three principles in its design, converting federalism's insoluble problem of ambiguous boundaries and competitive governments into opportunities for society.

In this book I have proposed a theory of how a constitution builds institutions to achieve the apparently contradictory tasks of strength and adaptability, and does so with imperfect institutions. In the following paragraphs, I describe a series of specific problems to be solved in any federal design and the system characteristics that overcome them. I have summarized these design principles in Table 8.1. Rather than make recommendations about particular safeguards, I have focused on their functions. This functional approach makes it easier to adjust the constitution to fit the society it purports to organize. Constitutions cannot be one-size-fits-all. Even if every federation had the same priorities, safeguards are context-dependent; their capacity depends on the willingness, and ability, of the agents who comprise them. In a community with a history of judicial corruption or executive deference, judicial safeguards may fail to motivate as well as they would in communities without this history. Language differences, differences in legal codes, and even population settlement history may cause particular safeguards to be more or less capable. This context sensitivity does not mean that we need to abandon a scientific understanding of how institutions affect performance, but it does mean that we need to alter our focus from proper names of institutions to the functions each might perform.

Table 8.1. *The Robust Federation: Design Principles*

Problem	Remedy Principle
Incomplete coverage of opportunism	COVERAGE: Pay attention to full scope; don't ignore any transgression type. Not all safeguards cover all types of transgressions.
Ineffective safeguard	COMPLEMENTARITY: Recognize that safeguards vary in punishment capacity. Pair safeguards with complementary force to bolster performance.
Unreliable safeguard response	INSURANCE: Build redundant system of safeguards with duplicate functions and unrelated (independent) errors when the effects of punishment are mild.
Overly frequent sanctions	CONFIRMATION: Build the system to confirm the observation of an apparent transgression when the severity of punishment is high.
Adapting the distribution of authority	EXPERIMENTATION: Build the system of safeguards with varying tolerances to condone mild transgressions but disallow more significant transgressions; all experimentation is subject to punishment.
Identification of socially beneficial adjustments	FEDERALISM CONSENSUS: Encourage the emergence of a federal culture by building a system of interdependent safeguards to structure deliberation and spread information about common perceptions.

The first challenge of constitutional design is to ensure balance between the federal and state governments by providing complete coverage of all three transgression categories. In Chapter 3, I defined three broad categories of opportunism based on the transgressing government, and in Chapter 5, I demonstrated how isolated safeguards may be incomplete in their coverage of these opportunism types. Structural safeguards, for example, generally affect only the federal government, and as such cannot prevent state shirking or burden-shifting. Incomplete constitutional safeguards may be worse than none at all: incompleteness may exacerbate imbalances that intergovernmental retaliation alone could not correct. Complementary safeguards provide more complete coverage.

A second issue, also related to compliance, focuses on the diversity of the safeguards' punishment capacity, examined in Chapter 6. Some safeguards have mild effects. The court, for example, can do very little by way of punishment without force to back it up. While it is a good deterrent of minor transgressions, it is not forceful enough to deter major transgressions. Intergovernmental retaliation is a severe threat, with the potential to escalate into exit attempts; its severity makes governments hesitant to use it to punish all but the most flagrant of deviations. The diversity in punishment capacity is both a hazard and an opportunity. Alone, intergovernmental retaliation will not diminish minor transgressions. While each is singly insufficient, the mild judicial safeguards and severe intergovernmental safeguards complement one another, boosting compliance.

Third, every safeguard is imperfect (Chapter 7). Safeguards are staffed by people with many competing priorities; it is possible and in some cases likely that maintenance of a balanced distribution of authority is only a secondary motivation. Sometimes these competing priorities cause more than innocent errors, introducing systematic flaws in a safeguard's responses. Safeguards may therefore be too tolerant or not tolerant enough, or they may be biased in the way that they interpret behaviors. Insurance is a form of redundancy that includes multiple safeguards that duplicate one another's function but have uncorrelated causes of failure. Insurance improves safeguard reliability: a second safeguard may react if the first fails.

Fourth, improving the reliability of responses can pose problems itself if the improvement increases the frequency of a severe punishment. The system should have a way to confirm the observed behavior before triggering a harsh punishment. This point underscores one of the greatest difficulties in designing a robust federation: the system must vary in sensitivity and reaction depending on the severity of noncompliance. When sanctions are of low cost, second safeguards act as insurance: when the sanctions are severe, a second safeguard can confirm the transgression before any punishment is levied. Redundancy that confirms an observation is as important for safeguards with severe consequences as insurance is for the milder safeguards.

Disagreement about minor transgressions is healthy; it helps to overcome the fifth challenge facing federations—the need to adapt the rules. If boundary stretching is prevented entirely, then the federation will cease to explore alternatives, perhaps missing opportunities to improve the authority allocation. The robust system of safeguards resolves the tension between flexibility and commitment. The safeguards close ranks when opportunism is egregious, but often disagree about the boundary's precise placement. A mild transgression may trigger multiple safeguards, albeit each imperfectly and with mild consequences. Their low levels of punishment, as well as their imperfection, introduce just enough flexibility to allow marginal exploration of the policy space. This process will lead to incremental adaptation of the rules. Large adjustments continue to require considerable consensus.

Sixth, the system's robustness is improved if popular safeguards emerge. Popular safeguards are ineffective for small acts of deviation, which are too easily justifiable to a public unconcerned with the finer points of procedure. But as the opportunism grows, so does the public's concern and its ability to coordinate its response. More flagrant acts of opportunism are more likely to be met by a common interpretation. The emergence of this common public perception about the boundaries of authority between federal and state governments is sometimes referred to as a federal culture. While it is unlikely to be present at a federation's founding, it is fed when the mild safeguards resolve disputes; public disagreements spread information about general points of agreement and contention.

By extension, just as a federal system may support democracy, democracy may improve the federal system. Popular safeguards serve as a firewall between the mild institutional safeguards and the potentially more severe intergovernmental retaliation. Democratic federations may be even more robust because intergovernmental retaliation requires democratic support, providing a healthy hesitation desired before engaging in intergovernmental retaliation, with its escalating, potentially irreversible consequences. Popular safeguards may also make it possible for intergovernmental retaliation to resist escalation, punishing with small in-kind gestures and protests.

Public defense of the federation is not necessarily articulated; it is not even necessarily a conscious process. As in Ostrom's work, the system's design enables the citizens to behave as if they were making a conscious decision to regulate the complex system of federalism. It may be hard thing to define, this citizen expectation, this respect for the union, this federal culture. But we can say that it was absent when no one criticized Jackson for not backing the Supreme Court against Georgia, but had developed by the time that Eisenhower sent troops to enforce the

Supreme Court's judgment against Arkansas 125 years later.[2] It is fed when Germans support their Government's decision to accept the *Cassis de Dijon* judgment[3] but not present when no one challenges Russia's President Putin for minimizing the effect of the Governors.

No knot is impermeable to the sharp blade of a tyrant's knife. The knot is protected only when the knife is prevented from reaching it, a defense that comes from the people's dedication to the existence of the federal problem on its own terms. When the people reject any unraveling of the knot that reformulates the problem, they resist opportunistic accumulations of power. When the public values federalism, the federation is truly robust and tyranny's threat weakened.

It is impractical, and perhaps theoretically impossible, to design the perfect federation given the variety of goals the federation might help a society to achieve, the different weights that every citizen places on each, and the changing prioritization of those goals over time. Even if a constitutional designer did know what the people wanted and could anticipate future changes, she would still have to acknowledge the imprecision of social science's understanding of how to calibrate the distribution of authority to meet these goals. Governments search to improve policy solutions, and in their search bump up against the boundaries of their authority. Flexible boundaries accommodate, even enable, the mild experimentation necessary for prudent adjustments, while the system of safeguards deters grander manipulations. It is through the complex interactions of the distributed parts that a sensible whole might emerge. The system of complementary safeguards enables this process, making the robust federation conceivable in a single moment, as well as over time.

---

[2] *Worcester v. Georgia*, 31 U.S. 515 [1832]; *Brown v. Topeka Board of Education* 347 U.S. 483 [1954], the showdown was in 1957.
[3] Case 120/78 [1979] E.C.R. 649.

References

Alesina, Alberto and Enrico Spolaore. 1997. "On the Number and Size of Nations." *Quarterly Journal of Economics* 112(4):1027–56.

Alesina, Alberto and Enrico Spolaore. 2003. *The Size of Nations*. Cambridge, MA: MIT Press.

Alesina, Alberto, Enrico Spolaore, and Romain Wacziarg. 2000. "Economic Integration and Political Disintegration." *American Economic Review* 90(5): 1276–96.

Alter, Karen J. 2001. *Establishing the Supremacy of European Law: The Makings of an International Rule of Law in Europe*. New York: Oxford University Press.

Amoretti, Ugo M. and Nancy Bermeo, eds. 2004. *Federalism and Territorial Cleavages*. Baltimore: The Johns Hopkins University Press.

Anderson, Benedict. 1991. *Imagined Communities: Reflections on the Origin and Spread of Nationalism,* Revised Edition. London: Verso.

Axelrod, Robert M. 1984. *The Evolution of Cooperation*. New York: Basic Books.

Axelrod, Robert and Michael D. Cohen. 2000. *Harnessing Complexity: Organizational Implications of a Scientific Frontier*. New York: Free Press.

Baker, Lynn A. and Mitchell N. Berman. 2003. "Getting off the *Dole*: Why the Court Should Abandon Its Spending Doctrine, and How a Too-Clever Congress Could Provoke It to Do So." *Indiana Law Journal* 78:459–541.

Bakke, Kristin and Erik Wibbels. 2004. "Inequality, Ethnic Diversity, and Conflict in Federal States." Presented at the American Political Science Association annual meeting, Chicago, IL, September 2–5, 2004.

Banting, Keith and Richard Simeon, eds. 1983. *And No One Cheered: Federalism, Democracy, and the Constitution Act*. Toronto: Methuen.

Bednar, Jenna. 2003. "The Madisonian Scheme to Control the National Government," in Samuel Kernell, ed., *James Madison: Theory and Practice of Republican Government*. Stanford: Stanford University Press.

Bednar, Jenna. 2006. "Is Full Compliance Possible? Conditions for Shirking with Imperfect Monitoring and Continuous Action Spaces." *Journal of Theoretical Politics* 18(3):345–73.

Bednar, Jenna. 2007a. "Valuing Exit Options." *Publius: The Journal of Federalism* 37(2):190–208.

Bednar, Jenna. 2007b. "Credit Assignment and Federal Encroachment." *Supreme Court Economic Review* 15:285–308.

Bednar, Jenna and William N. Eskridge, Jr. 1995. "Steadying the Court's 'Unsteady Path': A Theory of Judicial Enforcement of Federalism." *Southern California Law Review* 68:1447–91.

Bednar, Jenna, John Ferejohn, and Geoff Garrett. 1996. "A Political Theory of European Federalism." *International Review of Law and Economics* 16: 279–95.

Bednar, Jenna and Scott E. Page. 2007. "Can Game(s) Theory Explain Culture? The Emergence of Cultural Behavior within Multiple Games." *Rationality and Society* 19(1):65–97.

Beer, Samuel H. 1993. *To Make a Nation: The Rediscovery of American Federalism.* Cambridge, MA: Belknap Press.

Bendor, Jonathon. 1985. *Parallel Systems: Redundancy in Government.* Berkeley: University of California Press.

Bermeo, Nancy. 2004. "Conclusion: The Merits of Federalism." in Bermeo and Amoretti, eds., *Federalism and Ethnic Cleavages.* Baltimore: The Johns Hopkins University Press.

Besley, Timothy and Anne Case. 1995. "Incumbent Behavior: Vote-Seeking, Tax-Setting and Yardstick Competition." *American Economic Review* 85(1): 25–45.

Boix, Carles. 2003. *Democracy and Redistribution.* New York: Cambridge University Press.

Bolton, Patrick and Gerard Roland. 1996. "Distributional Conflicts, Factor Mobility, and Political Integration." *American Economic Review* 86(2): 99–104.

Bolton, Patrick and Gerard Roland. 1997. "The Breakup of Nations: A Political Economy Analysis." *Quarterly Journal of Economics* 112(4):1057–90.

Borck, Rainald. 2002. "Jurisdiction Size, Political Participation, and the Allocation of Resources." *Public Choice* 113(3–4):251–63.

Börzel, Tanja and Madeleine O. Hosli. 2003. "Brussels Between Bern and Berlin: Comparative Federalism Meets the European Union." *Governance* 16(2): 179–202.

Brancati, Dawn. 2006. "Decentralization: Fueling the Fire or Dampening the Flames of Ethnic Conflict and Secessionism?" *International Organization* 60:651–85.

Bueno de Mesquita, Bruce, Alastair Smith, Randolph M. Siverson, and James D. Morrow. 2003. *The Logic of Political Survival.* Cambridge, MA: MIT Press.

Bui, Linda T.M. 1998. "Gains from Trade and Strategic Interaction: Equilibrium Acid Rain Abatement in the Eastern United States and Canada." *American Economic Review* 88(4):984–1001.

Burley, Anne-Marie and Walter Mattli. 1993. "Europe Before the Court: A Political Theory of Legal Integration." *International Organization* 47: 41–76.

Burstein, Melvin L. and Arthur J. Rolnick. 1995. "Congress Should End the Economic War Among the States." *The Region* (Report of the Federal Reserve Bank of Minneapolis), http://minneapolisfed.org/pubs/ar/ar1994.cfm

Buta, Maximo. 1957. "Intervenciones Federales 1853–1943," in Carlos Maria, Bidegain, *Materiales para el Estudio de la Reforma Constitucional Vol. VI, La Intervencion Federal.* Buenos Aires: Comision de Estudios Constitucionales.

Bzdera, Andre. 1993. "Comparative Analysis of Federal High Courts: A Political Theory of Judicial Review." *Canadian Journal of Political Science* 26(1):3–29.

Cairns, Alan C. 1971. "The Judicial Committee and Its Critics." *Canadian Journal of Political Science* 4(September):301–44.

Cameron, Charles and Lewis Kornhauser. 2005. "Modeling Law: Theoretical Implications of Empirical Methods." Paper prepared for presentation at the conference "Modeling the Law" at the NYU Law School, October 2005.

Carty, R.K., ed. 1992. *Canadian Political Party Systems: A Reader.* Toronto: Broadview Press.

Chandra, Kanchan. 2005. "Ethnic Parties and Democratic Stability." *Perspectives on Politics* 3(2):235–52.

Chhibber, Pradeep and Ken Kollman. 1998. "Party Aggregation and the Number of Parties in India and the United States." *American Political Science Review* 92(2):329–42.

Chhibber, Pradeep and Ken Kollman. 2004. *The Formation of National Party Systems: Federalism and Party Competition in Canada, Great Britain, India, and the United States.* Princeton: Princeton University Press.

Choper, Jesse. 1977. "The Scope of National Power vis-a-vis the States: The Dispensability of Judicial Review." *Yale Law Journal* 86:1552–621.

Chwe, Michael Suk-Young. 2001. *Rational Ritual: Culture, Coordination, and Common Knowledge.* Princeton, NJ: Princeton University Press.

Clarke, Harold D. and Allan Kornberg. 1994. "The Politics and Economics of Constitutional Choice: Voting in Canada's 1992 National Referendum." *Journal of Politics* 56(4):940–62.

Cohen, Michael. 1981. "The Power of Parallel Thinking." *Journal of Economic Behavior and Organization* 2(4):285–306.

Cohen, Michael D. 1984. "Conflict and Complexity: Goal Diversity and Organizational Search Effectiveness." *American Political Science Review* 78(2):435–51.

Cooter, Robert D. 2000. *The Strategic Constitution.* Princeton, NJ: Princeton University Press.

Crémer, Jacques and Thomas R. Palfrey. 1996. "In or Out? Centralization by Majority Vote." *European Economic Review* 40:43–60.

Crémer, Jacques and Thomas R. Palfrey. 1999. "Political Confederation." *American Political Science Review* 93(1):69–83.

Crémer, Jacques and Thomas R. Palfrey. 2002. "An Equilibrium Model of Federal Mandates." Caltech manuscript.

Crombez, Christophe. 1997. "The Co-Decision Procedure in the European Union." *Legislative Studies Quarterly* 22(1):97–119.

Cross, Frank B. 2002. "The Folly of Federalism." *Cardozo Law Review* 24:1–59.

Dahl, Robert A. 1957. "Decision-Making in a Democracy: The Supreme Court as a National Policy-Maker." *Journal of Public Law* 6:279–95.

Dahl, Robert A. 2002. *How Democratic is the American Constitution?* New Haven, CT: Yale University Press.

Daughety, Andrew F. and Jennifer F. Reinganum. 2000. "Appealing Judgments." *RAND Journal of Economics* 31(3):502–25.

Diaz-Cayeros, Alberto. 2006. *Federalism, Fiscal Authority and Centralization in Latin America.* New York: Cambridge University Press.

Diermeier, Daniel. 1995. "Commitment, Deference, and Legislative Institutions." *American Political Science Review* 89(2):344–55.

Diermeier, Daniel and Keith Krehbiel. 2003. "Institutionalism as a Methodology." *Journal of Theoretical Politics* 15(2):201–32.

Dillinger, William and Steven Webb. 1999. "Fiscal Management in Federal Democracies: Argentina and Brazil." Policy Research Working Paper 2121, World Bank, Washington, DC.

Dinan, Desmond. 2004. *Europe Recast: A History of the European Union.* Boulder: Lynne Reiner Publishers.

Dion, Stéphane. 1996. "Why is Secession Difficult in Well-Established Democracies? Lessons from Quebec." *British Journal of Political Science* 26(2): 269–83.

Dixit, Avinash and John Londregan. 1998. "Fiscal Federalism and Redistributive Politics." *Journal of Public Economics* 68(2):153–80.

Donahue, John D. 1997. "Tiebout? Or Not Tiebout? The Market Metaphor and America's Devolution Debate." *Journal of Economic Perspectives* 11(4):73–81.

Dorf, Michael C. and Barry Friedman. 2000. "Shared Constitutional Interpretation." *Supreme Court Review* 2000:61–107.

Dougherty, Keith L. 2001. *Collective Action Under the Articles of Confederation.* Cambridge, UK: Cambridge University Press.

Downs, George W. and David M. Rocke. 1995. *Optimal Imperfection? Domestic Uncertainty and Institutions in International Relations.* Princeton, NJ: Princeton University Press.

Elazar, Daniel J. 1962. *The American Partnership: Intergovernmental Cooperation in the Nineteenth Century United States.* Chicago: University of Chicago Press.

Elazar, Daniel J. 1987. *Exploring Federalism.* Tuscaloosa: University of Alabama Press.

Elkins, David J. and Richard Simeon, eds. 1980. *Small Worlds: Provinces and Parties in Canadian Provincial Life.* Toronto: Methuen.

Ely, John Hart. 1980. *Democracy and Distrust: A Theory of Judicial Review.* Cambridge, MA: Harvard University Press.

Enrich, Peter D. 1996. "Saving the States from Themselves: Commerce Clause Constraints on State Tax Incentives for Business." *Harvard Law Review* 110:377–468.

Epstein, David and Sharyn O'Halloran. 1999. *Delegating Powers: A Transaction Cost Politics Approach to Policy Making Under Separate Powers.* New York: Cambridge University Press.

Epstein, Lee and Jack Knight. 1998. *The Choices Justices Make.* Washington, DC: CQ Press.

Erikson, Robert S. and Mikhail G. Filippov. 2001. "Electoral Balancing in Federal and Sub-national Elections: The Case of Canada." *Constitutional Political Economy* 12(4):313–31.

Eskridge, William N., Jr. and John Ferejohn. 1994. "The Elastic Commerce Clause." *Vanderbilt Law Review* 47(October):1355–400.

Fearon, James D. and David D. Laitin. 1996. "Explaining Interethnic Cooperation." *American Political Science Review* 90(4):715–35.

Ferejohn, John A. 1974. *Pork Barrel Politics: Rivers and Harbors Legislation, 1947–1968.* Stanford: Stanford University Press.

Fernandez, Raquel and Dani Rodrik. 1991. "Resistance to Reform: Status Quo Bias in the Presence of Individual-Specific Uncertainty." *American Economic Review* 81(5):1146–55.

de Figueiredo, Rui J.P. and Barry R. Weingast. 2005. "Self-Enforcing Federalism." *Journal of Law, Economics, and Organization* 21(1):103–35.

Filippov, Mikhail, Peter C. Ordeshook, and Olga Shvetsova. 2004. *Designing Federalism: A Theory of Self-Sustainable Federal Institutions.* Cambridge, UK: Cambridge University Press.

Fligstein, Neil. 2008. *Euroclash: The EU, European Identity, and the Future of Europe.* Oxford University Press.

Foner, Eric. 1970. *Free Soil, Free Labor, Free Men: The Ideology of the Republican Party Before the Civil War.* Oxford: Oxford University Press.

Frey, Bruno S. and Alois Stutzer. 2004. "The Role of Direct Democracy and Federalism in Local Power." Unpublished manuscript, University of Zurich, October 2004.

Friedman, Barry. 1993. "Dialogue and Judicial Review." *Michigan Law Review* 91(4):577–682.

Friedman, Barry. 1997. "Valuing Federalism." *Minnesota Law Review* 82: 317–412.

Friedman, Barry. 2005. "The Politics of Judicial Review." *Texas Law Review* 84:257–337.

Fudenberg, Drew, David Levine, and Eric Maskin. 1994. "The Folk Theorem with Imperfect Public Information." *Econometrica* 62(5):997–1039.

Funston, Richard. 1975. "The Supreme Court and Critical Elections." *American Political Science Review* 69(3):795–811.

Gaines, Brian J. 1992. "Balancing or Bandwagons? Links Between National and Provincial Votes in Canada." Unpublished manuscript, Stanford University, on file with the author.

Gaines, Brian J. and Christophe Crombez. 2004. "Another Look at Connections Across German Elections." *Journal of Theoretical Politics* 16(3):289–319.

Garrett, Geoffrey. 1992. "International Cooperation and Institutional Choice: The European Community's Internal Market." *International Organization* 46:533–60.

Garrett, Geoffrey. 1995. "The Politics of Legal Integration in the European Union." *International Organization* 49:171–81.

Gehlbach, Scott. 2007. "Electoral Institutions and the National Provision of Local Public Goods." *Quarterly Journal of Political Science* 2(1):5–25.

Gibson, Edward L. 2004. "Subnational Authoritarianism: Territorial Strategies of Political Control in Democratic Regimes," presented at the Annual Meetings of the American Political Science Association, Chicago.

Gibson, Edward L. and Tulia Falleti. 2004. "Unity by the Stick: Regional Conflict and the Origins of Argentine Federalism," in Gibson, ed., *Federalism and Democracy in Latin America*. Baltimore: The Johns Hopkins University Press, pp. 226–54.

Gilligan, Thomas W. and Keith Krehbiel. 1987. "Collective Decisionmaking and Standing Committees: An Informational Rationale for Restrictive Amendment Procedures." *Journal of Law, Economics, & Organization* 3(2): 287–335.

Gilligan, Thomas W. and Keith Krehbiel. 1989. "Asymmetric Information and Legislative Rules with a Heterogenous Committee." *American Journal of Political Science* 33(2):459–90.

Goldstein, Leslie Friedman. 2001. *Constituting Federal Sovereignty: The European Union in Comparative Context*. Baltimore: The Johns Hopkins University Press.

Gomez, Rosendo A. 1947. *Federal Intervention in Provincial Government in Argentina 1860–1930*. Master of Arts Thesis, University of Minnesota.

Gray, Virginia. 1973. "Innovation in the States: A Diffusion Study." *American Political Science Review* 67:1174–85.

Green, Edward J. and Robert H. Porter. 1984. "Noncooperative Collusion Under Imperfect Information." *Econometrica* 52(1):87–100.

Greenstone, Michael and Enrico Moretti. 2003. "Bidding for Industrial Plants: Does Winning a 'Million Dollar Plant' Increase Welfare?" NBER Working Paper No. 9844.

Hafer, Catherine and Dmitri Landa. 2007. "Public Goods in Federal Systems." *Quarterly Journal of Political Science* 2(3):253–75.

Halberstam, Daniel. 2006. "Comparative Federalism and the Role of the Judiciary," in Keith Whittington, Daniel Kelemen, and Gregory Caldiera, eds., *Oxford Handbook of Law and Politics* London: Oxford University Press.

Hale, Henry E. 2005. "The Makeup and Breakup of Ethnofederal States: Why Russia Survives While the USSR Fell." *Perspectives on Politics* 3(1): 55–70.

Hardin, Garrett. 1968. "The Tragedy of the Commons." *Science* 162: 1243–8.

Hardin, Russell. 1989. "Why a Constitution?" in B. Grofman and D. Whitman, eds., *The Federalist Papers and the New Institutionalism*. New York: Agathon.

Hatfield, John William. 2007. "Federalism, Taxation, and Economic Growth." Stanford University Graduate School of Business manuscript.

Hayek, Friedrich 1939. "The Economic Conditions of Interstate Federalism." *New Commonwealth Quarterly* 5(2):131–49.

Hix, Simon. 1999. *The Political System of the European Union*. New York: Palgrave.

Hogg, Peter. 1979. "Is the Supreme Court of Canada Biased in Constitutional Cases?" *Canadian Bar Review* 57:721–39.

Hooghe, Liesbet and Gary Marks. 2001. *Multi-Level Governance and European Integration*. New York: Rowman & Littlefield Publishers, Inc.

Hong, Lu and Scott E. Page. 2004. "Groups of Diverse Problem Solvers can Outperform Groups of High-Ability Problem Solvers." *Proceedings of the National Academy of Sciences* 101(46):16385–9.

Hong, Lu and Scott E. Page. 2005. "Interpreted and Generated Signals." University of Michigan manuscript.

Horowitz, Donald L. 1985. *Ethnic Groups in Conflict*. Berkeley: University of California Press.

Hutchings, Vincent L. 2003. *Public Opinion and Democratic Accountability: How Citizens Learn About Politics*. Princeton: Princeton University Press.

Iaryczower, Matias, Sebastian Saiegh, and Mariano Tommasi. 1999. "Coming Together: The Industrial Organization of Federalism." CEDI (Centro de Estudios para el Desarrollo Institucional) Working Paper No. 30.

Inman, Robert P. 2002. "Transfers and Bailouts: Enforcing Local Fiscal Discipline with Lessons from U.S. Federalism," in J. Rodden, G. Eskeland, and J. Litvack., eds., *Decentralization and the Challenge of the Hard Budget Constraint* Cambridge, MA: MIT Press.

Inman, Robert P. 2001. "Transfers and Bailouts: Institutions for Enforcing Local Fiscal Discipline." *Constitutional Political Economy* 12(2):141–60.

Inman, Robert P. 2007. "Federalism's Values and the Value of Federalism." University of Pennsylvania manuscript.

Inman, Robert P. and Daniel L. Rubinfeld. 1992. "Fiscal Federalism in Europe: Lessons from the United States Experience." *European Economic Review* 36(2–3):654–60.

Inman, Robert P. and Daniel L. Rubinfeld. 1996. "Designing Tax Policies in Federalist Economies: An Overview." *Journal of Public Economics* 60:307–34.

Inman, Robert P. and Daniel L. Rubinfeld. 1997a. "Making Sense of the Antitrust State Action Doctrine: Resolving the Tension Between Political Participation and Economic Efficiency." *Texas Law Review* 75:1203–99.

Inman, Robert P. and Daniel L. Rubinfeld. 1997b. "Rethinking Federalism." *Journal of Economic Perspectives* 11(4):43–64.

Inman, Robert P. and Daniel L. Rubinfeld. 2000. "Federalism." *Encyclopedia of Law and Economics* V:661–91. Cheltenham, UK: Edward Elgar.

Jones, Mark, Pablo Sanguinetti, and Mariano Tommasi. 2000. "Politics, Institutions, and Fiscal Performance in a Federal System: An Analysis of the Argentine Provinces." *Journal of Development Economics* 61:305–33.

Kedar, Orit. 2004. "The Micro Foundations of (Vertically) Divided Government: Evidence from Germany." Paper delivered at the Annual Meeting of the American Political Science Association, Chicago, IL, September 2004.

Knight, Jack and James Johnson. 1994. "Aggregation and Deliberation: On the Possibility of Democratic Legitimacy." *Political Theory* 22(2):277–96.

Kollman, Ken. 2003. "The Rotating Presidency of the European Council as a Search for Good Policies." *European Union Politics* 4(1):51–74.

Kollman, Ken, John H. Miller, and Scott E. Page. 2000. "Decentralization and the Search for Policy Solutions." *Journal of Law, Economics, and Organization* 16(1):102–28.

Kornhauser, Lewis A. 1992. "Modeling Collegial Courts I: Legal Doctrine." *Journal of Law, Economics, and Organization* 8(3):441–70.

Kramer, Larry. 1994. "Understanding Federalism." *Vanderbilt Law Review* 47:1485–561.

Kramer, Larry D. 2000. "Putting the Politics Back into the Political Safeguards of Federalism," *Columbia Law Review* 100:215–93.

Kramer, Larry D. 2004. *The People Themselves: Popular Constitutionalism and Judicial Review*. New York: Oxford University Press.

Kreps, David M. 1990. *A Course in Microeconomic Theory*. Princeton: Princeton University Press.

Kreps, David M., Paul Milgrom, John Roberts, and Robert Wilson. 1982. "Rational Cooperation in the Finitely Repeated Prisoners' Dilemma." *Journal of Economic Theory* 27(2):245–52.

Landau, Martin. 1969. "Redundancy, Rationality, and the Problem of Duplication and Overlap." *Public Administration Review* 29(4):346–58.

Laskin, Bora. 1978. "Judicial Integrity and the Supreme Court." *Law Society Gazette* 12:116–21.

Lemco, Jonathan. 1991. *Political Stability in Federal Governments*. New York: Praeger Publishers.

Levy, Jacob. 2007. "Federalism, Liberalism, and the Separation of Loyalties." *American Political Science Review* 101(3):459–77.

Lindert, Peter H. 1996. "What Limits Social Spending?" *Explorations in Economic History* 33(1):1–34.

Linz, Juan J. and Alfred Stepan. 1996. "Toward Consolidated Democracies." *Journal of Democracy* 7(2):14–33.

Lohmann, Susanne, David W. Brady, and Doug Rivers. 1997. "Party Identification, Retrospective Voting, and Moderating Elections in a Federal System: West Germany, 1961–1989." *Comparative Political Studies* 30(4):420–49.

Lok Sabha Secretariat (India). 1996. *President's Rule in the States and Union Territories*, 6th Edition. New Delhi: Government of India Press.

Lowry, Robert, James Alt, and Karen Ferree. 1998. "Fiscal Policy Outcomes and Electoral Accountability in American States." *American Political Science Review* 92(4):759–74.

Lupia, Arthur and Mathew D. McCubbins. 1998. *The Democratic Dilemma: Can Citizens Learn What They Need to Know?* Cambridge: Cambridge University Press.

Maddox, William P. 1941. "The Political Basis of Federation." *American Political Science Review* 35(6):1120–7.

Madison, James. 1999. *Writings*. Jack N. Rakove, ed. New York: Library of America.

March, James G. 1991. "Exploration and Exploitation in Organizational Learning." *Organization Science* 2(1):71–87.

Marks, Gary. 1992. "Structural Policy in the European Community," in Alberta Sbragia, ed., *The Political Consequences of 1992 for the European Community*. Washington, DC: The Brookings Institution, pp. 191–224.

Mattli, Walter and Anne-Marie Slaughter. 1995. "Law and Politics in the European Union: A Reply to Garrett." *International Organization* 49:183–90.

McCoy, Thomas R. and Barry Friedman. 1988. "Conditional Spending, Federalism's Trojan Horse." *Supreme Court Review* 1988:85–127.

McGarry, John and Brendan O'Leary, eds. 1993. *The Politics of Ethnic Conflict Regulation: Case Studies of Protracted Ethnic Conflicts*. London: Routledge.

McKay, David. 2004. "William Riker on Federalism: Sometimes Wrong but More Right than Anyone Else?" *Regional and Federal Studies* 14(2):167–86.

McWhinney, Edward. 1982. *Canada and the Constitution 1979–1982: Patriation and the Charter of Rights*. Toronto: University of Toronto Press.

Mickey, Robert W. 2009. *Paths Out of Dixie: The Democratization of Authoritarian Enclaves in America's Deep South, 1944–72*. Princeton: NJ: Princeton University Press.

Mikos, Robert. 2007. "The Populist Safeguards of Federalism." University of California at Davis manuscript.

Milgrom, Paul R., Douglass North, and Barry R. Weingast. 1990. "The Role of Institutions in the Revival of Trade: The Medieval Law Merchant, Private Judges, and the Champagne Fairs." *Economics and Politics* 1:1–23.

Moe, Terry M. 2005. "Power and Political Institutions." *Perspectives on Politics* 3(2):215–33.

Molinelli, Guillermo, Valeria Palanza, and Gisela Sin. 1999. *Congreso, Presidencia y Justicia: Materiales para su Estudio*. Buenos Aires: Temas Editorial.

Montinola, Gabriella, Yingyi Qian, and Barry R. Weingast. 1995. "Federalism, Chinese Style: The Political Basis for Economic Success in China." *World Politics* 48(1):50–81.

Moravscik, Andrew. 1991. "Negotiating the Single European Act: National Interests and Conventional Statecraft in the European Community." *International Organization* 45:19–56.

Morlan, Robert L. 1984. "Municipal vs. National Election Voter Turnout: Europe and the United States." *Political Science Quarterly* 99(3):457–70.

Mueller, Dennis C. 1996. *Constitutional Democracy*. New York: Oxford University Press.

Mueller, Dennis C. and Thomas Stratmann. 2003. "The Economic Effects of Democratic Participation." *Journal of Public Economics* 87(9):2129–55.

Musgrave, Richard A. 1997. "Devolution, Grants, and Fiscal Competition." *Journal of Economic Perspectives* 11(4):65–72.

Mutz, Diana C. 1998. *Impersonal Influence: How Perceptions of Mass Collectives Affect Political Attitudes*. Cambridge, MA: Cambridge University Press.

Myerson, Roger B. 2006. "Federalism and Incentives for Success of Democracy." *Quarterly Journal of Political Science* 1(1):3–23.

Nicolini, Juan Pablo, Josefina Posadas, Juan Sanguinetti, Pablo Sanguinetti, and Mariano Tommasi 2000. "Decentralization, Fiscal Discipline in Subnational Governments, and the Bailout Problem: The Case of Argentina." Washington: Inter-American Development Bank.

North, Douglass C. 1990. *Institutions, Institutional Change, and Economic Performance*. Cambridge: Cambridge University Press.

Oates, Wallace. 1972. *Fiscal Federalism*. New York: Harcourt Brace Jovanovich.

Oates, Wallace. 1993. "Fiscal Decentralization and Economic Development." *National Tax Journal* 46:237–43.

Oates, Wallace. 1999. "An Essay on Fiscal Federalism." *Journal of Economic Literature* 37(3):1120–49.

Olson, Mancur. 1969. "The Principle of 'Fiscal Equivalence': The Division of Responsibilities Among Different Levels of Government." *American Economic Review* (Papers and Proceedings) 59(2):479–87.

Olson, Mancur. 1993. "Dictatorship, Democracy, and Development." *The American Political Science Review* 87(3):567–76.

Ordeshook, Peter C. 1995. "Institutions and Incentives." *Journal of Democracy* 6(2):46–60.

Ordeshook, Peter C. 1996. "Russia's Party System: Is Russian Federalism Viable?" *Post-Soviet Affairs* 12(3):145–17.

Ordeshook, Peter C. and Emerson Niou. 1998. "Alliances Versus Federations: An Extension of Riker's Analysis of Federal Formation." *Constitutional Political Economy* 9(4):271–88.

Ordeshook, Peter C. and Olga Shvetsova. 1995. "If Madison and Hamilton were Merely Lucky, What Hope is there for Russian Federalism?" *Constitutional Political Economy* 6(2):107–26.

Ostrom, Elinor. 1990. *Governing the Commons: The Evolution of Institutions for Collective Action*. New York: Cambridge University Press.

Ostrom, Elinor. 1999. "Coping with Tragedies of the Commons." *Annual Review of Political Science* 2:493–535.

Ostrom, Elinor. 2005. *Understanding Institutional Diversity*. Princeton: Princeton University Press.

Ostrom, Vincent. 1971. *The Political Theory of a Compound Republic*. Lincoln: University of Nebraska Press.

Ostrom, Vincent. 1991. *The Meaning of American Federalism: Constituting a Self-Governing Society*. San Francisco: Institute for Contemporary Studies.

Page, Scott E. 1997. "An Appending Efficient Algorithm for Allocating Public Projects with Positive Complementarities." *Journal of Public Economics* 64(3):291–321.

Page, Scott E. 2007. *The Difference: How the Power of Diversity Creates Better Groups, Firms, Schools, and Societies*. Princeton, NJ: Princeton University Press.

Parikh, Sunita and Barry R. Weingast. 1997. "A Comparative Theory of Federalism: India." *Virginia Law Review* 83(7):1593–615.

Park, Albert, Scott Rozelle, Christine Wong, and Changqing Ren. 1996. "Distributional Consequences of Reforming Local Public Finance in China" *China Quarterly* 147(September):751–78.

Parikh, Sunita A. and Barry R. Weingast. 2003. "Partisan Politics and the Structure and Stability of Federalism, Indian Style." Working Paper, Stanford Center for International Development, Standford University.

Peltzman, Sam. 1992. "Voters as Fiscal Conservatives." *Quarterly Journal of Economics* 107(2):327–62.

Persson, Torsten and Guido Tabellini. 2003. *The Economic Effects of Constitutions*. Cambridge, MA: MIT Press.

Peterson, Paul E. 1995. *The Price of Federalism*. Washington, DC: Brookings.

Pettys, Todd E. 2003. "Competing for the People's Affection: Federalism's Forgotten Marketplace." *Vanderbilt Law Review* 56:329–91.

Pinder, John. 1991. *European Community: The Building of a Union*. Oxford: Oxford University Press.

Powell, G. Bingham. 2000. *Elections as Instruments of Democracy: Majoritarian and Proportional Visions*. New Haven, CT: Yale University Press.

Primus, Richard. 2006. "The Riddle of Hiram Revels." *Harvard Law Review* 119:1681–734.

Qian, Yingyi and Gerard Roland. 1998. "Federalism and the Soft Budget Constraint." *American Economic Review* 88(5):1143–62.

Qian, Yingyi and Barry R. Weingast. 1996. "China's Transition to Markets: Market-Preserving Federalism, Chinese Style." *Journal of Policy Reform* 1:149–85.

Qian, Yingyi and Barry R. Weingast. 1997. "Federalism as a Commitment to Preserving Market Incentives." *Journal of Economic Perspectives* 11(4):83–92.

Rabe, Barry G. 2004. *Statehouse and Greenhouse: The Emerging Politics of American Climate Change Policy*. Washington, DC: Brookings Institution Press.

Rakove, Jack N. 1996. *Original Meanings: Politics and Ideas in the Making of the Constitution*. New York: Alfred A. Knopf.

Rakove, Jack N. 1997. "The Origins of Judicial Review: A Plea for New Contexts." *Stanford Law Review* 49(5):1031–64.

Rakove, Jack N. 2002. "Judicial Power in the Constitutional Theory of James Madison." *William and Mary Law Review* 43(4):1513–47.

Rector, Chad. 2005. "Federation, International Organization, and Self-Sufficiency." Paper presented at the American Political Science Association meeting, Washington, DC, September 2005.

Riker, William H. 1955. "The Senate and American Federalism." *American Political Science Review* 49(2):452–69.

Riker, William H. 1964. *Federalism: Origin, Operation, Significance*. Boston: Little, Brown and Company.

Riker, William H. 1987. *The Development of American Federalism*. Boston: Kluwer.

Rodden, Jonathan. 2006. *Hamilton's Paradox: The Promise and Peril of Fiscal Federalism*. New York: Cambridge University Press.

Rodden, Jonathan and Susan Rose-Ackerman. 1997. "Does Federalism Preserve Markets?" *Virginia Law Review* 83(7):1521–72.

Rodden, Jonathan and Erik Wibbels. 2002. "Beyond the Fiction of Federalism: Macroeconomic Management in Multitiered Systems." *World Politics* 54: 494–531.

Rodden, Jonathan and Erik Wibbels. 2005. "Retrospective Voting, Coattails, and Accountability in Regional Elections." Paper presented at the Annual Meeting of the American Political Science Association, Chicago, IL.

Ross, C. 2003. "Putin's Federal Reforms and the Consolidation of Federalism in Russia: One Step Forward, Two Steps Back!" *Communist and Post-Communist Studies* 36:29–47.

Rubinfeld, Daniel P. 1997. "The Allocation of Government Authority: Commentary: On Federalism and Economic Development." *University of Virginia Law Review* 83: 1581–92.

Sah, Raaj Kumar and Joseph E. Stiglitz. 1985. "Human Fallibility and Economic Organization." *The American Economic Review* (Papers and Proceedings) 75(2):292–7.

Sah, Raaj Kumar and Joseph E. Stiglitz. 1986. "The Architecture of Economic Systems: Hierarchies and Polyarchies." *American Economic Review* 76(4): 716–27.

Saich, Tony. 2002. "The Blind Man and the Elephant: Analysing the Local State in China," in Luigi Tomba, ed., *East Asian Capitalism: Conflicts, Growth, and Crisis*. Milano: Feltrinelli.

Saiz, Martin and Susan E. Clarke. 2004. "Economic Development and Infrastructure Policy," in Virginia Gray and Russell L. Hanson, eds., *Politics in the American States*. Washington, DC: CQ Press, pp. 418–448.

Schauer, Frederick. 1991. *Playing by the Rules: A Philosophical Examination of Rule-Based Decision-Making*. London: Oxford University Press.

Schelling, Thomas C. 1978. *Micromotives and Macrobehavior*. New York: Norton.

Schofield, Norman. 1985. "Anarchy, Altruism and Cooperation: A Review." *Social Choice and Welfare* 2(3):207–19.

Segal, Jeffrey A. and Harold J. Spaeth. 2002. *The Supreme Court and the Attitudinal Model Revisited*. New York: Cambridge University Press.

Serrafero, Mario. 2000. "El Poder Ejecutivo y la Intervencion Federal a las Provincias." Universidad Argentina de la Empresa, Mimeo.

Shapiro, Martin. 1992. "The European Court of Justice," in Alberta M. Sbragia, ed., *Europolitics: Institutions and Policymaking in the "New" European Community*." Washington, DC: Brookings.

Shavell, Steven. 1995. "The Appeals Process as a Means of Error Correction." *Journal of Legal Studies* 24(2):379–426.

Sheppard, Robert and Michael Valpy. 1982. *The National Deal: The Fight for a Canadian Constitution*. Toronto: Fleet Books.

Shepsle, Kenneth A. 1989. "Studying Institutions: Some Lessons from the Rational Choice Approach." *Journal of Theoretical Politics* 1(2):131–47.

Simon, Herbert A. 1969. *Science of the Artificial*. Cambridge, MA: MIT Press.

Simon, Herbert A. 1985. "Human Nature in Politics: The Dialogue of Psychology with Political Choice." *American Political Science Review* 79(2): 293–304.

Skach, Cindy. 2005. "We, the Peoples? Constitutionalizing the European Union." *Journal of Common Market Studies* 43(1):149–70.

Smiley, Donald. 1983. "A Dangerous Deed: The Constitution Act, 1982," in Banting and Simeon, eds., *And No One Cheered*. Toronto: Methuen.

Smithey, Shannon. 1996. "The Effects of the Canadian Supreme Court's Charter Interpretation on Regional and Intergovernmental Tensions in Canada." *Publius: The Journal of Federalism* 26(2):83–100.

Snell, Ronald K. 2004. *State Balanced Budge Requirements: Provisions and Practice*. Denver: National Conference of State Legislatures.

Somin, Ilya. 2002. "Closing the Pandora's Box of Federalism: The Case for Judicial Restriction of Federal Subsidies to State Governments." *Georgetown Law Journal* 90:461–502.

Soss, Joe and David T. Canon. 1995. "Partisan Divisions and Voting Decisions: U.S. Senators, Governors, and the Rise of a Divided Federal Government." *Political Research Quarterly* 48(2):253–74.

Spiller, Pablo T. and Mariano Tommasi. 2007. *The Institutional Foundations of Public Policy in Argentina*. New York: Cambridge University Press.

Stepan, Alfred. 1999. "Federalism and Democracy: Beyond the U.S. Model." *Journal of Democracy* 10(4):19–33.

Strumpf, Koleman. 2002. "Does Government Decentralization Increase Policy Innovation?" *Journal of Public Economic Theory* 4(2):207–41.

Sunstein, Cass R. 2003. *Why Societies Need Dissent*. Cambridge, MA: Harvard University Press.

Teichman, Doron. 2005. "The Market for Criminal Justice: Federalism, Crime Control, and Jurisdictional Competition." *Michigan Law Review* 103: 1831–76.

Tiebout, Charles M. 1956. "A Pure Theory of Local Expenditures." *Journal of Political Economy* 64(5):416–24.

Ting, Michael M. 2003. "A Strategic Theory of Bureaucratic Redundancy." *American Journal of Political Science* 47(2):274–92.

Tocqueville, Alexis de. 1959. *The Recollections of Alexis de Tocqueville*. J.P. Mayer, ed. New York: Meridian Books. First published in 1893.

Tommasi, Mariano, Sebastian Saiegh, and Pablo Sanguinetti. 2001. "Fiscal Federalism in Argentina: Policies, Politics, and Institutional Reform." *Economia* 1(2):157–211.

Triesman, Daniel. 2007. *The Architecture of Government: Rethinking Political Decentralization*. New York: Cambridge University Press.

Trudeau, Pierre Elliott. 1993. *Memoirs*. Toronto: McClelland & Stewart.

Tsebelis, George. 2002. *Veto Players: How Political Institutions Work*. Princeton, NJ: Princeton University Press.

Tsebelis, George and Geoff Garrett. 1997a. "Agenda Setting, Vetoes, and the European Union's Co-decision Procedure." *Journal of Legislative Studies* 3(3):74–92.

Tsebelis, George and Geoff Garrett. 1997b. "More on the Co-Decision Endgame." *Journal of Legislative Studies* 3(4):139–43.

Vaillancourt, Francois. 1998. "The Economics of Constitutional Options for Quebec and Canada." *Canadian Business Economics* Winter: 3–14.

Vaughan, Frederick. 1986. "Critics of the Judicial Committee of the Privy Council: The New Orthodoxy and an Alternative Explanation." *Canadian Journal of Political Science* 19(3):495–519.

Volden, Craig. 1997. "Entrusting the States with Welfare Reform," in John Ferejohn and Barry R. Weingast, eds., *The New Federalism: Can the States be Trusted?* Stanford: Hoover Institution Press.

Volden, Craig. 2002. "The Politics of Competitive Federalism: A Race to the Bottom in Welfare Benefits?" *American Journal of Political Science* 46(2): 352–63.

Volden, Craig. 2003. "States as Policy Laboratories: Experimenting with the Childrens Health Insurance Program." Unpublished manuscript, Ohio State University.

Volden, Craig. 2005. "Intergovernmental Political Competition in American Federalism." *American Journal of Political Science* 49(2):327–42.

Von Neumann, John. 1956. "Probabilistic Logics and the Synthesis of Reliable Organizations from Unreliable Components," in C.E. Shannon and J. McCarthy, eds., *Automata Studies*. Princeton: Princeton University Press.

Walker, Jack L. 1969. "The Diffusion of Innovation Among the American States." *American Political Science Review* 63:880–99.

Watts, Ronald. 1999. *The Spending Power in Federal Systems: A Comparative Study*. Kingston, ON: Institution of Intergovernmental Relations, Queen's University.

Wechsler, Herbert. 1954. "The Political Safeguards of Federalism: The Role of the States in the Composition and Selection of the National Government." *Columbia Law Review* 54:543–60.

Weiler, J.H.H. 1991. "The Transformation of Europe." *Yale Law Journal* 100:2403–83.

Weiler, J.H.H. 2001. "Federalism and Constitutionalism: Europe's *Sonderweg*," in Kalypso Nicolaidis and Robert Howse, eds., *The Federal Vision: Legitimacy and Levels of Governance in the US and EU*. Oxford: Oxford University Press.

Weingast, Barry R. 1995. "The Economic Role of Political Institutions: Market-Preserving Federalism and Economic Growth." *Journal of Law, Economics, and Organization* 11:1–31.

Weingast, Barry R. 1996. "Institutions and Political Commitment: A New Political Economy of the Civil War Era." Unpublished manuscript, Hoover Institution, Stanford University.

Weingast, Barry R. 1997. "The Political Foundations of Democracy and the Rule of Law." *American Political Science Review* 91(2):245–63.

Weingast, Barry R. 1998. "Political Stability and Civil War: Institutions, Commitment, and American Democracy," in Robert H. Bates et al., eds., *Analytic Narratives*. Princeton, NJ: Princeton University Press.

Weingast, Barry R., Kenneth A. Shepsle, and Christopher Johnsen. 1981. "The Political Economy of Benefits and Costs: A Neoclassical Approach to Distributive Politics." *Journal of Political Economy* 89(4):642–64.

Whittington, Keith E. 1999. *Constitutional Construction: Divided Powers and Constitutional Meaning*. Cambridge, MA: Harvard University Press.

Williamson, Oliver E. 1985. *The Economic Institutions of Capitalism*. New York: Free Press.

Williamson, Oliver E. 1993. "Opportunism and Its Critics." *Managerial and Decision Economics* 14(2):97–107.

Williamson, Oliver E. 1998. "The New Institutional Economics: The Institutions of Governance." *The American Economic Review* 88(2):75–9.

Young, Robert A. 1994. "The Political Economy of Secession: The Case of Quebec." *Constitutional Political Economy* 5(2):221–45.

Zhang, Le-Yin. 1999. "Chinese Central–Provincial Fiscal Relationships, Budgetary Decline, and the Impact of the 1994 Fiscal Reform: An Evaluation." *China Quarterly* 157:115–41.

Ziblatt, Daniel. 2006. *Structuring the State: The Formation of Italy and Germany and the Puzzle of Federalism*. Princeton, NJ: Princeton University Press.

Index

continued from page iii

Raymond M. Duch and Randolph T. Stevenson, *The Economic Vote: How Political and Economic Institutions Condition Election Results*

Jean Ensminger, *Making a Market: The Institutional Transformation of an African Society*

David Epstein and Sharyn O'Halloran, *Delegating Powers: A Transaction Cost Politics Approach to Policy Making under Separate Powers*

Kathryn Firmin-Sellers, *The Transformation of Property Rights in the Gold Coast: An Empirical Study Applying Rational Choice Theory*

Clark C. Gibson, *Politicians and Poachers: The Political Economy of Wildlife Policy in Africa*

Avner Greif, *Institutions and the Path to the Modern Economy: Lessons from Medieval Trade*

Stephen Haber, Armando Razo, and Noel Maurer, *The Politics of Property Rights: Political Instability, Credible Commitments, and Economic Growth in Mexico, 1876–1929*

Ron Harris, *Industrializing English Law: Entrepreneurship and Business Organization, 1720–1844*

Anna L. Harvey, *Votes Without Leverage: Women in American Electoral Politics, 1920–1970*

Murray Horn, *The Political Economy of Public Administration: Institutional Choice in the Public Sector*

John D. Huber, *Rationalizing Parliament: Legislative Institutions and Party Politics in France*

John E. Jackson, Jacek Klich, and Krystyna Poznanska, *The Political Economy of Poland's Transition: New Firms and Reform Governments*

Jack Knight, *Institutions and Social Conflict*

Michael Laver and Kenneth Shepsle, eds., *Making and Breaking Governments: Cabinets and Legislatures in Parliamentary Democracies*

Michael Laver and Kenneth Shepsle, eds., *Cabinet Ministers and Parliamentary Government*

Margaret Levi, *Consent, Dissent, and Patriotism*

Brian Levy and Pablo T. Spiller, eds., *Regulations, Institutions, and Commitment: Comparative Studies of Telecommunications*

Leif Lewin, *Ideology and Strategy: A Century of Swedish Politics* (English Edition)

Gary Libecap, *Contracting for Property Rights*

John Londregan, *Legislative Institutions and Ideology in Chile*

Arthur Lupia and Mathew D. McCubbins, *The Democratic Dilemma: Can Citizens Learn What They Need to Know?*

C. Mantzavinos, *Individuals, Institutions, and Markets*

Mathew D. McCubbins and Terry Sullivan, eds., *Congress: Structure and Policy*

Gary J. Miller, *Managerial Dilemmas: The Political Economy of Hierarchy*